A HISTORY
of
VIDEO GAMES
IN
64
OBJECTS

DEY ST.
An Imprint of WILLIAM MORROW

★

A HISTORY

of

VIDEO GAMES

IN

64

OBJECTS

WORLD VIDEO GAME HALL OF FAME

CONTENTS

A NOTE FROM
THE WORLD VIDEO GAME
HALL OF FAME

This book represents more than ten years of work. In 2006, The Strong National Museum of Play had just completed a major expansion. We already had a world class collection of dolls, toys, games, and other artifacts of play, but it was obvious that the present and future of play was bound up in the growth of video games. Our museum staff began the work of collecting, preserving, and interpreting the history of video games. From a smattering of about a dozen artifacts, The Strong's collection of materials related to the history of electronic games has now grown to more than sixty thousand games and related artifacts and hundreds of thousands of archival materials documenting the growth of electronic gaming over the last half century.

Our work was motivated and guided by two tenets: First, we believed that video games would be the most important medium of the twenty-first century, just as the novel dominated the nineteenth century and film and television were the pre-eminent media of the twentieth century. Second, we predicted that historians and other scholars would want to study the rise of video games and their impact on society and culture, both individually and collectively. We have thus tried to expand our collection broadly and deeply, and we have been gratified that already scholars from all over the world have been coming to The Strong to research the history of electronic games.

In 2009, the museum's collection had grown large enough for us to establish the International Center for the History of Electronic Games (ICHEG). In 2015, the museum created the World Video Game Hall of Fame, which annually inducts video games that meet four criteria: icon-status, influence, longevity, and geographical reach. In the Hall of Fame's first three years, sixteen games were inducted: *Donkey Kong*, *Doom*, *Grand Theft Auto III*, *Halo: Combat Evolved*, *The Legend of Zelda*, *The Oregon Trail*, *Pac-Man*, *Pokémon Red* and *Green*, *Pong*, *The Sims*, *Sonic the Hedgehog*, *Space Invaders*, *Street Fighter II*, *Super Mario Bros.*, *Tetris*, and *World of Warcraft*.

This book is a celebration and an exploration of some of the most important items related to the history of video games that are currently at The Strong. We have been able to gather and preserve these materials thanks to the generosity of many donors, ranging from industry veterans and game companies to journalists, scholars, collectors, and everyday gamers who have given The Strong materials they have collected over the years. We are deeply grateful to each of these individuals and companies for their contributions to our ongoing preservation of video game history.

In many cases, the objects we photographed for this book represented one part of a larger history. There is no surviving copy of the original 1958 game "Tennis for Two," for example, but scientists at Brookhaven National Laboratory recreated it using the original designs and vintage equipment. That recreation is now on display at The Strong and seemed a fitting representation of that game's role in the history of electronic gaming.

Even as we have tried to focus on the history of video games, we have also been cognizant of how video games always exist in relation to the broader culture. That is why in this book we have tried to contextualize the histories, to write something more than an internal history of who created which game. Games arose in relation to broader social, cultural, and technological phenomena, and their development was often tied to deep social, economic, and political trends—such as the military's investments in computer technology during the Cold War or the social and cultural revolutions that convulsed society during the 1960s and 1970s.

And yet video games do not merely reflect culture and society; they also shape it. Today, as computers pervade our lives, it is worth remembering that it is through playing with games that we have become digital natives. Games shape the digital tools we use, condition our willingness to assume the mask of an avatar, and impact how we communicate and compete online, including across geographic and linguistic boundaries. As smartphones proliferate, it is ever more apparent that we are all gamers of some kind, and the mechanics and modes of these games are shaping the way we experience the world.

The objects in this book are not the only ones we could have chosen—in fact, there are many items in The Strong's collection that we regretted leaving out—but we believe these objects most effectively tell the story of electronic games and their impact on our culture. We hope you appreciate as much as we do how games, from the earliest pinball machines to *Pong* to *Pokémon Go*, have shaped and will continue to shape how we play for many years to come.

Jon-Paul C. Dyson, PhD

Jeremy K. Saucier, PhD

HUMPTY DUMPTY

(1947)

Gottlieb revolutionized pinball with the introduction of *Humpty Dumpty*, the first machine with electromechanical flippers. Many moral reformers who had once condemned the pastime as a gateway to gambling were partially mollified by the skill it now took to play. Nevertheless, a pinball ban remained in New York City until 1976. The interactive and complex nature of pinball gameplay paved the way for electronic games.

onsider the ubiquitous pinball machine, a staple of arcades and bowling alleys nationwide. Slip in a few quarters, pull back a spring-loaded plunger, and launch a metal ball into a minefield of bumpers, kickers, slingshots, targets, and saucers. It's hard to fathom how this charmingly old-fashioned machine could lay the foundation for video games, or how it could once have been seen as a threat to the moral fabric of America. To tell the history of pinball is to tell the history of twentieth-century American culture itself.

Pinball traces its roots to an eighteenth-century French parlor game called *bagatelle*, in which players flicked balls onto a flat board where they bounced off pins and into one of several scoring pockets—an ancestor of sorts to Plinko from *The Price is Right*. Modern pinball originated in 1931 with the pin games *Whiffle* and *Whoopee Game*, which were similar to *bagatelle* but used wooden cases and coin mechanisms that earned money for the arcade operator. Other early examples of pinball include *Baffle Ball* (1931), *Ballyhoo* (1932), and *World's Fair Jigsaw* (1933), a clever game featuring a jigsaw puzzle rendition of the 1933 Chicago World's Fair that flipped over its pieces as players scored. In 1936, Bally's *Bumper* revolutionized pinball by introducing the electrified coil scoring bumper, automatic ball removal from the playfield, and a score tracker—transforming pinball from a static game with a goal of avoiding pins to a game focused on bumping the ball across a playfield to accumulate points.

Yet a crucial difference separates these early games from modern pinball, one that would form the beating heart of video games: interactivity. Pinball games from the 1930s were essentially games of chance, with no player-operated flippers that could affect the trajectory of the ball. Early pinball games did not require much skill, which did not sit well with regulators during the Prohibition era who were crusading against gambling. So-called games of chance had been largely outlawed nationwide, but the coin-operated amusements industry found loopholes with jukeboxes, slot machines, gumball machines, and eventually pinball. Such machines, which lacked player interaction, were not unlike roulette and other banned forms of gambling. In 1942, New York City mayor Fiorello La Guardia outlawed pinball machines and denigrated pinball pushers as "slimy crews of tinhorns, well dressed and living in luxury on penny thievery." Pinball was seen as the gateway to gambling, one that corrupted children and set them along the path to drinking and prostitution. La Guardia made pinball raids a priority and was even photographed toppling seized pinball machines. As history has shown, La Guardia's crusade was part of a recurring pattern of moral panics in reaction to new forms of entertainment and media.

By the end of World War II, pinball machines were often consigned to seedy establishments like porn shops and dive-bar basements. But this began to change in 1947, when D. Gottlieb & Co. debuted *Humpty Dumpty*, designed by Harry Mabs, which for the first time featured electro-mechanical "flipper bumpers" that enabled players to launch and maneuver the ball. Compared to modern layouts, *Humpty Dumpty* was crude: the six flippers faced outward and were located on the sides of the playfield far above the bottom outhole, making gameplay tedious and difficult by today's standards. Nevertheless, now that players could aim, fire, and control the ball as it moved across the board, pinball manufacturers

WHAT IS A MORAL PANIC?

The anti-pinball crusade championed by New York City mayor Fiorello La Guardia and other officials across the United States is an example of a moral panic. A moral panic is when widespread fears of a new cultural form or activity greatly exceed the actual threat posed to society. Such panics can be about anything, but moral guardians have often set their sights on combating objects, activities, and the "folk devils" who create them. Pinball didn't cause the downfall of civilization, but games and new forms of media remain some of the easiest targets of moral reformers.

faced outward). Other manufacturers followed and the classic pinball configuration was quickly standardized. Later versions of pinball would vary in complexity—Bally's *Balls-A-Poppin* (1956), for instance, featured multi-ball play—but the hand-eye coordination and ability to aim were skills that players developed on one machine and could then transfer to other pinball games.

Pinball manufacturers sought to distance themselves from their gambling roots. Most machines bore a large FOR AMUSEMENT ONLY disclaimer. Municipalities increasingly began licensing pinball arcades, and in 1974, California's Supreme Court overturned the state's pinball ban. Two years later, the city council of New York voted to overturn La Guardia's infamous ban. Yet many moral guardians were still suspicious, worried that if pinball would not turn children into degenerate gamblers, it would still make them mindless illiterates who didn't do their homework.

Humpty Dumpty and *Triple Action* established a new layer of interactivity and complexity that—along with other pinball and penny arcade game conventions, such as starting a game with three lives, accumulating extra lives, and chasing high scores (often recorded by hand on notecards or on chalkboards)—would lay the foundation for video games. Players were not just watching a game unfold; they were actively taking part in it. And while *Humpty Dumpty*'s red plastic "flipper bumpers" and kitschy artwork may bear little resemblance to *Mortal Kombat* and the Grand Theft Auto series, the early history of pinball illustrates how critics expressed outrage over games long before the advent of the joystick.

began arguing that their products were "games of skill," not gambling machines. Slowly but surely, pinball entered the mainstream.

The following year, pinball manufacturer Genco continued pinball's evolution with *Triple Action*, designed by Steve Kordek, which featured the now-customary two flippers at the bottom of the playfield (though these flippers also

TENNIS
FOR TWO

(1958)

Guests to Brookhaven National Laboratory's annual Visitor's Day were amazed when they saw the first publicly demonstrated video game in 1958. Fifty years later, engineers at Brookhaven recreated it using an original Donner analog computer, complete with vintage transistors, fuses, and oscilloscope. Brookhaven loaned this to The Strong for display in 2017.

Residents of Brookhaven, New York, generally did not ask questions about the massive government lab that sat on the edge of town. It was the 1950s, the height of the Cold War, and most assumed that scientists were hard at work on top-secret weapons systems. Run by the Department of Energy, Brookhaven National Lab (BNL) specialized in nuclear and high-energy physics, and due to the secretive nature of its projects, was closed to the public except on Visitor's Day—a chance for the Brookhaven community to meet scientists and explore the grounds. Visitor's Day usually meant hastily-put-together photo and text displays showcasing projects from BNL's various lab divisions, but in 1958, the public was treated to something new: a 5½-inch DuMont cathode-ray oscilloscope connected to a Donner Scientific Company Model 30 vacuum-tube analog computer. On the oscilloscope's hazy screen was a virtual simulation of a tennis net, a court, and a ball. The scientists had rigged up the game so that visitors could interact with it via two external controllers, manipulating the trajectory of the ball as they served, returned, and volleyed with an opposing player. As it turns out, this drizzly October day in BNL's gymnasium was the first time the general public had ever witnessed a video game.

"Tennis for Two" was the brainchild of nuclear physicist William Higinbotham. A key member of the Manhattan Project, Higinbotham, along with J. Robert Oppenheimer, helped develop the timing circuits for the atomic bomb, even witnessing the Trinity nuclear test in the Jornada del Muerto desert. Yet he would become a leading crusader for adopting atomic energy for peaceful purposes and was the first chair of the Federation of American Scientists, a group that advocated for the nonproliferation of nuclear weapons. Higinbotham hoped to demystify BNL to the general public by creating a playable game that could "convey the message that our scientific endeavors have relevance for society."

"Tennis for Two" (a name that Higinbotham never used but derives from his description of it as a "tennis game for two to play") was powered by a small analog computer composed of resistors, capacitors, and relays. Images were displayed using an oscilloscope—a lab instrument that displays the waveform of electronic signals, similar to an electrocardiogram (EKG) machine at the doctor's office—and a cathode-ray tube like those used in black-and-white TVs. The instruments were officially used to calculate trajectories of bullets and intercontinental ballistic missiles (ICBMs), but when Higinbotham saw the brightly lit projectiles sweeping across the screen, it reminded him of tennis. So he created a version in which a "ball" left a trail as it bounced

between two paddles. Physicist Peter Takacs of BNL's instrumentation division, who fifty years later worked to re-create a playable version of "Tennis for Two," explained that:

The real innovation in this game is the use of those "new-fangled" germanium transistors that were just becoming commercially available in the late 1950s. Higinbotham used the transistors to build a fast-switching circuit that would take the three outputs from the computer and display them alternately on the oscilloscope screen at a "blazing" fast speed of 36 Hertz. At that display rate, the eye sees the ball, the net, and the court as one image, rather than as three separate images.

When the ball hit the ground, a relay was thrown, reversing polarity and allowing the ball to bounce and mirror its previous trajectory. Another relay could sense when the ball hit the net—which appeared on the screen as an upside-down *T*—while others governed the paddles. "Tennis for Two" was surprisingly sophisticated for its time, requiring players to carefully calibrate the moment and angle to swing the paddle or else risk hitting the ball into the net. The game was so popular that it returned for the following year's Visitor's Day, this time with a larger oscilloscope so crowds could have a better view of the gameplay. One of the visitors who played the game was a high school student named David Ahl. He would go on to become a

great popularizer of computers and write a best-selling anthology of computers, *101 BASIC Computer Games* (page 55).

Brookhaven staff took apart the game after the 1959 Visitor's Day, and they repurposed the oscilloscope and Donner analog computer for other projects more closely related to the mission of BNL. The game was seemingly lost to history. Higinbotham, who did not patent the game, later reflected that "it didn't seem likely that anyone would want to spend much time twisting the dials on rheostats to play this two-dimensional form of tennis." Due to the fact that the game received almost no publicity or support from BNL, the only remaining artifacts of the original installation are a few photographs, engineering schematics, and handwritten log entries.

It was only in 1997 that Takacs and his colleagues, celebrating the fiftieth anniversary of BNL, dug up the original schematics to re-create the game for yet another Visitor's Day. After scrounging some vintage parts and assembling the game according to Higinbotham's instructions, visitors were once more able to play "Tennis for Two" on a Donner analog computer and oscilloscope. Takacs's reconstruction is now on display at The Strong museum.

"Tennis for Two" might seem like just a blip on a cathode-ray oscilloscope, but its existence is testament to the fact that even in the most top-secret defense laboratories, even on machines designed to wage war and with minds paid to plot destruction, play can still be found—even if only for a few hours in a quiet Long Island gymnasium.

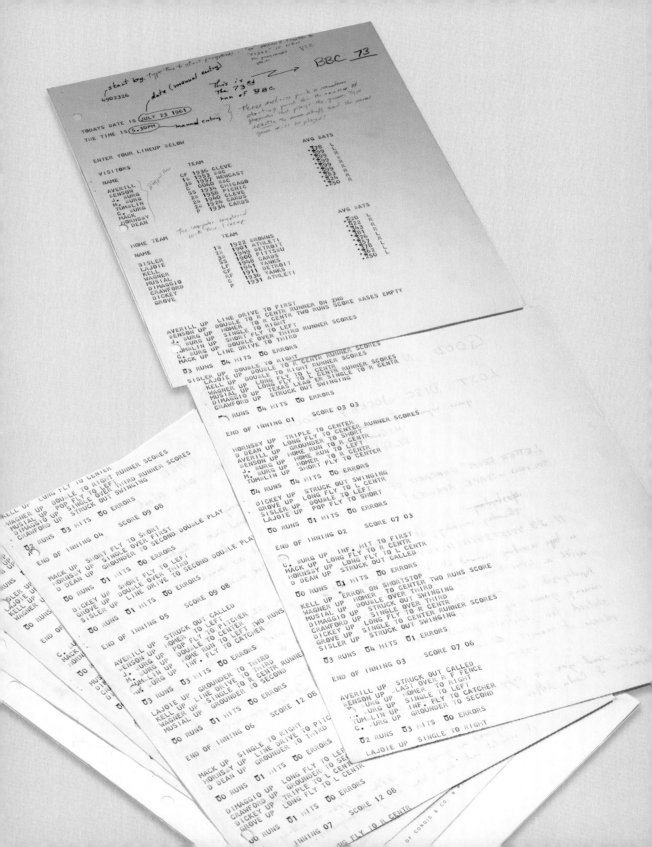

JOHN BURGESON'S
BASEBALL GAME

(1960)

There were numerous pen-and-paper baseball simulation games in the twentieth century, but John Burgeson's program was the first reenactment of baseball to use a computer. In 2012, he gave his papers related to the game to The Strong.

Before there were fantasy baseball, sabermetrics, and defensive shifts, there was an IBM 1620 mainframe computer and a man named John Burgeson, creator of the first-ever simulated baseball game.

At its heart, baseball is about numbers. More specifically, baseball is about *statistics*. A hitter's batting average predicts his future success at the plate, a pitcher's earned-run average measures his overall effectiveness, and a fielder's rate of errors correlates strongly with his likelihood of making an out. All sports rely on statistics, of course, but baseball is overflowing with them: 162 games per team per season with an average of 700 plate appearances for batters, 180 innings tossed for pitchers, and 3.8 pitches per at bat. Advanced sabermetrics with byzantine names like WAR, FIP, BABIP, xFIP, and wRC+ dissect the game into a spectrum only visible when using powerful computers, scrutinizing everything from bat launch angles to exit velocities.

Before front offices were ruled by stat geeks armed with supercomputers, most of the country experienced baseball through print newspapers. Box scores included simple statistics like hits, strikeouts, and home runs, allowing Americans to track the progress of their favorite stars. Tradeable baseball cards featured players' positions and career statistics. Growing up in Ohio in the 1940s, John and his brother, Paul, would simulate baseball using game boards, pieces, and randomizing devices such as spinners and dice to determine whether players smacked a triple, walked, or struck out. Throughout his childhood, Burgeson kept detailed records of his favorite players, diligently recording their statistics.

After college, he worked as a computer programmer at IBM. Around Christmas 1960, he caught the flu and stayed home from work. It was then he got the idea of combining his childhood love for baseball with his newfound love for computers. With help from his brother, Burgeson began coding a baseball program in the Symbolic Programming System (SPS) language, used at the time to run the IBM 1620 mainframe computer. The program was not a video game in the modern sense; players did not push buttons to crush homers or groove curveballs. Rather, they played the part of a baseball general manager: piecing together a lineup, assembling a pitching staff, and monitoring their team's progress over the course of a season. Burgeson used the program to simulate games involving players from disparate eras, from icons of the dead-ball era like Honus Wagner and Nap Lajoie to contemporary stars like Joe DiMaggio and Stan Musial.

The first simulations Burgeson and his brother ran produced absurdly lopsided results even by the standards of the '27 Yankees, with some teams creaming others by dozens of runs. The program also could not account for all of baseball's eccentricities—it did not understand, for instance, that the bottom of the ninth inning was not necessary when the home team was leading. But the brothers diligently refined the code until the program accounted for baseball's complex rules while accurately predicting how a team would perform based on the statistics of its players.

The simulation worked by inserting a punch card into the IBM mainframe, which would spit out printed instructions to choose a roster of nine out of a total of fifty preprogrammed players. After randomizing the remaining players into the opposing team, the computer would simulate a game, printing the results of each pitch slowly like ticker tape—successfully replicating not just the makeup of baseball, but the at-times glacial pace of a game. One particularly successful inning from July 23, 1961 began:

AVERILL UP LINE DRIVE TO FIRST

BENSON UP DOUBLE TO R CENTR RUNNER ON 2ND

J. BURG UP HOMER TO R CENTR TWO RUNS SCORE
    BASES EMPTY

M.BURG UP SINGLE TO RIGHT

This matchup pitted Earl Averill (1936 Cleveland Indians) and Rogers Hornsby (1924 St. Louis Cardinals) on one team, with Honus Wagner (1900 Pittsburgh Pirates), Stan Musial (1948 St. Louis Cardinals), and Joe DiMaggio (1941 New York Yankees) on the other. Averill and Hornsby's team won, twelve to eight, although the result was not surprising considering Burgeson stacked the home team with fictional ringers—two of whom were named after him and his brother—each sporting a .599 batting average. (Perhaps he wanted to make sure that team won since it also included two players from the Cleveland Indians, his favorite club.)

When Rege Cordic, a radio disc jockey from Pittsburgh, heard about Burgeson's program, he imagined the possibilities for a broadcast version of a simulated game. Using Burgeson's computer, he reenacted a matchup between long-dead superstars. For three evenings in the fall of 1961, listeners of Cordic's radio show listened to a marquee baseball game featuring a cross-generational who's who of stars including Willie Mays, Stan Musial, Honus Wagner, Lefty Grove, Joe DiMaggio, George Sisler, and Dizzy Dean.

While Cordic hoped to make this a recurring segment on his show, IBM management was less convinced that a baseball simulator constituted an appropriate use of its 1620 computer. At the height of the Cold War, IBM was determined to showcase the powerful national defense capabilities of its computers and likely felt that a gimmicky baseball program was not a proper ambassador for such a serious product. IBM executives demanded that Burgeson scrub the game from the 1620's memory banks. Hoping to change their minds, Burgeson pleaded in a letter:

I am sorry you have felt it necessary to remove novelty type programs from the library. In the economic struggle for survival our company faces, some of these programs have proven exceptionally useful in demonstration concepts rather than a specific application in a context understandable by a layman. The Baseball demonstrator program has been used often in this manner to illustrate the concept of computer simulation. As such, I consider it of high significance to the programming community.

The IBM corporate hierarchy's suspicion of Burgeson's baseball game foreshadowed the negative attitude of many corporate and educational institutions through the years toward the use of computers for gameplay. And yet, as Burgeson understood, often the best way of discovering new applications for a computer is to play with it. Today, there are hundreds of electronic baseball games, from high-res swing-fests like *MLB The Show 18* to number-crunching simulations such as *Baseball Mogul*. Despite their sophistication, these baseball games accomplish what John Burgeson did all the way back in 1961—take players out for a memorable trip to a ballgame that can be played anytime, anywhere, rain or shine.

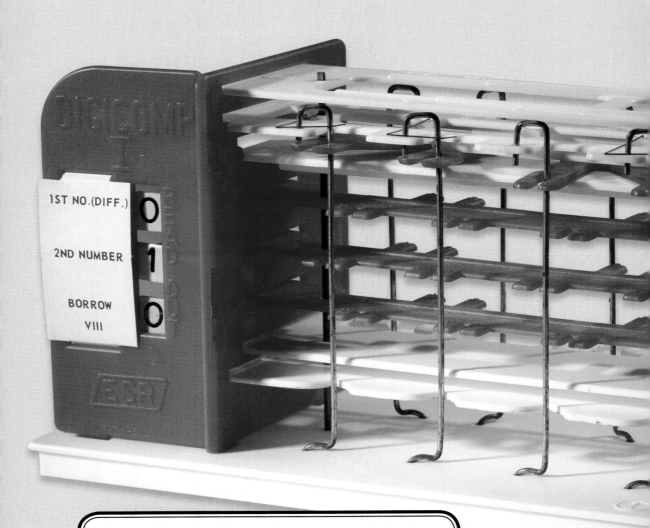

Girls and boys of the baby boom era could simulate a rocket countdown or play games with the "first digital computer in plastic."

DIGI-COMP COMPUTER

(1963)

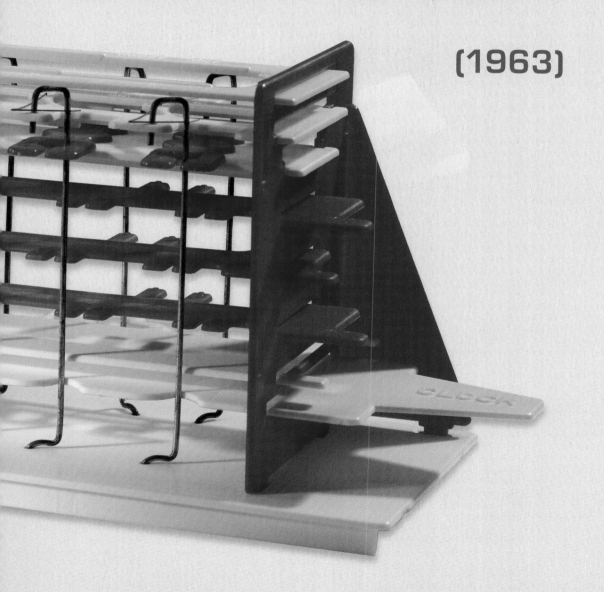

To children growing up in the 1960s, computers were exotic, otherworldly machines that guided rockets into space. They cost millions of dollars, took up entire rooms, and were operated by punch card–wielding astrophysicists. The possibility that kids could own a computer in their very own home seemed as distant as the moon itself. But what is a computer, exactly? Does it need to be electronic? Does it need to be capable of performing advanced calculations? Does it need a screen, or even a keyboard?

"If you have ever counted on your fingers YOU could be called a DIGITAL COMPUTER," the instruction manual for E.S.R. Inc.'s Digi-Comp I computer began. "The word *digit* means finger (or toe) and a computer is someone or something that does number work." At first glance, Digi-Comp was a far cry from the IBM 7090 mainframe computers that guided the Mercury and Gemini manned spaceflights. The IBM needed its own air-conditioned room; Digi-Comp could easily fit on a coffee table. Rather than using fifty thousand germanium alloy-junction transistors, Digi-Comp relied on three plastic flip-floppers as memory devices that could accept an input, remember it, and then output it on command. Instead of costing $2.9 million, Digi-Comp cost $4.99.

And yet, as the instructions proudly stated, Digi-Comp was still a computer. "[Digi-Comp] is a mechanical equivalent of an electronic, digital computer. With DIGI-COMP I you can PLAY GAMES, SOLVE RIDDLES, and DO ARITHMETIC in the same way as you would on a large digital computer." Measuring about a foot long and four inches high, it performed surprisingly sophisticated math despite its all-plastic construction. The packaging came with coding sheets and a manual explaining Digi-Comp's binary language, which could be programmed using "logic rods" positioned over the mechanical flip-floppers. Digi-Comp's flip-floppers were binary, able to be set in one of two positions. Because it contained three flip-floppers, Digi-Comp was technically a three-bit computer.

Users could program Digi-Comp by repositioning the logic rods along the flip-floppers using thin vertical wires. With cylindrical pegs, a user could control whether the logic rods moved in response to an input or were blocked. She then turned a separate control, called the "clock," which cycled the program in the same way your laptop's processor does—just at a tiny fraction of the speed.

The manual included many simple games and tasks Digi-Comp could perform. One program simulated a rocket launch from Cape Canaveral with a countdown timer and a preflight check of oxygen systems, ship controls, and radio systems. Another program simulated an elevator with a memory function allowing Digi-Comp to "remember" on which floor the elevator was presently sitting. One challenge tasked users with helping a bank manager recall the binary password to the vault, while another helped astronauts reenter Earth's atmosphere by correctly sequencing reentry procedures. Digi-Comp could even play a version of Nim, the ancient mathematical strategy game in which players take turns removing objects from three rows, with the loser taking the final object. Nim had been a favorite game for computer scientists to simulate on massive mainframes, but now kids could play it on their own personal computer at home.

Similar toys had long existed for other areas of technological advance. Erector Sets and Lionel trains introduced children to construction and the intricacies of railroads. Chemistry sets offered kids the chance to experiment as society was learning about "better living through chemistry," as the famous DuPont slogan went. Future physicists like Richard Feynman learned the properties of waves with crystal radio sets. But the beauty of Digi-Comp lay not just in the machine's simplicity, but in the great respect the makers had for young minds. Programming Digi-Comp required understanding binary, and children were challenged with learning this unintuitive language of ones and zeroes along with Boolean logic notations consisting of "true" and "false" statements. Digi-Comp's goal was not to idly amuse kids, but to engage them, to teach them, and to mold them into the scientific minds that would be necessary to change the world. "Everything you learn on Digi-Comp can be used on large electronic digital computers," the manual promised. Digi-Comp's simple binary language is the basis for how all computers then and now operate.

Digi-Comp also represented a great gender equalizer. Toys at the time, especially those geared toward math and the sciences, were highly gendered. Erector Sets and chemistry kits almost always featured young boys on the cover, while most toys marketed toward girls were dolls. One of the few intricate toys for girls was the Easy-Bake Oven—a first of many reminders of a woman's expected place in American society. Yet Digi-Comp's packaging featured a young boy and a young girl, both taking part in programming the machine.

In many ways, this reflected the reality of computing, for women were integral to the programming of computers from the very beginning. Admiral Grace Hopper headed many of the United States' computing initiatives and created COBOL, the programming language that became the engine of most business computing. In government and business, while men usually dominated the arenas of hardware design, women often did the painstaking work of designing, running, and debugging the programs that computers ran. Those who have seen the movie *Hidden Figures* will recognize the ways both men and women contributed to the computing revolution that transformed American society.

The Digi-Comp I was not able to send a man to the moon, but it did have the power, through play, to help children—boys and girls—master the new digital world with the flip of a few plastic switches.

SUMERIAN GAME

(1964)

During the Cold War, experts looked to computers to solve a teacher shortage and prepare students with the necessary skills to compete with the Soviet Union. Educators and computer scientists at IBM teamed up to create the first educational computer game, the *Sumerian Game*. Alexandra Johnson, daughter of cocreator Mabel Addis, donated these printouts to The Strong.

t might seem ironic that the progenitor for so many productivity-sapping simulation games—like *Sid Meier's Civilization* and *SimCity*—was born in the classroom.

The early 1960s was a time of convergence. After the launch of Sputnik in 1957, the United States and the Soviet Union were embroiled in a heated arms race to develop the newest, fastest, and smallest computerized technology. Computers, once the purview of science-fiction novels, were rapidly miniaturizing and now capable of guiding nuclear-tipped intercontinental ballistic missiles halfway around the world. Meanwhile, the previously sleepy field of mathematics vaulted from the theoretical to the very real. "We realize now that progress in technology depends on progress in theory," President John F. Kennedy told the National Academy of Sciences in 1963. "The most abstract investigations can lead to the most concrete results." Abstract ideas like game theory—the study of conflict and cooperation between rational decision-makers—suddenly became relevant with the advent of computerized modeling and the all-too-real possibility of nuclear war. The final addition to the puzzle was education. With the baby boom after World War II, more kids than ever were churning through the public school system. By the early 1960s, there simply were not enough teachers to go around. With a federal government laser-focused on science and technology, the hunt was on for a way to teach children the new age skills necessary to win the Cold War.

Enter the computer game: the unlikely intersection of technology, math, and education. The idea was that if teachers could not train the next American generals, statesmen, and scientists, then computers would have to. In 1962, IBM teamed up with the Boards of Coop-

erative Educational Services (BOCES) of Northern Westchester County, New York, to explore how computer simulation games could be used to educate students. Computer scientists and pioneering educators such as Mabel Addis collaborated to identify numerous possible topics, and after selecting ancient Mesopotamia, they created the *Sumerian Game*.

Using terminals in a BOCES center, students dialed in to a room-sized IBM 7090 mainframe computer. This was the same type of computer that engineers used to get astronauts into space. (Viewers of the movie *Hidden Figures* will remember that NASA employees struggled to squeeze it through the doorway.) The computer ran a program that consisted of fifteen thousand lines of code and let the students become king of Lagash, a city-state in ancient Sumer in the year 3,500 B.C. In 1965, after three years of development, twenty-six sixth-grade students from the Mohansic Elementary School in Yorktown Heights, New York, played the game for the first time.

The *Sumerian Game* presented students with an economic report of population, harvest, total farm land, and acres under cultivation. Players had to choose what to do during the spring and autumn growing seasons: *How many bushels of new grain should they place in storage? How much should they plant? How much should they feed their people?* Students then learned, based on their wise or foolish use of resources, whether their population had increased or decreased and if their harvest had grown. Wise rulers prospered. The goal was to teach students how to make rational choices that could affect the fates of millions while mastering the subject at their own pace with an individualized learning approach.

The *Sumerian Game* was not widely disseminated, as only a minute fraction of schools could afford to connect to the massive computers required to run the game. While the *Sumerian Game* may not have won the Cold War for America, its legacy lives on—notably in a variant strategy game *Hammurabi*, which was written around 1968 and cast players as the ancient Babylonian king Hammurabi, tasked with managing land resources and feeding citizens. The *Sumerian Game*, *Hammurabi*, and other early turn-based strategy games were forerunners to the educational game *The Oregon Trail* (page 33), which became ubiquitous in U.S. classrooms throughout the 1980s and '90s, as well as Sid Meier's wildly popular Civilization series.

It's hard to imagine today's graphically intensive real-time strategy games bearing any resemblance to the printouts from the *Sumerian Game*: frail, yellowing scrolls that now reside at The Strong museum and long ago weaved through bulky teletype terminals. They once belonged to teacher Mabel Addis, who helped develop the game. They are reminders that what the *Sumerian Game* lacked in mechanics it made up for with the same imagination that fueled twentieth-century America: that of building a society and caring for its people, of solving impossible problems, and above all else, of relentlessly pursuing the goal of progress.

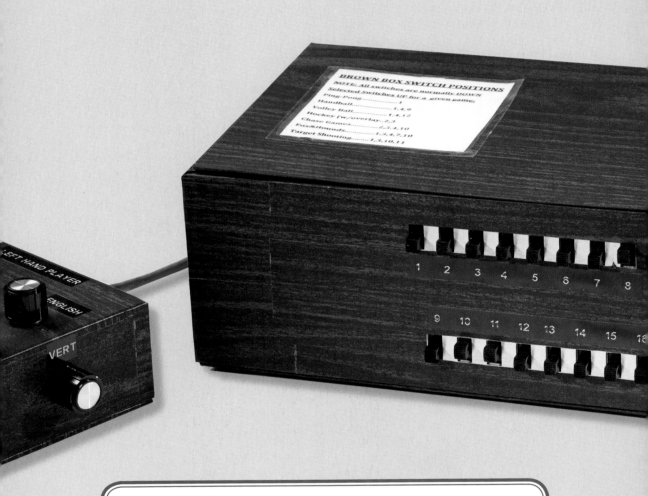

BROWN BOX SWITCH POSITIONS

NOTE: All switches are normally DOWN

Selected Switches UP for a given game:

Ping-Pong.................1
Handball..................1,4,9
Volley Ball...............1,4,12
Hockey (w/overlay..2,3
Chase Games...........2,3,4,10
Fox&Hounds.............1,3,4,7,10
Target Shooting........1,3,10,11

LEFT HAND PLAYER

ENGLISH

VERT

When Ralph Baer, the famed inventor and engineer, first developed a simple paddle game for television in the late 1960s, he had no idea how large the video game industry would grow. In 2010, he personally recreated his "Brown Box" prototype home video game for The Strong.

RALPH BAER'S
BROWN
BOX

(1967)

The console that paved the way for today's home video games was not born in the arcade or in some top-secret Defense Advanced Research Projects Agency (DARPA) laboratory. Rather, the very first home video game system was a simple brown box painstakingly assembled by a man named Ralph Baer.

Ralph Baer all his life had the ability to overcome obstacles. Born in Germany in 1922 to Jewish parents, he was thrown out of school by Nazis and forced to work menial jobs. While toiling at a shoe factory, he invented a machine that automated several tedious processes—an early sign of his ingenuity. Baer later taught himself English and managed to flee Germany with his family shortly before *Kristallnacht*, the Night of Broken Glass, when Nazi paramilitary forces smashed store windows and looted property owned by Jews in November 1938. The family made its way to New York, where the autodidactic Baer spent afternoons studying in the New York Public Library and taking electronics classes. After serving for two years in the army, he attended the American Institute of Technology in Chicago on the G.I. Bill and graduated with a degree in television engineering.

Baer quickly found work in the electronics industry in New York. In 1951, he was working at Loral Electronics, which was attempting to break into the emerging television market. (TVs were invented in the late 1920s and had steadily improved, but development was halted during World War II, when most manufacturers were supporting the war effort.) Baer was hard at work designing Loral's TV when he had an idea: What if TVs could offer a fun, interactive component in addition to their broadcast capabilities?

His bosses promptly said no, but Baer kept the idea in the back of his mind.

Televisions swiftly became a staple of American homes. While barely six thousand TVs were in use in 1946, nearly twelve million had been produced by 1951, and by 1955 half of all American homes had one. In 1966, Baer was the manager of the Equipment Design division at Sanders Associates, a defense industry contractor and the largest employer in New Hampshire. While at a bus station in New York City, his television game idea suddenly returned to him. He quickly jotted down some notes and rushed to his office. Now the head of his division, Baer finally had the clout to execute his idea. His department did not deal with televisions, but he was surrounded by brilliant engineers eager to learn new technologies. With the blessing of his supervisor and $2,500 of company money at his disposal, Baer tapped several technicians to experiment with interactive TV games. The operation eventually took over a secret former library space on the fifth floor of Sanders Associates Canal Street building in Nashua, New Hampshire—what Baer called his own personal "skunk works."

Baer's work proceeded slowly. At first the team was unable to engineer its device, which connected to a television via an input, to produce legible images on the screen. But by 1968, Baer and his team were able to display crisp points that could be moved with a controller. With this rudimentary interactivity, they designed simple games such as volleyball, ping-pong, handball, hockey, mazes, and soccer. They even built a "light gun," which allowed players to shoot targets on the screen—very sophisticated technology for the time and the precursor to Nintendo's famed *Duck Hunt* light gun introduced in 1984.

Due to technological limitations, Baer's console could only display three moveable dots on a black screen. For "graphics," players had to attach colored transparent plastic overlays to the screen, such as a tennis court or the outline of a maze.

Baer dubbed his invention the "Brown Box," named for the faux wood self-adhesive vinyl hastily applied to the box's siding to make it seem more appealing to investors. He presented the product to executives at Sanders Associates, who agreed that it could be very profitable. But as a defense contractor specializing in radar technology, Sanders had no idea how to market a consumer product—let alone launch an entirely new industry. Throughout 1969, Baer demonstrated the Brown Box to TV manufacturers including RCA, Sylvania, Motorola, and GE. While executives were impressed by the technology, they saw video games as a clever hack, not an industry that would one day be worth billions of dollars. Finally, in 1971, Magnavox agreed to license the Brown Box from Baer and Sanders Associates, releasing the Odyssey—the first-ever commercial home video game console—the following year. (For more information about the Magnavox Odyssey, see page 40.)

The Brown Box, which Baer put together with the help of assistants Bill Rusch and Bill Harrison, would launch an electronic-game industry that fifty years later had global sales of roughly $100 billion. Yet Baer continued to invent. In 1978, he created *Simon*, the famed Milton Bradley electronic memory game that became a pop culture phenomenon during the 1970s and '80s (page 103). His other game inventions include *Super Simon*, *Maniac*, and *Computer Perfection*. He was the recipient of the National Medal of Technology in 2006, and upon his death in 2014, Baer had acquired more than one hundred international patents.

Baer had a nose for how technology could be applied in new ways. His mind worked continuously, churning out ideas from home video games to talking doormats to his pioneering use of digitized faces in the arcade game *Journey*. Baer never lost the engineer's delight in taking machines apart and using the pieces to build entirely new ones. Many engineers endlessly tinker with new technologies, but Baer was practical and knew that a product should be profitable, even if that meant using a cheaper, two-generation-old chip instead of the latest one. In his later years, he donated many of his papers to The Strong and visited numerous times, delighting in the opportunity to beat staff members at a game of tennis played on a copy of the Brown Box he gave to the museum. Baer stayed sharp to the end. Even when his body was failing him, he continued to invent, build new toys, and study the latest tech.

So how could a self-taught refugee turned defense-industry contractor launch a multibillion-dollar industry with zero experience in electronic games? "A piece of Jewish chutzpah," Baer liked to say. "I just did it."

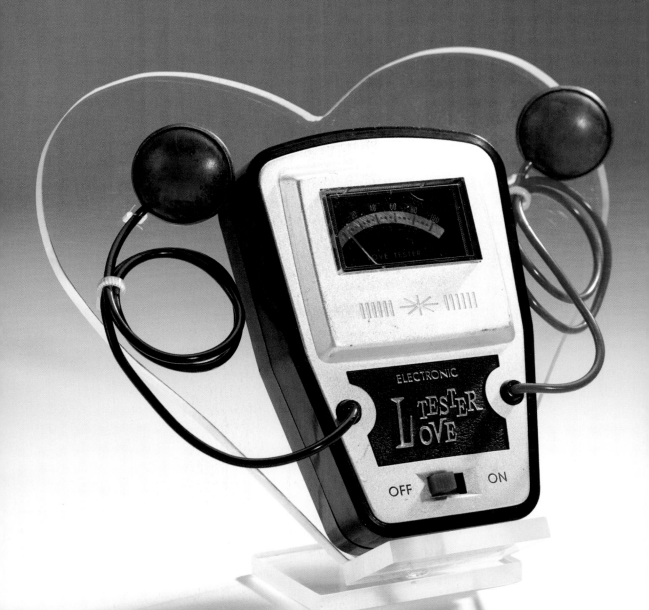

NINTENDO LOVE TESTER

(1969)

Long before Nintendo designer Gunpei Yokoi created the Game Boy, he crafted this playful way for young lovers to quantify their romantic compatibility.

n a small, dark side street in Kyoto, Japan, near several yakuza strongholds, is a modest three-story stone structure with an engraved plaque: "The Nintendo Playing Card Co." The building, constructed in 1933, is often referred to as Nintendo's first headquarters. In fact, the company first set up shop almost half a century before in an adjacent two-story building, now the site of a parking lot. Nintendo today is one of the most successful video game companies of all time with blockbuster franchises such as Super Mario Bros. and The Legend of Zelda, but the company traces its roots back long before the advent of electronic games.

In a sense, Nintendo's story begins all the way back in 1633, when Japan, fearing that its culture was being overrun by Europeans, closed off all contact with the West. Almost immediately the government banned playing cards, many of which originated in Portugal and were popular among gamblers. Japan continued to crack down on gambling over the next two centuries, but in 1886 it sanctioned *Hanafuda*, or "flower cards." To deter gambling, *Hanafuda* were marketed as word-association games and lacked the numbers typical playing cards had; they were instead decorated with pictures of animals and flowers. However, inventive players almost immediately developed ways to associate points with image combinations, and *Hanafuda* soon became synonymous with gambling.

Three years after the Japanese government officially sanctioned *Hanafuda*, a young entrepreneur named Fusajiro Yamauchi founded the Kyoto-based Nintendo Playing Card Co. By then, *Hanafuda* was a popular pastime for New Year's festivities, although the cards' success was largely driven by illicit gambling rings—and, by extension, the preeminent Japanese organized

crime syndicate, the yakuza. (The name *yakuza*, in fact, originally meant "useless individuals," derived from the worst possible hand in a version of *Hanafuda* called *Oicho-Kabu*.) While the origin of the name *Nintendo* is unclear, some point out that *nin* derives from *ninkyodo*, meaning "chivalrous way"—a tenet to which yakuza members of the time believed themselves to adhere.

As demand for *Hanafuda* grew, Yamauchi hired assistants and rapidly expanded his business. Playing cards remained the core of Nintendo's business throughout the early twentieth century. After World War II decimated the Japanese economy, Nintendo—now run by Yamauchi's grandson, Hiroshi Yamauchi—scraped together business by supplying the occupying American troops with playing cards. As the company sought a modern identity, it experimented with other ventures such as soups, pens, building blocks, taxis, bowling alleys, skeet shooting, instant rice, a TV network, and primitive photocopiers. The company managed to stay afloat by securing the rights to Disney playing cards, and in stark contrast to Nintendo's family-friendly image of today, the company dabbled in adult-oriented cards featuring Marilyn Monroe and other models.

In 1966, Nintendo ventured into the toy industry with plastic extendable tongs known as the Ultra Hand, designed by the assembly-line engineer Gunpei Yokoi during his free time. Surprisingly, the Ultra Hand sold more than one million units, helping Nintendo stave off financial ruin. Eyeing an opportunity in the toy market, Nintendo executives plucked Yokoi from the maintenance team and set him up designing novelties such as Rubik's Cube–like puzzles, a miniature remote-controlled vacuum cleaner, a baseball-throwing machine, and a "Love Tester."

Released in 1969 for "young ladies and men," Nintendo's Love Tester was an electromechanical device that claimed to quantify how much two people loved each other. To compute their love, two users held hands while separately grasping metal sensors. Measuring heart rates—or as Nintendo called it, the "love quotient"—the Love Tester spit out a score between one and one hundred. The gadget was a big seller for Nintendo and was one of the few products to be marketed and sold outside of Japan. In the slightly more jaundiced Western market, Nintendo sold the Love Tester as the "Lie/Love Detector," able to measure the "strength of love ability" while pulling double duty as a lie detector.

Hanafuda and the Love Tester may not have a direct connection to today's video games, but they illustrate the meandering, bizarre paths play companies traveled before the advent of electronic games. Sega, for instance, began life as a slot-machine manufacturer in Hawaii, while the arcade-game maker Namco initially operated kiddie rides on the roof of a department store in the city of Yokohama, Japan. After nearly a century of experimenting, Nintendo finally dis-covered its niche with electronic games in the 1970s and would eventually strike gold with the coin-operated arcade game *Donkey Kong* in 1981 (page 141) and its famous NES console in 1985 (page 182). But Nintendo never forgot its roots, and to this day it faithfully prints the same *Hanafuda* cards on which the play company originally built its empire. Throughout its many iterations, Nintendo has never been afraid to take risks, from playing cards to love testers. Epitomizing this adaptability, Gunpei Yokoi, who created the Love Tester, would later create Nintendo's Game & Watch handheld LCD games, the directional pad for NES consoles, the Game Boy, and even produced critically acclaimed game series including Metroid and Kid Icarus.

Through all of its products, from the wildly successful to the disastrous, Nintendo has remained a play company at heart. "The Love Tester came from me wondering if I could somehow use this to get girls to hold my hand," Yokoi admitted not long before his death in 1997. "I wound up holding hands with quite a few girls thanks to it."

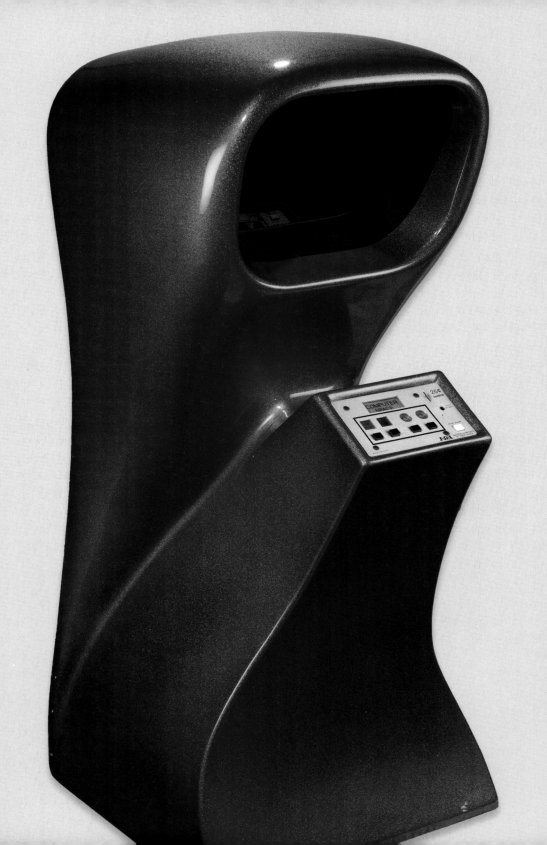

COMPUTER SPACE

(1971)

Nolan Bushnell, the cofounder of Atari, launched his video game career with *Computer Space*, the first arcade video game. Despite the futuristic styling, many consumers found it confusing and difficult to play, but it paved the way for successors such as *Pong*.

When you think of arcade games, you likely conjure images of classic video games like *Pac-Man*, *Space Invaders*, and *Defender*. Yet arcades existed long before the advent of electronic games. Arcade games were largely electromechanical and coin-operated—some could tell your fortune or divine your love interests, some cleverly used lights and music to simulate a battle, while others used rear-image projection to produce moving animations on a screen. So-called penny arcades, which housed these early video game ancestors along with staples like pinball, were ubiquitous in American culture throughout the twentieth century. Then, in 1971, along came *Computer Space*—the first mass-produced video game—and the DNA of arcade games was forever changed.

The story begins in 1964, when a student at the University of Utah named Nolan Bushnell came across *Spacewar!*, the brainchild of MIT engineers. *Spacewar!* was a rudimentary video game consisting of two spaceships engaging in a dogfight in outer space, both controlled by human players. Based on Newtonian physics, the game was extremely sophisticated for its time, but playable only on $20,000 vector displays and $120,000 DEC PDP-1 mainframe computers—more than $1 million in today's dollars. *Spacewar!* was therefore only accessible to computer hackers at well-endowed universities. When Bushnell sat in front of the monitor and navigated his spaceship around space, blasting torpedoes at his enemy while avoiding the gravity well of a star, he formed the kernel of an idea.

Bushnell, a game lover at heart, worked summers as a manager at the Lagoon Amusement Park in Farmington, Utah, overseeing the coin-operated games. He enjoyed the shooting galleries, pinball machines, and other crude electromechanical amusements, but understood the awesome immersive potential of computer games. What if *Spacewar!* could one day be played by ordinary people at an arcade? Instead of paying millions of dollars for a mainframe computer, people could merely deposit a quarter to experience the thrill of intergalactic combat.

Bushnell knew computers were still too expensive and too large, so he filed away the idea. In 1968, he moved to California to begin work at Ampex, a leading audio/video recording company. Sitting across from Bushnell was thirty-one-year-old Ted Dabney, and the two immediately bonded over their love of board games. Bushnell eventually brought his friend to see *Spacewar!*. Dabney was unimpressed by the clunky interface, but understood his friend's vision for a coin-operated video game. Much had changed in only a few short years: The company Data General had just released a $4,000 minicomputer called the Nova that could fit inside a cabinet. Consumer-level video games were tantalizingly within reach.

Of course, $4,000 was still an enormous sum of money for two lowly engineers, and Bushnell discovered that the Nova lacked the computing power for a playable video game. Dejected, he and Dabney gave up hope. But then a curious thing happened three months later, when Bushnell was watching television. TVs of the day had to be routinely synced with analog signals or else the image would scroll off the screen, reappearing at the top or bottom. Viewers had to frequently adjust a vertical "hold" knob to sync the signal and keep the image steady. Bushnell realized that this interaction could be the basis for an electronic video game.

Dabney managed to cobble together a rudimentary circuit board that allowed users to move a virtual object around a television screen with buttons. This simple interface could form the basis of a combat game like *Spacewar!*. With a workable idea, the duo needed money, and they needed a manufacturer. When Bushnell mentioned this predicament to—of all people—his dentist, he remarked that one of his patients worked for Nutting Associates, a local arcade game company. Bushnell immediately called this person up to discuss his idea. Nutting was not in good shape; its meager business was almost entirely dependent on an old computerized quiz game. Desperate for a new source of revenue, the fledgling company agreed to license Bushnell and Dabney's technology and hire them as employees.

They developed a coin mechanism, a power supply, a control panel, and a rudimentary sound system, then assembled a wooden cabinet to house it all. The hardest element was figuring out how to rotate the player's ship on the screen, a problem Bushnell eventually solved using simple circuit-board diodes arranged to represent the actual shape they formed on the screen. Bushnell and Dabney presented their finished product to Nutting in 1971. The game was incredibly crude by today's standards, but was a marvel of ingenuity for the time. A player controlled a rocket as it attempted to fire at flying saucers, all while thrusting and rotating to avoid enemy fire. The ship was controlled with four buttons: one for firing, one for thrusting, and two for rotating left and right. Bushnell dubbed the game *Computer Space*.

Taking design cues from the bridge control panels of *Star Trek*'s starship *Enterprise*, the company designed a zany cabinet for *Computer Space* that looked nothing like the square pinball cases and electromechanical arcade games that were staples of arcades. Boasting sleek, curvy, futuristic, brightly colored fiberglass, *Computer Space* looked like a control panel from an alien ship. With a nation still enamored by the Apollo moon missions, *Computer Space* invited players to enter their own virtual spacecraft and wage war in the heavens.

Despite the giant technological leaps made, *Computer Space* was a commercial disappointment. The game's cabinet was so exotic that it looked out of place in bowling alleys, bars, and arcades; the ship controls were difficult to master, while gameplay was frustrating and tedious. The missiles moved painfully slowly and players had to wait until one connected or left the screen before firing another. Nutting managed to sell around a thousand units, but it was not the blockbuster phenomenon Bushnell and Dabney had hoped for. With its wacky exterior and complex controls, *Computer Space* was too far ahead of its time, appealing more to university students familiar with *Spacewar!* than working-class barflies. But Bushnell and Dabney already had bigger and better plans. With their earnings from *Computer Space*, the duo would found Atari the following year. Their first product, *Pong* (page 49), would change the gaming world forever.

Despite its flaws, *Computer Space* kick-started a movement that would transform the pinball arcade into a video game arcade. It established the blueprint for all future arcade video games: a large cabinet complete with speakers and a control panel enclosing the circuit boards and monitor. As the archetype of the video arcade game industry, *Computer Space* holds a unique place in the history of electronic games.

THE OREGON TRAIL

(1971)

Generations of American social studies students have learned about Westward expansion through a timeless game called *The Oregon Trail*. First created for middle-school students in 1971, it was later ported to the Apple II and other personal computers. The pioneering game entered the World Video Game Hall of Fame in 2016.

YOU HAVE DIED OF DYSENTERY. This catchphrase emblazoned on a neon-green image of an ox-pulled wagon has lived a second life as one of the all-time great internet memes. People of a certain generation, of course, instantly associate that crude 8-bit image with their middle-school computer lab, and specifically the game *The Oregon Trail.*

If one sign of a great game is staying power, then *The Oregon Trail* has reigned for over forty years, long outliving the computer platforms on which it was originally introduced. Those who went to school during the 1980s and '90s will likely remember the mechanics of *The Oregon Trail,* an educational game designed to teach students about nineteenth-century life on the 2,170-mile Oregon Trail, which connected the Missouri River to the Oregon valleys. Passing through the Plains states of Nebraska and Kansas, the Platte River valley, the treacherous Rocky Mountains, and the lush farmlands of Northern California and Oregon, the trail was a literal and figurative cross-section of America itself. By the 1860s, the trail had guided approximately four hundred thousand settlers, farmers, ranchers, miners, and adventure-seekers to new lands of opportunity.

Fast-forward a century to 1971. One day at Carleton College, a tiny liberal arts school in Northfield, Minnesota, student-teacher Don Rawitsch asked his fellow seniors Paul Dillenberger and Bill Heinemann, "Can't we do something with the computer in my history class?" The "computer" Rawitsch mentioned was a very crude one by modern standards: a teletype machine with no monitor, hooked up to a mainframe computer via phone line. Nevertheless, the three friends realized that a simple text-based game could still teach students about the Oregon Trail.

"Instead of shaking dice to determine how far you went," Heinemann recalled, "the program could take into consideration how much you spent on your oxen and your wagon and how much of a load you were carrying."

The gameplay was quite primitive. Students dialed in their instructions on the electromechanical typewriters. Players hunted by furiously typing "BANG," "POW," or "WHAM." If they typed fast enough and did not misspell any words, the computer spit out a response onto a ream of paper—"Full bellies tonight"—and players were rewarded with food for their travel party. They were also required to manage their resources—food, bullets, clothing, and cash—as they made their way westward, occasionally having to drive off bandits, fix broken wagons, find lost children, or hunker down during inclement weather. When party members died, players were helpfully asked: "Do you want a fancy funeral?" and "Do you want a minister?" In the early versions of the game, no one actually died of dysentery, but they did die of pneumonia, injuries, snake bites, and gun shot. It was hard migrating across country.

The game was a hit with students, who learned team-building skills. The best typists sat in front of the computer, while other members monitored supplies and navigated along with a map. But like other early text-based computer games, such as the *Sumerian Game* (page 17), *The Oregon Trail* was limited by the massive mainframe computers required to run it; most schools simply lacked the space and money to house them or even to connect to them. The game might have been abandoned after Rawitsch, Dillenberger, and Heinemann finished their student teaching, but Rawitsch kept a physical copy of the code. In 1974, he went to work for the Minnesota Educational Computing Consortium (MECC), the first state-funded organization to provide widespread access to games and other computer software for educational purposes. During Thanksgiving 1974, Rawitsch painstakingly transcribed eight hundred lines of codes onto MECC computers. Suddenly, *The Oregon Trail* was available on a MECC mainframe that schools across the state could access with teletype machines.

By the late 1970s, computers were miniaturizing at a rapid pace. In 1978, a year after Steve Wozniak and Steve Jobs developed the Apple II, representatives of MECC saw the computer and recognized that its relative affordability, surprising power, and appealing color graphics made it a perfect fit for the classroom. MECC placed a large order for the computers and continued to increase that order by thousands every year until MECC became the largest seller of Apple computers, providing the fledgling computer-maker a crucial stake in the educational-computing market. (This relationship was so important that Apple cofounder Steve Jobs himself flew to Minnesota to deliver the keynote address at a 1982 MECC conference.)

In 1979, MECC ported *The Oregon Trail* to the Apple II. Programmers created a crude graphical interface that allowed players to hunt by shooting at graphics of deer, bison, and rabbits "dashing" across the screen. The game grew enormously popular as schools across the country purchased Apple II computers. By 1983, MECC was making so much money with *The Oregon Trail* and several hundred other educational games that Minnesota turned it into a for-profit company. In 1994, MECC went public, raising $22 million. By that point, *The Oregon Trail* powerhouse comprised nearly one-third of MECC's $30 million annual revenue. Over the years, programmers at MECC refined and enhanced *The Oregon Trail* with new animations and mini-games to take advantage of improvements in computer processing speed, graphics, and sound. These changes kept the game fresh for players who still loved the basic challenge of helping nineteenth-century pioneers make it safely across the country.

The Oregon Trail succeeded because it was simple, yet challenging, and endured because MECC invested the resources to keep it updated and fresh. Students throughout the 1980s, 1990s, and 2000s all played different versions of the game but came away with the same interactive history of America. For the majority of children who didn't have home computers, *The Oregon Trail* was often not only the first computer game they played, but also their first introduction to computers. Most important, for the first time, people could develop a bond with this strange box full of wires. When little Joey died of dysentery, it meant something. When the cart overturned while fording the river, it was devastating. Like no other game before it, *The Oregon Trail* transported players to an entirely new world, if only for third-period history class.

Today, there are many other historical simulations and many more opportunities for teachers to use games in the classroom. But nearly a half-century after its creation, *The Oregon Trail* still stands out as one of the most effective simulation games ever made. When children stock their supplies, load up their wagon, and head west, they begin to understand the challenges of western migration, build valuable decision-making skills, and have fun. And hopefully no one dies of dysentery along the way.

Rolling Stone reported on how hippies, rock-n-rollers, and radicals of all stripes were reshaping America in the 1960s and 1970s. The magazine recognized the countercultural impact of the computer in this article on the first "Space War Olympics."

"SPACEWAR:
FANATIC LIFE AND SYMBOLIC DEATH AMONG THE COMPUTER BUMS"
IN *ROLLING STONE*

(1972)

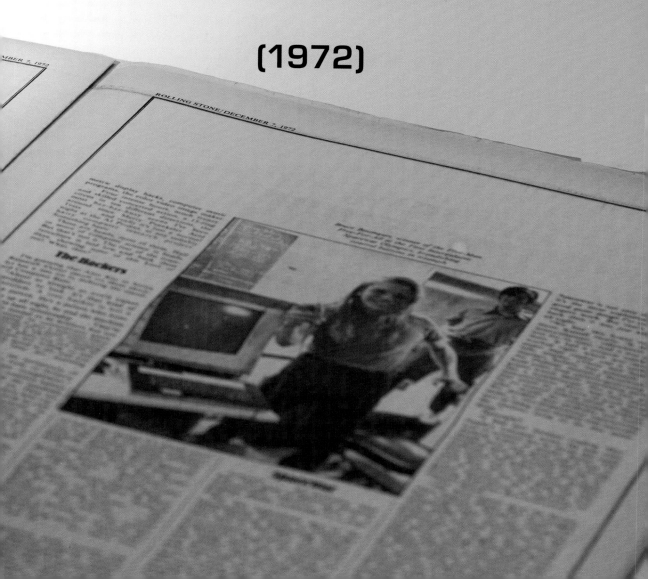

Since 2011, the Valve Corporation has hosted a contest called The International, and starting in 2014, it has been held at the seventeen-thousand-seat KeyArena in Seattle, Washington, the former home of the SuperSonics NBA franchise. The International is not a sporting event, however—at least not in the traditional sense. Rather, it is an *eSports* event in which teams of gamers wage battle in the video game *Dota 2*. Released by Valve in 2013, *Dota 2* is a stand-alone sequel to the popular *Warcraft III* mod *Defense of the Ancients*. In 2016, the winner of The International—a China-based team called Wings Gaming—took home more than $9 million, while the total prize pool clocked in at more than $20 million. All told, the global eSports industry generated nearly $500 million in 2016 and counts hundreds of millions of fans who collectively watched more than six billion hours of professional gaming—and the industry continues to enjoy double-digit growth each year.

Nearly half a century ago, however, few people had heard of video games, and no one watched gaming tournaments. The most affordable computers still cost hundreds of thousands, if not millions, of dollars, and most were room-sized and operated by major research institutions. Computer code was cold, clinical, and nearly impossible to decipher without at least one advanced degree.

In 1962, at the Massachusetts Institute of Technology, computer scientist Steve "Slug" Russell wrote *Spacewar!* for the newly developed PDP-1 computer. *Spacewar!* was not a top-secret Cold War plan to wage galactic battle against the Russians, but a video game—one of the first ever. The game featured two spaceships—a "needle" and a "wedge"—engaging in a dogfight while avoiding the gravitational pull of a star. Following the laws of Newtonian physics, *Spacewar!* was quite sophisticated, even allowing players to harness principles such as gravity assist to gain a speed advantage on their opponent. Using torpedoes, two players fought until one was destroyed. *Spacewar!* became extremely popular on university campuses throughout the 1960s and was the inspiration for later commercial video games such as *Computer Space* (page 29) and *Asteroids* (page 121). As his game grew more popular, Russell realized the commercial potential for video games, likening them to "the most advanced, imaginative, expensive pinball machine the world has seen."

By 1972, when Stewart Brand decided to stage a *Spacewar!* competition, the game had been around for roughly a decade. Brand was the editor of the *Whole Earth Catalog*, an American counterculture magazine and product catalog that revered self-sufficiency and ecology. He was well in-tune with the iconoclastic spirit pervading the Bay Area—and for many, that meant computers. "I discovered that drugs were less interesting than computers as a way to expand your consciousness," he told *Rolling Stone* in 2016. Although he could scarcely operate a computer himself, Brand was enamored with the ability of these machines to create alternative worlds.

While touring college campuses in the 1960s, he routinely came across the same phenomenon: *Spacewar!*. Young engineering students would cluster around multimillion-dollar PDP-1 computers, blasting one another with missiles and hosting small tournaments. Brand was also fascinated by how the students, in the same do-it-yourself mentality with which he infused the *Whole Earth Catalog*, were designing their own mods to the game, such as cloaking devices and a hyperspace feature (later borrowed by Atari for *Asteroids*).

In 1972, the Stanford University artificial-intelligence lab had just upgraded to the cutting-edge PDP-10 computer, and engineers immediately churned out an amped-up version of *Spacewar!* with improved graphics and new features such as mines and an ability for five players to battle simultaneously. When Brand visited Stanford, his alma mater, he had just been hired by *Rolling Stone* to write a story about the burgeoning computer community. Suddenly, Brand had an idea: What if the article could revolve around a *Spacewar!* tournament? He could think of no better way to introduce the masses to hacker culture than with the ultimate hacker game itself.

Brand convinced the lab's executive officer, Les Earnest, to close it down for one evening for the First Intergalactic *Spacewar!* Olympics, where the best *Spacewar!* players would wage battle in front of an audience feasting on pizza and beer. On the night of the tournament, Brand arrived with *Rolling Stone*'s soon-to-be-famous photographer, Annie Leibovitz, who snapped away at the latest computer tech that for years had remained hidden in the bowels of Stanford's AI lab, including robotic arms and prototype digital cameras.

Brand explained the action to readers unfamiliar with the game: "Five different space ships, each with a dot indicating torpedo tubes are loaded, five scores, each at zero, a convincing starfield, and four space mines orbiting around a central sun, toward which the spaceships are starting to fall at a correctly accelerating rate." He described the competitors' ships as "twisting, converging, evading, exploding," while transcripts of his tape recorder depict some of the first-ever gamer coordination and trash talk:

Good work, Tovar.
Revenge. Clickclick clickclick
Cease fire. Clickclickclick.
Ohhhhhh NO! You killed me, Tovar.
I'm sorry. Clickclickclick
Being partners means never having to say you're sorry. Clickclickclick
Get him! Get the mother!
Clickclick-clickclickclick
Awshit. Get tough now.

The spoils of war were not quite as lucrative as Valve's *Dota 2* tournament. Instead of $9 million, the First Intergalactic *Spacewar!* Olympics awarded the eventual winner—a computer engineer named Bruce Baumgart—a free subscription to *Rolling Stone* and a few leftover slices of pizza.

"Spacewar: Fanatic Life and Symbolic Death Among the Computer Bums" by Stewart Brand was published in the December 1972 issue of *Rolling Stone*, the flagship publication of American youth. Brand's article on *Spacewar!* was punctuated with advertisements for *The Connoisseur's Handbook of Marijuana* and *The Art of Erotic Massage*. While the public associated computers with slide rule–wielding engineers involved in the moon landings and secret Defense Department programs, Brand described an anarchic, free-wheeling gamer culture that presaged American youth's impending love affair with video games and the embrace of the computer as the ultimate toy. Just one month earlier, Atari had released *Pong*, soon to take the country by storm and spark a revolution in play. In many ways, Brand's article was the opening salvo for that movement, which would forever shape American culture.

"Ready or not," the article began, "computers are coming to the people."

MAGNAVOX
ODYSSEY

(1972)

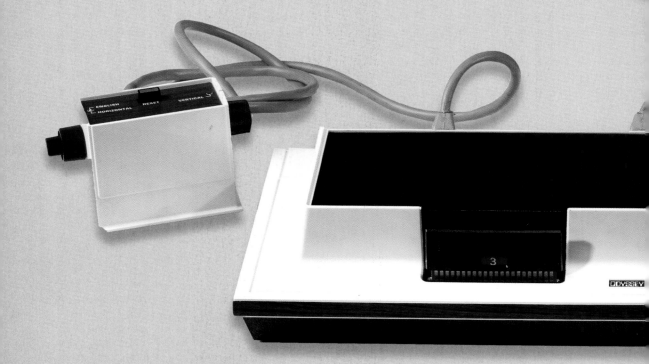

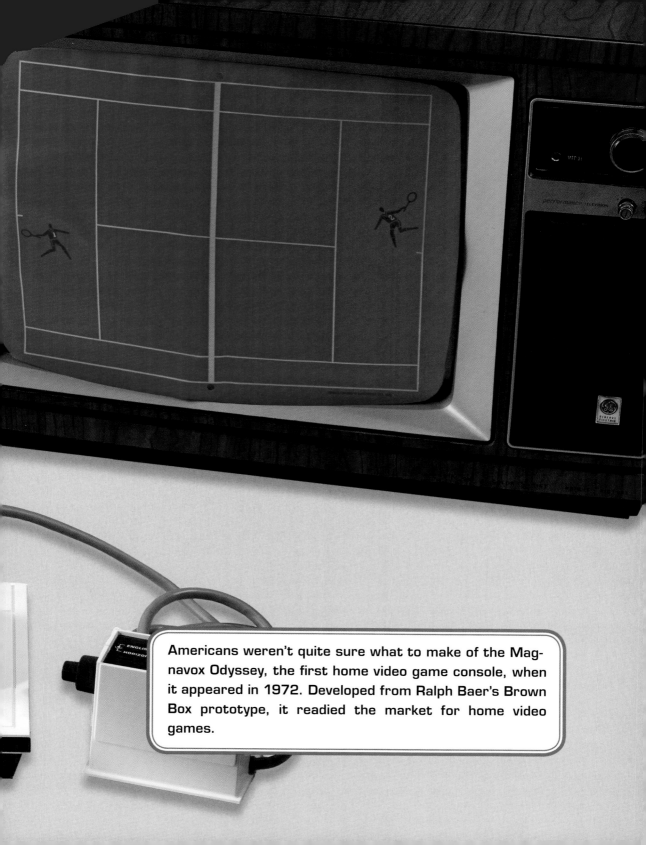

Americans weren't quite sure what to make of the Magnavox Odyssey, the first home video game console, when it appeared in 1972. Developed from Ralph Baer's Brown Box prototype, it readied the market for home video games.

Can you name the first home video game console?

Most people would guess the Atari 2600 (page 86). While it was the first wildly successful console, it was not the first. In fact, the first home console came five years before, and it was produced by the television manufacturer Magnavox.

The story of the Odyssey begins not in some top-secret Magnavox laboratory, but in Nashua, New Hampshire, at the headquarters of a defense contractor called Sanders Associates. Throughout the late 1960s, engineer Ralph Baer and his team toiled away in a converted library room to produce the Brown Box—a prototype game system named for its faux wooden vinyl siding. The finished product was rudimentary but revolutionary: It allowed two players to control dots on a TV screen using controllers. There were limited graphics and no sound, but plastic overlays could be attached to the screen to provide visual context. (For more about Ralph Baer and the Brown Box, see page 21.)

Sanders Associates had zero experience selling consumer electronics, let alone video games, so they decided to license Baer's Brown Box to a TV manufacturer. While executives from RCA, Magnavox, Sylvania, Motorola, and GE were impressed with the technology, they couldn't possibly imagine video games becoming a billion-dollar industry. Yet Baer did not give up, tirelessly traveling the country to showcase the Brown Box. Baer finally caught a break when an executive named Bill Enders left RCA to become a marketing vice president at Magnavox. Enders had witnessed one of Baer's demonstrations while at RCA and was blown away, but he couldn't convince his boss to license the product. Once at Magnavox, he asked the marketing team to take a second look at the console they had already rejected.

In 1970, Baer and his colleague Lou Etlinger flew to Magnavox's headquarters in Fort Wayne, Indiana. Baer attached the Brown Box to a nineteen-inch TV and showcased various games, including ping-pong and the light gun. Baer later said that none of the executives besides Enders were impressed with the device except for one: Gerry Martin, a vice president for television marketing. Martin understood that while the Brown Box was crude, it represented a huge opportunity for television sets. It took nearly a year for Martin to persuade his bosses to license the technology, but the deal was inked in March 1971.

Magnavox then had to decide how to adapt the Brown Box for mass production. Color TVs were increasingly common during the early 1970s, yet Magnavox decided to keep the console monochromatic to save money. The original Brown Box also had sixteen switches that had to be set in a specific sequence for each game; this modified the internal circuitry of the Brown Box, allowing the console to display different components and react differently to controller input. Magnavox removed the switches and opted for a simplified system of removable "game cards." Unlike later game cartridges that contained game data, game cards were merely composed of printed circuit boards. Many games used the same cards but simply required different overlays.

While testing the console, Magnavox dubbed its console the "Skill-O-Vision," which was later changed to "Odyssey." The finished Odyssey was a trapezoidal, black-and-white colored box powered by six C-cell batteries, while an included RF switchbox enabled players to connect the console to their TV. The two rectangular controllers contained knobs used to control dots on the screen.

Magnavox also sold a light gun accessory, usable with the game "Shooting Gallery," allowing players to shoot moving targets. (Very much resembling an actual rifle, many today might consider Magnavox's light gun in poor taste, unlike the decidedly more family-friendly shooter built by Nintendo for *Duck Hunt*.)

Though revolutionary at the time, the Odyssey required a significant amount of imagination to play. There was no sound, and games relied on the use of plastic overlays that clung to the TV screen with static electricity, transforming the display into a football field, a casino, a tennis court, or even a haunted house. Because gameplay was limited to moving three dots on the screen, players had to keep score themselves, and in some cases, set their own rules. The system even came packaged with scorecards, dice, poker chips, and other physical props to supplement the limited graphics.

Magnavox released the Odyssey in September 1972. It performed modestly, selling nearly one hundred thousand units in its first year despite initially only being available in Magnavox boutiques, a decision made to entice consumers into buying Magnavox TVs. Baer later complained that Magnavox's advertising misled people into believing they had to purchase Magnavox televisions in order to run the Odyssey, a claim backed up by some anecdotal reports about salesmen insisting customers purchase a TV along with the console.

But the Odyssey mainly suffered from an intrinsic problem: people did not understand what video games were. Some had experience playing the first-ever video arcade game, *Computer Space* (page 29), but the public largely did not comprehend the concept of electronic games, let alone one they could play on their TV. Shortly before the Odyssey was released, Magnavox set up a promotional segment on *What's My Line?*, a popular gameshow in which celebrity panelists questioned a contestant in order to determine his or her occupation. When the Magnavox representative played the Odyssey on the show and described to the panel what he was doing, the panelists were stumped; they could not fathom the idea of playing interactive electronic games. By Christmas 1972, Magnavox had produced 130,000 units and 20,000 light guns. All told, the Odyssey sold approximately 350,000 units by the time it was discontinued in 1975.

Due to technical limitations, the Odyssey was not a great system. But it was the first, and it showcased the potential of home video games. In some ways, the Odyssey was a victim of its release date—*Pong*, which helped establish the arcade video game market in 1972 (page 49), was launched two months after the Odyssey. Despite limited sales, Magnavox's creation was a pioneering device that brought video games to homes at a time when most people did not understand what video games were.

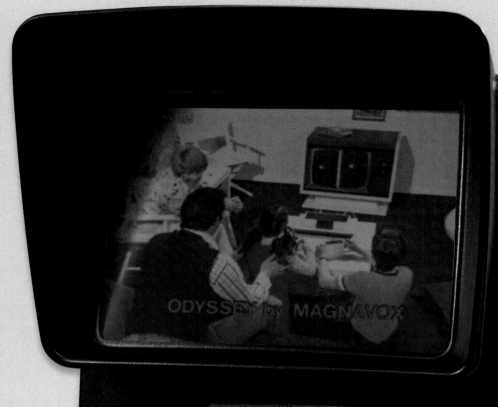
ODYSSEY by MAGNAVOX

United Visuals
CORPORATION

magnavox
mini theater

MAGNAVOX
MINI
THEATER

(1972)

The idea of playing games on a television, not simply watching them, surprised American consumers. Magnavox created marketing films and display kiosks to familiarize people with the idea.

How do you sell a product to a public that has no idea what your product does?

Car salesmen might struggle to explain to customers why they need automatic moisture-sensing windshield wipers, proximity warning systems, and anti-rust undercoating, but they don't need to explain why their customers need a car. Likewise, electronics salesmen can pitch smart TVs and high-fidelity sound systems without having to explain what a television set is. But what about when the product is entirely new? The late Apple CEO Steve Jobs famously quipped that "People don't know what they want until you show it to them." In other words, with good marketing and salesmanship, you can sell anything to anyone.

Magnavox was bullish on the future of video games, but how could it sell its Odyssey console (see page 41)? For one, consumers would have to experience the product up close. Select Magnavox boutiques soon featured a Magnavox Mini Theater—a kiosk with a small projector spooled up with an 8mm promotional film about the Odyssey. Rather than teach every Magnavox salesman how to pitch the Odyssey, the Magnavox marketing department relied on the five-minute film to describe what video games were, what the Odyssey could do, and how simple it was to hook up.

"Families who are content to let television do its thing often find themselves at its mercy for a choice of entertainment," the film's narrator began, "while people who want television to do their thing entertain themselves with Odyssey." Acutely aware that pinball and other coin-operated games were seen by many parents as unwholesome distractions played in dark, unsavory arcades and bars, Magnavox deliberately positioned the Odyssey as a safe, at-home product that a family could enjoy together. The film peered through a snow-covered window at a smiling, white, middle-class family in the safety and comfort of the most important space of the post-World War II home: the family room. Mother, father, and children gathered not around a fireplace, but instead in front of the new electronic hearth of television and a home video game console. The film showcased numerous kid-friendly and educational games including "Simon Says," "Cat and Mouse," and a geography game titled "States," as well as adult-oriented ones such as "Shooting Gallery" (which used the specialty light gun) and "Roulette." The subtext of the film was clear: video games are to become part of our domestic space—wholesome, educational, and entertaining for the entire family.

The Magnavox Mini Theater borrowed a concept that had long been a feature of retail stores. Before the 1880s, few businesses arranged products or store spaces to appeal to shoppers. By the early twentieth century, however, following the lead of Philadelphia merchant John Wannamaker and other merchandising pioneers, retailers of all stripes redecorated their stores using glass cases, mirrors, color schemes, specialty lighting, interior displays, and show windows to entice customers to stop in, even if they weren't planning on buying anything. Not surprisingly, visuals played an important role in selling home video games from the beginning.

As video games took hold in American culture, companies needed to do less explaining and more *showing*. In the late 1980s, Nintendo expanded the untapped potential of video game visual merchandising displays with "The World of

Nintendo," a store-within-a-store that promoted the Nintendo product line with logo signage, banners, software and hardware displays, and game demonstration modules. As a 1988 Nintendo Merchandising Program pamphlet claimed, "It's a cosmic fact: 70% of all retail sales result from in-store decisions based on a product's visual appeal."

Whether or not that is a "cosmic fact," merchandising displays became important sites for first introducing and then selling video games to the public. While sales of the Magnavox Odyssey were modest, the Mini Theater became a kind of template for how video games were sold to Americans in retail stores. Today, consumers can still play the latest home game consoles on demonstration units in merchandising displays at many retail and toy stores, although if recent reports are any indication, retail brick-and-mortar stores may one day go the way of the Magnavox Odyssey.

With consumers increasingly choosing online giants like Amazon.com over malls and other physical locations, the Mini Theater is not just a window into how Americans once bought video games, but how they bought everything.

PONG

PONG

(1972)

"Avoid missing ball for high score." These simple instructions go far to explain why Atari's *Pong* was so universally intuitive, such a commercial success, and a member of the inaugural class of the World Video Game Hall of Fame.

What makes a successful video game?

Game designers have been agonizing over this question for decades. Does it need cutting-edge graphics to wow players into a fantastic virtual world? Does it need simple controls? A good story? To Nolan Bushnell, the answer was simple: "All the best games are easy to learn and difficult to master. They should reward the first quarter and the hundredth."

Bushnell's first venture with video games taught him the truth of this maxim. His creation in 1971 of the world's first mass-produced video game—*Computer Space* (page 29)—was a marvel of ingenuity, but it was deeply flawed: Players controlled their ship with four buttons—one to thrust, one to fire, and two for rotating left and right—which made gameplay laborious. If the mark of a good game is to be easy to learn and difficult to master, then the game failed on both accounts. But *Computer Space* is also seen as a successful failure, one that motivated Bushnell and his partner, Ted Dabney, to investigate the philosophy of games themselves. They learned about console engineering, about gameplay, and about the idiosyncratic arcade business. Bushnell and his team later said that *Computer Space* was "a historical blueprint of how all arcade games to follow would be made."

With their meager royalties from *Computer Space*, Bushnell and Dabney left Nutting Associates, who had produced and distributed the game, to form their own company, Syzygy Engineering. (A *syzygy* is straight-line configuration of three celestial bodies in a gravitational system. Bushnell, a space fanatic, liked the name.) When the team discovered that "Syzygy" was already incorporated in California by a roofing contractor, Bushnell drew inspiration from another passion: board games—specifically the ancient Chinese strategy game *Go*. He settled on "atari," a *Go* term that describes when a player's stones are in imminent danger and are "about to become engulfed" by the opposing player. Atari Inc. was incorporated on June 27, 1972.

As their first employee, Bushnell and Dabney hired a former colleague from their days at the audiovisual conglomerate Ampex: twenty-two-year-old Al Alcorn. An electrical engineer by trade, Alcorn was drawn to Bushnell's charisma and ambition, and he even accepted a $200-per-month pay cut in return for 10 percent of the company. He was also drawn to Bushnell's repeated promises of enormous contracts Atari had won—although, as he later learned, Bushnell merely *hoped* to win them. Nevertheless, Alcorn was smitten.

Given Alcorn's expertise with transistors, integrated circuits, and other analog tech—at the time, microprocessors were still far too expensive to be commercially viable—Bushnell initially wanted him to work on a racing game. But then Bushnell abruptly changed his mind. "We were going to build a driving game," Bushnell told *Playboy* in 1983. "But I thought it was too big a step for him to go from not knowing what a video game was to that. So I defined the simplest game I could think of, which was a tennis game, and told him how to build it." In later years, Bushnell claimed he developed the idea of *Pong* from early PDP-1 computers he had played during college.

Bushnell's explanation may not be the entire story. In May 1972, he visited Burlingame, California, to witness Magnavox's demonstration of its Odyssey home video game console. One of the games he saw was none other than table tennis. The Odyssey was a very rudimentary video game system, but its patents formed the basis of Magnavox's years-long lawsuit against Atari claiming that *Pong* infringed upon its intellectual property. Most damningly for Atari, it came out that Bushnell had signed the guest book when he had first seen the Odyssey demonstration. Atari would eventually settle for $1.5 million and grant Magnavox a license for all technology produced by Atari from June 1976 to June 1977.

Did Bushnell come up with the idea for *Pong* by himself or did he lift the idea from Magnavox? No one will ever know for sure. Nevertheless, Alcorn slaved away at creating a table tennis game for Atari, eventually producing a unique product that would forever change American culture. Since microprocessors were not yet viable options for video games, Alcorn had to rely on the same analog tricks that Bushnell devised with *Computer Space*—namely, hacking the vertical and horizontal sync controls on televisions to create an interactive experience. Learning from his previous failure, Bushnell supposedly instructed Alcorn to produce a simple game "that any drunk in any bar can play." While *Computer Space* required users to master Newtonian physics and four separate flight controls, Alcorn's ball game merely required having had a childhood.

Alcorn finished his prototype within a few months. The gameplay is, of course, now the stuff of legend: Players controlled an in-game paddle by moving it vertically across one side of the screen, competing against either the computer or a second player. The ball was hit back and forth until one player missed, scoring a point for her opponent. The first player to eleven points won. The instructions hastily posted on the very

first *Pong* arcade console in 1972 were even more succinct: AVOID MISSING BALL FOR HIGH SCORE.

Pong contained not a single line of computer code; Alcorn relied on his expertise in transistors and circuits to improve on Bushnell's old *Computer Space* schematics. Yet he was able to create a surprisingly sophisticated game, complete with sound effects and realistic physics. For instance, the center of the paddle would return balls at a leisurely ninety-degree angle, but the paddle edges would return them at sharp, unpredictable trajectories. Meanwhile, the ball accelerated the longer it remained in play, making gameplay much more challenging. Alcorn set up the *Pong* prototype with a $75 black-and-white Hitachi television, while Dabney designed a crude wooden case with a tacky wooden veneer—a far cry from the curvy, futuristic fiberglass case that had housed *Computer Space.*

Bushnell and Alcorn brought *Pong* to Andy Capp's Tavern in Sunnyvale, California, a mecca for billiards, pinball, and electromechanical arcade games. Bushnell had used some of his profits from *Computer Space* to buy pinballs and electromechanical driving games, and he had placed them in a variety of locations. Andy Capp's was one of the bars on the company's "route" where these games were placed. The denizens of Andy Capp's came to drink, smoke, and play games. If *Pong* could succeed here, Bushnell reasoned, it could succeed anywhere. Bushnell and Alcorn installed the *Pong* prototype on top of a wine barrel. A couple of curious drunks wandered over to play it and the game's success was launched. According to legend, two guys showed up at the bar one morning not to drink, but to play *Pong*— they were supposedly engineers from a rival firm hoping to copy the game's design. Within a few

KNOCKING OFF PONG

One way to measure a game's influence is to chart how often it's been copied. Beginning in late 1972, many manufacturers who had never even thought of creating a video game began producing a parade of *Pong* clones. *Computer Space* manufacturer Nutting Associates offered the first copy at the end of 1972: a sparkling, brown-and-tan fiberglass cabinet titled *Computer Space Ball*. Over the next three years, dozens of *Pong* imitators and variants appeared, including Allied Leisure's *Paddle Battle*, For-Play Manufacturers' *Rally*, Ramtek's *Volly*, Midway's *Winner*, Chicago Coin's *TV Ping Pong* and *TV Tennis*, Williams' *Paddle Ball*, Taito's *Elepong*, Sega's *Pong Tron*, Meadows Games' *Flim-Flam*, and Exidy's *TV Pinball*. Atari may have sold thousands of *Pong* cabinets themselves, but tens of thousands more poured out of other factories. Imitation may be the sincerest form of flattery, and in the case of Atari's ball-and-paddle video game *Pong*, it also helped jumpstart an industry.

weeks, *Pong* had become so popular that Alcorn found the coin mechanism stuffed with quarters and had to design a more robust one that could handle the deluge of coins. Soon it was clear: *Pong* could be big. Very big.

With *Computer Space*, Bushnell had agreed to a licensing deal with the arcade game manufacturer Nutting Associates. But Bushnell knew that *Pong* had what *Computer Space* did not—simple and addicting gameplay—and correctly foresaw that it would become enormously popular. Atari could manufacture *Pong* itself and keep all the profits, but it had to secure financing. This proved difficult, as arcade games were still seen skeptically by a public who continued to associate pinball with seedy porn shops and organized crime (page 2). Finally, Bushnell secured a modest loan from Wells Fargo for $50,000—far less than he had hoped for.

Atari opened its "factory" in an abandoned roller-skating rink in Santa Clara. Their workforce was not exactly state of the art—Bushnell mustered his crew from local unemployment centers, some of whom were drug addicts or petty thieves who attempted to steal the *Pong* televisions. At first, Atari was manufacturing barely ten units a day and suffered rampant quality-control problems. But within months, it was churning out nearly one hundred arcade games per day while keeping production costs around $300.

Pong was a smash hit that signaled the beginning of America's love affair with video games. Bushnell toured California pitching *Pong* to local arcades, who could not buy enough cabinets. *Pong's* $1,200 price tag was steep, but with the game taking in an average of $200 per week in quarters, arcade operators saw them as a gold mine. *Pong* swept the country by storm, eventually selling some thirty-five thousand units. Bushnell knew he had to keep the game fresh, so Atari pumped out various coin-operated sequels such as *Pong Doubles* (1973), *Barrel Pong* (1973), *Super Pong* (1974), *Quadrapong* (1974), *Rebound* (1974), and *Puppy Pong* (1974).

Pong made Bushnell and Dabney rich, and soon it also made video arcade games become a new pastime; this new video game form was a social lubricant formed from transistors and circuits that united jocks and geeks and Americans from all walks of life. Everyone of a certain age has a *Pong* story, and Bushnell claims that thousands of people have told him they met their spouse playing it. The game was primitive but refined, and endlessly playable. *Pong* may not have been the first video arcade game—and it was also not the first video game modeled on table tennis—but like Edison's light bulb and Ford's Model T, it was the exemplar. *Pong*'s X factor was its simplicity and its accessibility. "Avoid missing ball for high score" was all players needed to be told; the rest was left up to the imagination.

$7.50

BASIC
COMPUTER
GAMES

Edited by David H. Ahl

digital

101 BASIC COMPUTER GAMES

(1973)

People learn best through play. David Ahl's compilation of simple computer games provided computer code and play-throughs of programs in the BASIC language. Readers became programmers when they typed in the instructions in their own machines.

During the early 1970s, the public was for the first time grasping the awesome potential of computers. NASA had completed six moon landings that relied on room-sized computers, while video arcade games—most notably *Pong* (page 49)—were sweeping the nation. But to most people, computers were still boxes of wires and gizmos commanded by elite engineers. The possibility that ordinary people could use a computer, let alone program one themselves, was preposterous.

Around this time, a new class of computers called minicomputers were growing popular. While less powerful than traditional mainframes, minicomputers were powered by the latest single-chip CPU microprocessors and generally sold for under $25,000. While certainly not "mini" by today's standards, minicomputers required only a large cabinet, making them far more versatile than their room-sized brethren. For the first time, schools, midsize businesses, and other non-elite organizations could harness the power of a computer.

While computers were becoming cheaper and smaller, they remained complex in usability. Most ran 1950s-era programming languages, particularly COBOL and FORTRAN. COBOL, released in 1959, was the product of a Department of Defense–spearheaded project aiming to create a portable programming language for data processing. Widely adopted by 1968 (and still in use today by many large businesses), COBOL was inaccessible to most amateur programmers due to its verbosity and lack of customization. FORTRAN, meanwhile, was developed by IBM in the 1950s for scientific and engineering applications. Especially effective at numeric computation, FORTRAN became the preeminent language for supercomputers, weather prediction, fluid dynamics, crystallography, and other sophisticated applications requiring extensive computing power. Like COBOL, FORTRAN was also difficult to learn and generally inaccessible to those without advanced degrees.

It was in this computing climate that Digital Equipment Corporation (DEC) hired David Ahl as a marketing consultant to develop its educational products line. DEC was a major player in the computer industry, manufacturing minicomputers, software, and peripherals for corporations and research institutions. (DEC was eventually purchased by Compaq in 1998, which, at the time, was the largest merger in the history of the computing industry.) With degrees in electrical engineering and business administration and a PhD in educational psychology, Ahl was uniquely qualified to market computers to education professionals, who generally lacked the coding prowess to operate them. Ahl began editing DEC's newsletter, *EDU*, which highlighted the educational applications for minicomputers. With the success of *Pong* and other arcade games, Ahl realized that computer games were an excellent entry point into computer programming, and *EDU* regularly published code for simple games that could be played on DEC products.

Ahl understood that his clients were struggling with advanced programming languages like COBOL and FORTRAN, so he began experimenting with a relatively new language called BASIC (an acronym for Beginner's All-Purpose Symbolic Instruction Code), which was developed during the mid-1960s at Dartmouth College as a way to teach non-engineering students how to use computers. Compared to the complex jargon of legacy programming languages, BASIC used simple commands such as PRINT to output text and numbers to teletype terminals or screens; IF and THEN statements to regulate decision making; FOR and NEXT to run loops; and END to conclude programs. In many ways, the BASIC language was the genesis for personal computing, democratizing computers by allowing users to write simple programs for everyday purposes.

BASIC was not without its critics. Seasoned programmers ridiculed the language as "spaghetti code" whose user-friendly interface gunked up computers with needless characters and commands. BASIC's most zealous opponent was Edsger Dijkstra, a famed Dutch scientist who helped bring computers from their theoretical realm into true scientific applications. "It is practically impossible to teach good programming to students that have had a prior exposure to BASIC," Dijkstra grumbled in a 1975 essay. "As potential programmers, they are mentally mutilated beyond hope of regeneration."

Nevertheless, BASIC would become the foremost computing language by the mid-1970s. At DEC, Ahl began porting games into the BASIC language and publishing the code in *EDU*. As the newsletter gained popularity, students learning BASIC sent Ahl their own games, leading him to publish an anthology with DEC titled *101 BASIC Computer Games*. Ahl believed very deeply in the educational power of games, writing in the book's preface:

Newton's second law is probably the furthest thing from the mind of a person sitting down to play ROCKET. However, when the player finally lands his LEM [Lunar Excursion Module] successfully on the moon, the chances are very good that he has discovered something about gravity varying inversely with the mass of the LEM and the distance from the moon.

101 BASIC Computer Games included games such as BATNUM, where players matched wits in a battle of numbers versus the computer; BOMBER, a World War II bombing game; BLKJAC, a Las Vegas blackjack game; and CHOMP, where two or more players ate cookies while avoiding poisoned biscuits. (All program titles had no more than six letters, since that was all most computers could handle for file names.) Many games were designed by Ahl, while others were developed by college and even high-school students. By 1974, the book had sold some ten thousand copies.

Inspired by the burgeoning BASIC community, Ahl pressed DEC to invest in developing personal microcomputers that people could use in their own homes, but his superiors were content with the educational market. Frustrated, Ahl left DEC in 1974 to start the magazine *Creative Computing*, one of the very first publications intended for home computer enthusiasts. *Creative Computing* positioned itself firmly in the vanguard of the home computer revolution. Older minicomputers were too large and cost-prohibitive for most people to buy, but the first microcomputers managed to shrink processing power onto fingernail-sized chips, dramatically reducing their size and cost. Computing functions that were once the purview of large circuit boards were now available on tiny integrated circuits. And these microcomputers almost universally ran the BASIC programming language.

Ahl purchased the rights to *101 BASIC Computer Games* from DEC and republished the book with new games. As the home computer market exploded, Ahl printed many new editions of his book and translated it into six languages. *101 BASIC Computer Games* became the first computer book to sell one million copies, and every self-respecting computer nerd had at least one dog-eared paperback of Ahl's book lying around.

As Ahl wrote in the preface to *101 BASIC Computer Games*, "This is not the first collection of computer games and simulations nor will it by any means be the last." By championing the BASIC programming language, Ahl helped democratize computers for the masses. You did not need a PhD to operate a computer, nor did you need a million-dollar mainframe computer. You just needed an imagination and a willingness to learn. "The main objection to games as a learning tool seems to be the fact that it's largely unguided learning and potentially wasteful of computer time," Ahl wrote. "However, the educational value of games can be enormous—not only in their playing but in their creation."

Ahl's belief that everyone could learn to code was prescient, and with *101 BASIC Computer Games*, he gave people the tools to do this and the examples to mimic.

BOMBER

FLY A WORLD WAR II BOMBER

Description

In this program, you fly a World War II bomber for one of the four protagonists of the war. You then pick your target or the type of plane you are flying. Depending upon your flying experience and the quality of the enemy defenders, you then may accomplish your mission, get shot down, or make it back through enemy fire. In any case, you get a chance to fly again.

Program Author

This program was somewhat modified at DIGITAL. The original author is:

David Sherman
Curtis Junior High School
Sudbury, MA 01776

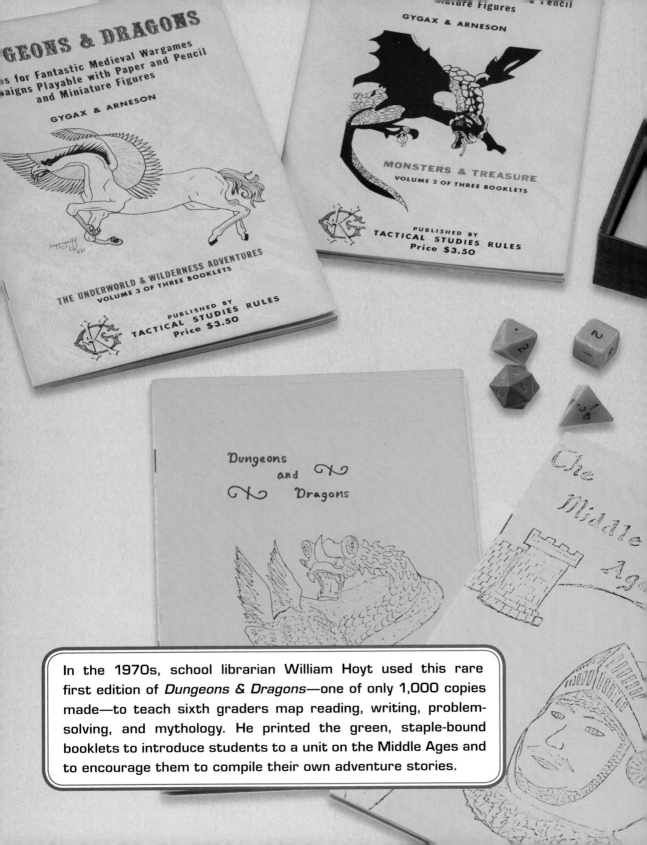

In the 1970s, school librarian William Hoyt used this rare first edition of *Dungeons & Dragons*—one of only 1,000 copies made—to teach sixth graders map reading, writing, problem-solving, and mythology. He printed the green, staple-bound booklets to introduce students to a unit on the Middle Ages and to encourage them to compile their own adventure stories.

DUNGEONS
& DRAGONS

(1974)

or many kids growing up in the 1970s, freedom meant a brand-new bike— ideally one with enough speeds to conquer any hill in the neighborhood. For others, freedom meant the keys to Dad's Buick for the night. But for the geeks of the world, freedom meant *Dungeons & Dragons*.

Some might wonder how a tabletop game, especially one so dependent on a pen, paper, and dice, represents a cornerstone of video game history. Today, more people subscribe to *World of Warcraft* than played pen-and-paper *D&D* in its heyday, while tens of millions more play other fantasy role-playing games on computers and consoles. Yet *Dungeons & Dragons* not only inspired thousands of computer role-playing games, but it shaped the basic game mechanics—the DNA of gameplay—of a significant proportion of later games.

It all began with a group of friends in Lake Geneva, Wisconsin, playing with toy soldiers. Calling themselves the International Federation of Wargamers (IFW), they enjoyed recreating famous battles such as Waterloo and Gettysburg with topologically accurate maps— reenactments that could take hours and days to complete. Known as kriegspiel, this sort of toy-based war-gaming was developed in the early nineteenth century by a Prussian officer named Georg Leopold von Reiswitz. (According to some accounts, the Prussians used kriegspiel to plan the Franco–Prussian War before they decimated the French troops in the mid-nineteenth century.)

The IFW was actually a fairly large group, with as many as seven hundred members mostly clustered in the American Midwest. The Lake Geneva–based chapter was led by Gary Gygax, who was particularly fond of medieval warfare and created an IFW subgroup called the Castle & Crusade Society. Gygax organized skirmishes using a mix of soldier classes who had varying strengths and weaknesses. (Crossbowmen, for instance, had excellent attack ratings but poor armor.) But over time the group grew bored of their medieval reenactments, and Gygax sought to spice up the gameplay. A fan of fantasy novels, he began injecting fantastical elements into IFW skirmishes, such as dragons, elves, and wizards who summoned fireballs.

Codeveloped with a friend, hobby-shop owner Jeff Perren, Gygax's fantasy twist became so popular that he started a company called Guidon Games. Operating out of Gygax's basement, the company in 1971 published *Chainmail: Rules for Medieval Miniatures*, which included a supplemental guide for introducing Tolkien-esque gameplay elements. Around this time Gygax met Dave Arneson, a fellow IFW member who ran a subgroup out of the University of Minnesota. Arneson had created a popular *Chainmail* variation where players snuck into a castle, and Gygax was intrigued by the intimacy of playing as an individual warrior instead of overseeing a vast army. The duo created new immersive scenarios that included castle maps and role-playing features that transported players to imaginative worlds. Over time, the gameplay featured fewer large-scale battles, focusing instead on storytelling, dark dungeons, monsters, and treasures.

Gygax and Arneson put together what they called "The Fantasy Game," adding in innovative features like "hit points" to determine how injured a player was and "experience points" that allowed players to grow more powerful over time. When coming up with names for the game, which by then heavily featured fantastical underground lairs, Gygax's daughter supposedly selected "Dungeons and Dragons" from the list of titles they were considering. Gygax and Arneson tried selling their game to publisher Avalon Hill, but the company did not believe there was a market. One of the most influential games of all time might have died a quiet death if not for a bold decision: Gygax published *Dungeons & Dragons* himself.

He poured most of his money into a new company called Tactical Studies Rules (TSR), and was soon joined by Arneson and two other investors, Don Kaye and Kevin Blume. The team worked feverishly to create a commercial version of their game, which now bore little resemblance to its wargaming roots. Players assumed the roles of characters with unique sets of strengths and weaknesses. Variables included race, such as elf or human; class (occupation), like fighting-man or magic user; and an ethical "alignment," such as law or chaos, which governed certain aspects of role-playing. One player was designated to be the "dungeon master," responsible for enforcing the rules of the game (or making up his or her own when necessary), narrating the storyline, and presiding over interactions with monsters. Each game was called an "adventure," and numerous adventures could be linked together into a "campaign."

D&D became immensely popular. Tactical Studies Rules sold nearly one thousand copies by the end of 1974—a blockbuster by wargaming standards—and thousands more in 1975. Growth continued exponentially throughout the late 1970s and early 1980s, even as Gygax and Arneson battled over creative credit. (Arneson eventually left the company and sued for royalties he believed he was owed.) *D&D* swiftly outgrew its creators in ways that were not even perceivable at the time. When Gygax and Arneson adapted their rules for miniature play to a fantasy environment, they created numeri-

cal systems for calculating countless aspects of fantasy play, from the increases in experience players gained from slaying opponents and finding treasure to the likelihood that a combatant's blow would strike an opponent. The highly statistical nature of *D&D* lent itself well to computers that produced random numbers as well as dice and calculated charts of hit probabilities quicker than a *D&D* dungeon master.

Consider these common features of fantasy computer games: hit points, experience points, levels, character races and classes, the need to acquire personal possessions like armor and weapons, and the impetus to fight progressively fiercer monsters. Video games adapted these conventions and many more, directly or indirectly, from pen-and-paper versions of *Dungeons & Dragons*. *D&D*'s influence extends far beyond just fantasy games; the numerical measurement and representation of many game components, from health in a first-person shooter such as *Doom* to the hunger and hygiene motives of *The Sims*, also descend from *D&D*'s mechanics, even if a sword or a sorcerer never appears in any of these titles. Indeed, many early video game developers got their start by making their own *D&D* campaigns.

Yet the game's true impact lies in how it sparked players' imaginations as they created characters and set out on adventures. Players' love for *Dungeons & Dragons* derived not from its statistical mechanics, but from the pretend worlds it made possible. The game immersed players in these worlds, lost them in adventures and crusades, and inspired them to try and replicate that experience on computers. For countless young players, *Dungeons & Dragons* opened imaginative landscapes every bit as thrilling as those accessible with a bicycle.

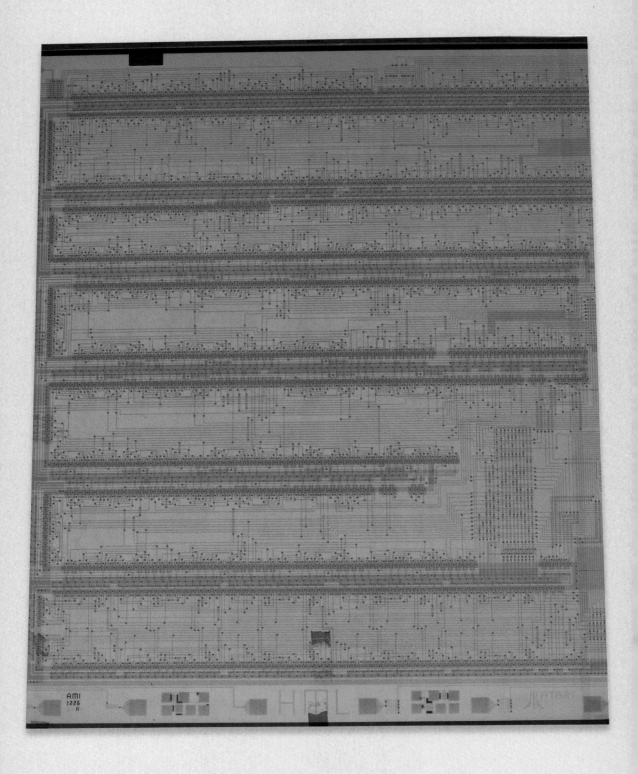

HOME PONG

(1975)

Atari designer Harold M. Lee developed the subtle tracery of this computer-chip plot that was used to manufacture *Home Pong.* Note his initials at the bottom.

The year is 1974. America is in full-blown *Pong* fever. Atari has sold more than eight thousand units, making it a staple of arcades, bars, and restaurants nationwide. (For more about the original *Pong*, see page 49.)

But Nolan Bushnell, Atari's founder, was worried. While *Pong* was wildly successful, it was based on outdated technology. Instead of a computer chip, *Pong* was powered by transistor-transistor logic (TTL)—analog tech that was rapidly becoming obsolete even by standards of the time. Computerized microprocessors promised cutting-edge graphics and gameplay far beyond what was possible with circuits and transistors. Bushnell had always dreamed of using computers in his consoles, yet they remained prohibitively expensive.

Atari was also competing with a slew of copycat products hoping to capitalize on the *Pong* craze. One prominent example was manufactured by Marx Toys in 1974. Hoping to beat other manufacturers to the chase, Marx hastily put together a crude electromechanical replica of *Pong* called *TV Tennis*. Instead of producing a video game console like the Odyssey that attached to a TV, Marx sold a small plastic box that looked like a TV with oversized knobs on the lower corners that could play a *Pong* clone. The knobs controlled paddles on either side that bounced a careening "ball" back and forth over the screen. In reality the "ball" was simply a light bulb at the end of a mechanical arm. *TV Tennis* was a cleverly designed piece of hardware, but a poor reproduction of actual video game play.

Eyeing the modest success of these clones designed to operate in the living room rather than the arcade, Bushnell understood that home video

games were the future and directed his team at Atari to begin researching home consoles. One idea was to shrink the analog technology used in *Pong* into a console similar to the Odyssey, but Bushnell and Al Alcorn—the chief architect of the original *Pong*—were more interested in digitizing the game with a single computer chip. This could mean sound effects, a score counter, and most tantalizingly, color graphics. But to digitize *Pong* would require integrated circuit (IC) chips—expertise that no one at Atari possessed.

Alcorn had an idea. Earlier in 1974, an Atari employee named Harold Lee left the company after growing tired of designing traditional TTL-powered arcade games. Before he was hired at Atari, Lee worked at Standard Microsystems designing microchips for calculators and other electronics, and Atari's 1960s-vintage tech bored him. Alcorn realized that if Atari were to shrink *Pong* down to a microchip, they would have to coax Lee back to the company. He contacted Lee and asked him a simple question: "Can *Pong* be put on a chip?" When Lee replied that it could, Alcorn immediately hired him back as an outside consultant operating out of his own outfit called MOS Sorcery. As his headquarters, Lee chose a tiny cabin located in a Christmas tree farm in the hills of Los Gatos, California.

He began methodically drawing up a chip design on drafting paper, occasionally emerging from his woodland sanctuary to bring a completed section to Alcorn, who worked with his wife to wrap the circuits into a largescale model. After many rounds of debugging, Alcorn and Lee produced a working "golden schematic" consisting of a rat's nest of wires and circuits crammed inside a pedestal. All that was left was to shrink it down to about the size of a thumbnail.

This was no easy feat, as it required creating a large-scale integrated circuit chip, a new technology onto which tens of thousands of transistors could be squeezed. To do this, Atari required cutting-edge computer-aided design (CAD) software, which only a handful of firms offered. Lee recommended Applicon Inc., one of the very first companies to produce CAD technology. Alcorn and Lee found an Applicon machine in Palo Alto, which they rented for $80 per hour at night to save money. Shrinking *Pong* onto microscopic wafers was laborious—a tiny mistake meant an entire night of work was lost. Yet the design was finally completed, and Atari quickly contracted with three chip producers in Silicon Valley— American Microsystems, MOS Technology, and Synertek—to mass produce *Pong*'s brain.

Atari put together a basic design consisting of a brown plastic box attached to two knob controllers, which two players used to control their respective paddles. Running on four D-cell batteries, the console attached to any TV with a coaxial cable, and was even playable in color.

The Atari engineers—predominantly male and notoriously lewd—dubbed it "Darlene" after an attractive female coworker. In the end, the company simply reverted to the *Pong* name for the home version.

The only remaining problem was to mass produce and sell the product. Atari had zero experience selling consumer products, so they needed a retail partner. Alcorn and Gene Lipkin, Atari's new head of marketing, flew to New York in January 1975 to showcase *Home Pong* at the New York Toy Fair. Alcorn and Lipkin expected the process of finding a retail partner to be easy; after all, *Pong* was the hottest game in the country. Instead, retail executives were skeptical of Atari's ability to mass produce a consumer product. Producing thousands of arcade games was one thing, but building hundreds of thousands of home consoles was quite another. After being turned down by Radio Shack and other prominent retailers, Alcorn and Lipkin returned to California to rethink their strategy.

By chance, they spied an advertisement for

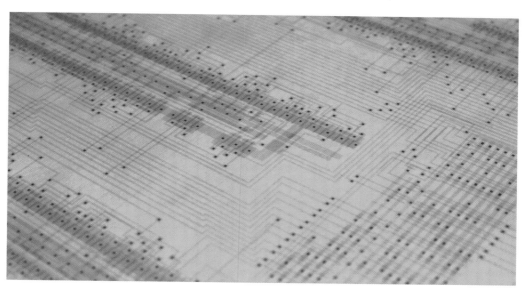

the Magnavox Odyssey in the sporting goods section of a Sears catalog. Sears' departments at the time were largely autonomous, and the sporting goods department, run by a colorful executive named Tom Quinn, was taking risks that other departments were not. In fact, just months earlier, the Sears television department had turned Atari down. On a whim, Lipkin decided to cold call Quinn and pitch him *Home Pong*. Two days later, Quinn was standing in Atari's lobby to discuss terms.

The deal was contingent on a *Home Pong* demonstration for Quinn's team in Chicago. Lipkin and Alcorn hauled their prototype to the Sears Tower and nervously connected it to a TV set in front of a large audience of executives. Alcorn hit the power button . . . and nothing happened. The TV screen continued to hiss static. Franti-

cally, he fiddled with the console until he realized the problem: one of the most powerful transmitters in the world sat atop the Sears Tower, right over their heads, and it was blasting away on the same channel *Home Pong* was designed to operate on. He switched the channel output on the console and the game functioned perfectly.

Sears demanded it sell *Home Pong* under its own "Tele-Games" brand, while Atari insisted its logo also appear on the device—a highly unusual move considering Sears's bargaining power. They eventually reached a compromise: Tele-Games appeared in bright yellow lettering at the top of the device, while an Atari logo was awkwardly slapped onto the power button. Atari agreed to let Sears sell *Home Pong* exclusively during the 1975 holiday season (but not after), and Sears lined up financing for Atari's new fac-

Sears, Roebuck and Company, the nation's leading retailer, introduced consumers to *Home Pong* in its 1975 Christmas Wishbook catalog. Manufactured by Atari, Sears featured it in its sporting goods section under the Tele-Games label.

tory through its own bank. Sears also provided manufacturing and quality-control expertise, enabling Atari to produce seventy-five thousand units by November 1975.

Priced at $99.99, *Home Pong* was a massive success, flooding Atari's coffers with much-needed cash that would seed the development of the famed 2600 console (page 86). Sears sold nearly one hundred fifty thousand Tele-Games–branded *Home Pong* systems during the holiday season, easily becoming its most successful product. Atari would later release its own version of *Home Pong*, along with a slew of sequels including *Pong Doubles*, *Super Pong*, and *Ultra Pong*.

The unlikely marriage between a scrappy video game upstart and a behemoth retailer represented a key moment in the history of video games. Consumers who had never set foot inside an arcade could now read about and purchase a home video game system in the ubiquitous Sears catalog, a copy of which could be found in nearly every American home. After flipping through basketballs, footballs, baseball uniforms, tents, sleeping bags, bikes, and rifles, Americans nationwide came across a glorious full-page ad for *Home Pong*. "Ma, I want *Pong* for Christmas" became the rallying cry for an entire generation. With a foothold in the consumer market and a powerful microchip at its disposal, Atari was the undisputed king of games.

BREAKOUT

(1976)

Before Steve Jobs and Steve Wozniak founded Apple, the duo developed Atari's successful brick-smashing game, *Breakout.*

Steve Jobs had only days to deliver on a promise, and he was getting worried.

Most people remember Jobs, who died of cancer in 2011 at age fifty-six, as the visionary CEO of Apple. But in 1975 he was a lowly technician at Atari. He had been hired two years earlier by Atari's founder, Nolan Bushnell, and *Pong* creator Al Alcorn. Atari was an idiosyncratic company, willing to take a chance on Jobs, who would become Atari employee No. 40. According to legend, Jobs insisted that his strict fruitarian diet meant his body was so pure that he did not have to shower or wear deodorant; his coworkers did not agree, and Atari management relegated him to the night shift. Bushnell, however, later suggested that this arrangement was more pragmatic. Aware of the close relationship Jobs had with engineer (and later Apple cofounder) Steve Wozniak, who was working during the day at Hewlett Packard, Bushnell claimed in 2014 that "If I put Jobs on the night shift, I'd get two Steves for the price of one. A very good business proposition." Indeed, the affable Wozniak often visited Jobs at night to play games and lend his talents to various projects.

In late 1975, Bushnell decided that he wanted a new, vertically oriented version of *Pong*, but instead of volleying with an opponent, players would use their paddle to bounce a ball against a wall of bricks, depleting them one at a time. He and two Atari managers, Alcorn and Steve Bristow, sketched out the concept for what would be called *Breakout* and assigned Jobs to create a prototype. Hoping to minimize production costs, Bushnell instructed Jobs to keep the number of expensive transistor-transistor logic (TTL) chips

as low as possible—most Atari games required between 150 and 170—and even offered him a bonus for each chip he could reduce from the original *Pong* design. Jobs accepted the challenge and promised he would deliver a prototype in four days.

The only problem was that Jobs was not a good enough engineer to complete the task. Wozniak, however, was an expert at reducing chip counts, and Jobs offered to split the bonus with him if he could complete the prototype in four days. (Jobs failed to mention that he had suggested to Atari the crushing deadline so he could keep longstanding travel plans.) Wozniak agreed, and the two set to work. Wozniak pored over the *Breakout* design while at his day job at Hewlett-Packard, then came to Atari at night to assemble the circuit board. Jobs provided him no sketches; Wozniak worked entirely off his friend's conceptual idea. "We worked day and night," Wozniak later said. "We both got the sleeping sickness, mononucleosis." Jobs put together the "breadboard" on which the circuits were laid, while Wozniak handled the tedious, and far more difficult, work of assembling the circuits, not to mention designing the gameplay.

Jobs delivered a working *Breakout* prototype in four days, as promised. The design used an astoundingly low forty-six TTL chips, good for a bonus of $5,000. Jobs, however, pocketed the money to fund his travel and told Wozniak that the bonus was a mere $700, and so his friend only received $350 despite his tireless effort. (Wozniak would not learn about the bonus for another ten years.) Atari, ultimately, was unable to use Wozniak's exact design; by relentlessly eliminating as many chips as possible, he had engineered a board that was too compact and complicated to be mass produced. Jobs, not willing to divulge the extent of Wozniak's contribution, was unwilling to help Atari engineers decipher the prototype. As Alcorn later said,

"Since Jobs didn't really understand [*Breakout*] and didn't want us to know that he hadn't done it, we ended up having to redesign it before it could be shipped."

KEE GAMES

As Nolan Bushnell expanded his Atari empire throughout the mid-1970s, he ran into a problem: he couldn't get his games into enough arcades. For years, pinball-arcade operators relied on a complex web of distributors and other middle men to secure a generous share of game receipts. These arrangements remained in place into the era of electronic arcade games, and Bushnell found that arcades would not sign deals without a major distributor acting as an intermediary. Moreover, many arcades had signed exclusivity deals with distributors, meaning certain regions would always remain out of Atari's reach.

To circumvent this problem, Bushnell hatched a scheme with his neighbor Joe Keenan. In September 1973, Keenan started a company called Kee Games, which produced near carbon copies of Atari titles. *Elimination* (1973), for instance, was a clone of Atari's *Quadrapong*, *Formula K* (1974) was a clone of *Gran Trak 10*, and so on. To the outside world, Kee Games looked like a competitor trying to claw away Atari's market share. In reality, Kee Games was a wholly owned subsidiary of Atari—a fact that was shrouded from the public. In effect, this allowed Atari to vastly increase its revenue stream by selling the same game to multiple distributors. To ham up the "competition" between the companies, Bushnell even transferred some of his engineers to Kee Games and released press releases condemning Keenan for poaching his employees.

Soon Kee Games had a number of its own hits, including *Tank!* (1974), in which players navigated tanks through mazes while shooting other tanks and avoiding mines. With Kee Games titles succeeding, sometimes at the expense of its financially troubled parent company, Bushnell in late 1974 announced an official "merger" between the two companies. Fortunately for Bushnell, by this point most arcades were abandoning the traditional pinball distribution model, with operators realizing that exclusivity deals were limiting the number of hit games they could offer and the number of paying customers who played them.

Breakout's gameplay was quite simple. The game began with eight rows of bricks, with each two rows a different color, descending from yellow to green to orange to red. Players used the moveable paddle and the sides of the screen to bounce a ball and knock down one brick at a time. If the paddle missed a rebound, the player lost a turn. A novel feature of *Breakout* was a rudimentary difficulty curve; as a player knocked away more bricks, the paddle shrank and the ball picked up speed. Atari eventually managed to create a mass-producible version of Wozniak's design, and *Breakout* was introduced to arcades in April 1976. It was an immediate hit that became one of Atari's most successful titles until *Asteroids* in 1979 (page 121).

Although Wozniak deserves most of the credit for *Breakout*, Jobs's fingerprints are all over its design. In many ways the game epitomizes his career: *Breakout* is elegantly simple, a hallmark trait of Jobs' design sense from the first Apple computers to the Macintosh, iPod, iPhone, and iPad. After delivering *Breakout* to Atari, he realized that he was not cut out to be an engineer, toiling away with circuit boards and soldering irons. He could never match Woz-

niak's mechanical genius, but Jobs would hone another type of genius, one that could coax the very best out of others with a cocktail of encouragement, cajoling, and coercion—sometimes all at the same time. Just as he inspired Wozniak's marathon struggle to build Atari's iconic brick-blasting game, Jobs squeezed every ounce of effort from his employees to build his Apple empire.

As he would later say after a lifetime of successes and failures, "Sometimes life is going to hit you in the head with a brick. Don't lose faith."

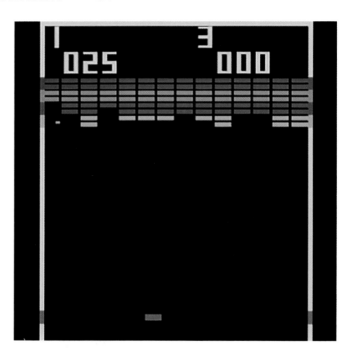

BREAKOUT WAS INTRODUCED TO ARCADES IN APRIL 1976. IT WAS AN IMMEDIATE HIT THAT BECAME ONE OF ATARI'S MOST SUCCESSFUL TITLES.

FAIRCHILD CHANNEL F

(1976)

Designer Jerry Lawson made home video game consoles infinitely expandable by leading the creation of the first interchangeable game cartridge. His family donated this prototype of *Math Quiz I* to The Strong.

For decades, home video games have operated on a simple premise: you install a cartridge or a disc into a console and hit the power button. This allows players to switch between, say, *Madden NFL* and *Call of Duty* in a matter of seconds. And yet the very first home video game consoles lacked this critical feature. *Home Pong* (1975), for instance, could only play a variation of Atari's popular table tennis arcade game, and the Magnavox Odyssey (1972), which came hardwired with a handful of games, used cartridges only to change how dots moved on the television screen. Many assume the first commercial console with true interchangeable games was the Atari 2600, but the technology actually arrived a year earlier with a long-forgotten yet immensely important console called the Fairchild Channel F.

The Channel F's tale actually begins in the late 1960s with a bowling alley equipment supplier called American Machine and Foundry (AMF), an early pioneer of electronic score-keeping systems. After AMF moved its research-and-development team from Stamford, Connecticut to North Carolina, an offshoot of engineers led by Norman Alpert and Wallace Kirschner decided to leave the company and start their own firm, the Alpex Computer Corporation. After dabbling with electronic cash registers, Alpex took a risk with the emerging video game market. Noting that the most popular games of the early 1970s, such as *Pong*, were based on outmoded circuitry, Alpex sought to develop a microprocessor-based system that could outmuscle its competition. By 1974, when the Magnavox Odyssey was still the only player in the home console market, Alpex began designing a console based around the Intel 8008

microchip, building simple prototype games such as hockey, table tennis, and tic-tac-toe. Alpex called their creation "RAVEN," for "Remote Access Video Entertainment."

As Alpex's stable of games increased, one thing became clear: players would need a simple way to change between games. Computers at the time generally used magnetic tape and other cumbersome storage methods, but Alpex employed the latest-generation Erasable Programmable Read-Only Memory that could be miniaturized onto a circuit board and crammed into a cartridge. After raiding Radio Shack, Kirschner put together a five-inch by three-inch prototype cartridge enclosing a circuit board and memory chip that slotted into the RAVEN console with a twenty-five-pin connector. By separating the system from the game media, Alpex could create an entirely new revenue stream by encouraging consumers to purchase the latest and greatest game long after purchasing the console.

The only problem was finding a deep-pocketed business partner who could distribute and market Alpex's revolutionary video game system. After failing to convince TV manufacturers Zenith, Sylvania, Motorola, and RCA, Alpert and Kirschner approached the semiconductor manufacturer Fairchild. A pioneer developer of integrated circuits, Fairchild was a major distributor of microprocessors for mainframe computers and had recently begun venturing into the consumer market with digital watches, pocket calculators, and other gadgets. A Fairchild representative, Shawn Fogarty, was impressed by Alpex's technology and told a colleague, Gene Landrum, to evaluate the technology and produce a feasibility report. "I want you to go to

Connecticut," Fogarty told Landrum, "and I am going to send this engineer with you—this guy Lawson—and I want you to look at this thing and decide if we will buy it."

"This guy Lawson" was Jerry Lawson, Fairchild's electronics expert and one of the few African-American engineers in Silicon Valley. As a boy Lawson delighted in playing with unusual toys, especially an Irish mail handcar his father gave him. Later he played with ham radios and built and sold walkie-talkies. Self-taught, Lawson read and experimented throughout his life with everything from radio, radar, and television to lasers, astronomy, and science fiction. His curiosity eventually brought him from his hometown of Queens, New York, to Silicon Valley's Fairchild Camera and Instrument Corp. Here Lawson discovered the first arcade video game, *Computer Space* (page 29), inspiring him to create "Demolition Derby," a coin-operated video game he built in his garage. Completed in early 1975 using Fairchild's new F8 microprocessors and tested in a nearby pizza parlor, "Demolition Derby" was among the earliest microprocessor-driven games. When word of Lawson's game reached Fairchild management, the executives offered him a new position as head of the company's video products division—a group tasked with creating what would eventually become the Channel F.

Jerry Lawson's work badge.

GERALD A. LAWSON
FAIRCHILD
CAMERA AND INSTRUMENT
CORPORATION
41339
Employee Number

Lawson's first task was to convert the RAVEN from an Intel-based chip to a Fairchild F8 microprocessor. He also scrapped the prototype's clunky keyboard controls for a far more intuitive joystick. After studying Lawson's changes, Landrum determined that Fairchild could successfully market the console to consumers and recommended that his bosses officially license the technology. They did, and the RAVEN officially became the Fairchild Video Entertainment System (VES), later redubbed the Channel F (short for "Channel Fun"). Under Lawson's supervision, Fairchild miniaturized the Channel F into a box that could easily nestle beside a living room TV set. The team also had to perfect the removable cartridge system, a task Fairchild delegated to a mechanical engineer named Ron Smith, who had created the first-ever pocket calculator prototype with a removable memory module while working at National Semiconductor. Lawson and Smith reworked the memory internals while industrial designer Nick Talesfore created the plastic cartridge exterior, a design he would base on eight-track tapes.

Fairchild debuted the Channel F in June 1976, at the Consumer Electronics Show in Chicago. The company eventually released twenty-seven games for the system, including *Hockey*, *Tennis*, *Shooting Gallery*, *Math Quiz I*, *Video Blackjack*, and *Pinball Challenge*. The graphics were crude by modern standards but advanced for the time, able to display four background colors per line of resolution, and the F8 chip allowed for human vs. computer matches—a first for home consoles. Lawson's final design featured the industry's first digital home-game joysticks with more degrees of movement than any other controller of the time and the first pause button (labeled HOLD)

to allow players to freeze a game in progress. The Channel F performed well at first, selling some two hundred fifty thousand units by 1977. However, the release of the more advanced and better marketed Atari 2600 in September of that year saw dwindling sales for the Channel F. Fairchild attempted to regain its market share with the Channel F System II in 1978, but Atari's juggernaut console with its growing stable of hit games, including *Breakout*, *Adventure*, and *Space Invaders*, simply became too powerful, and Fairchild sold its Channel F division to Zircon International after selling about three hundred fifty thousand units.

The Channel F is often viewed as a footnote in the history of video games, but its influence persists to this day. The console revolutionized gameplay by providing consumers with the potential for an ever-growing list of individual games to purchase and play in a market previously dominated by dedicated *Home Pong* consoles. The game cartridge also allowed many new game developers to thrive. During the early 1980s, Lawson left Fairchild and founded Videosoft, a promising engineering and game-design company that created many innovations, such as the first three-dimensional video games (with the use of 3-D glasses). In 1984, the company released its novel *Color Bar Generator* utility cartridge for the Atari 2600. Unfortunately, the company closed down in the wake of the video game industry crash and recession that lasted from 1983 until 1985. But the video game cartridge lived on. Companies like Nintendo and Sega would sell tens of millions of cartridge-based home consoles, handheld systems, and games in the 1980s and 90s. And although the proliferation of CD-ROM and digital-download technologies has all but wiped out cartridges, the model of using consoles as platforms to play an endless amount of games remains a pillar of the video game market.

Much like the Channel F itself, Lawson's pioneering work was largely forgotten. But before he passed away in April 2011, the International Game Developers Association's Minority Special Interest Group honored him for his contributions to the gaming industry. Spanning from the early 1970s through the middle 1990s, The Strong museum's Gerald A. "Jerry" Lawson Collection illustrates those contributions and preserves some of his most significant work with Fairchild and Videosoft.

DEATH RACE

(1976)

Inspired by the movie *Death Race 2000*, this game shocked critics by letting players run down stick figures (which the creators called "gremlins"). Today it's hard to see what the panic was all about.

Sick and morbid," the National Safety Council (NSC) said in reference to the game *Death Race*. In the wake of the game's release, *60 Minutes* devoted an entire show to analyzing the psychological effects of video games, while behavioral psychologist Gerald Driessen of the NSC's research department argued that the game could lead to widespread violence:

> **In this game a player takes the first step to creating violence. The player is no longer just a spectator. He's an actor in the process . . . I'm sure most people playing this game do not jump in their car and drive at pedestrians . . . But one in a thousand? One in a million? And I shudder to think what will come next if this is encouraged. It'll be pretty gory.**

Death Race, released more than twenty years before *Grand Theft Auto*, a favorite punching bag of today's moral guardians, holds the famous—or infamous, depending on your point of view—distinction of sparking the first-ever organized protest over a video game and setting off a virulent video game moral panic that persists to this day.

The year was 1975, and America was in a cultural crisis. Two years earlier, the last U.S. troops exited Vietnam, a war that claimed more than fifty-eight thousand American lives while dampening the belief that American-style democracy could flourish around the globe. Consumers were still recovering from the 1973 oil crisis, which saw petroleum prices more than quadruple, provoking mass rationing and shattering naive assumptions that our natural resources were limitless. Meanwhile, the U.S. economy was mired in stagflation, unemployment, and recession.

Throughout all of this, books and movies turned darker. Gone were the 1950s patriotic Cold War allegories and 1960s escapism. Stephen King's 1978 novel *The Stand* imagined a bleak post-apocalyptic landscape after a superflu kills off most of the world's population, while the 1976 film *Logan's Run* examined overpopulation and humanity's overreliance on technology. Pushing the envelope over what was acceptable on screen, the 1975 film *Death Race 2000*, directed by Paul Bartel and starring David Carradine and Sylvester Stallone, portrayed the United States government restructured into a violent totalitarian regime. To pacify the population, the government organized the murderous Transcontinental Road Race in which drivers won points for running over pedestrians in souped-up rigs.

While the film was panned by critics for its graphic depictions of violence—Roger Ebert famously awarded it zero stars—its dystopic social satire made it a cult hit. Many were turned off by what they perceived as the film's glorification of violence, citing, for instance, how victims like the elderly and infirm gained drivers the most points. But others saw *Death Race 2000* as wickedly funny and a scathing take on the degradation of American society. Despite its modest haul at the box office, *Death Race 2000* sparked an enormous debate over the boundaries of free speech in cinema and youth access. Moral guardians believed that America's increasingly violent films were explicitly intended for impressionable children.

It was in this cultural context that arcade-game manufacturer Exidy decided to exploit the controversy surrounding *Death Race 2000* by releasing a video game version. This was the latest in a wave of games hoping to cash in on popular movies; a year earlier, for instance, Atari released *Shark Jaws* in the wake the 1975 blockbuster film *Jaws*. Like Atari, Exidy did not obtain a license from the film's producers; the company designed its game to be thematically similar to *Death Race 2000* without running afoul of copyright laws. Yet the connection was obvious: the arcade cabinet sported two steering wheels and a prominent "Death Race" logo. *Death Race* was adorned with colorful, macabre artwork featuring ghoulish Grim Reaper imagery designed to capture players' imaginations as much as the gameplay itself.

Up to two players, each with a steering wheel, gas pedal, and shift lever, controlled cars on screen and were tasked with running over "gremlins" to score points. When hit, the gremlins screamed and were replaced by tombstones, which became obstacles for the remainder of the game. Due to the primitive monochrome graphics, the gremlins resembled human stick figures. Combined with the game's title, this led some players to believe they were actually killing pixelated humans.

Despite Exidy's insistence that players were killing monsters, not human figures, *Death Race* sparked a firestorm of controversy. The NSC and other organizations condemned the game for its abject violence, while news outlets like the *New York Times* and *NBC News* breathlessly reported on the growing scandal. Even Atari piled on, eyeing an opportunity to position itself in the "family-friendly" market; Nolan Bushnell, Atari's founder, later said that his company "had an internal rule that we wouldn't allow violence against people. You could blow up a tank or you could blow up a flying saucer, but you couldn't blow up people." This wasn't true of course; Atari's *Outlaw*, released in 1976, was a Western-style shooting game where players drew a gun as fast as possible to shoot criminals.

Why did *Death Race* attract so much con-

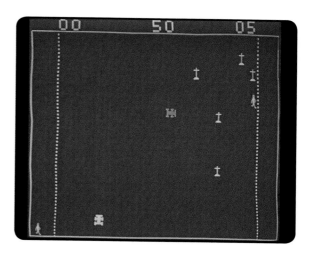

troversy while similarly violent games were ignored by America's moral guardians? After all, *Outlaw* along with other games such as *Crash 'n Score, Cops 'n' Robbers,* and *Jet Fighter* explicitly featured human-on-human violence yet never attracted the same degree of outrage. More important, as game scholar Carly A. Kocurek writes, *Death Race* "did not follow culturally accepted narratives of violence, such as military or police violence, or the Western . . . *Death Race* did not fit within these violent realities, instead presenting a fictional landscape that most closely echoed the reality of the pedestrian hit-and-run accident." In other words, John Wayne picking off bandits with his Colt Single Action Army revolver was one thing, but mowing down innocent pedestrians with cars was quite another.

In a decade defined by disarray, *Death Race* was yet another cultural breach for a nation experiencing the whiplash of Vietnam, high gas prices, and economic downturn. Just like its spiritual successor, *Grand Theft Auto* (page 259), *Death Race* took America and video games into uncharted waters, blurring the line between mainstream violence and moral repugnance, while further redefining the very definition of a video game.

ATARI

VIDEO COMPUTER SYSTEM

(1977)

No home gaming system did more to introduce Americans to the joys of video games than Atari's Video Computer System, which became known as the 2600. Its graphics may have been crude, but its impact was immense.

Atari Inc. was fighting a war on all fronts. The game company had made transistor-transistor logic (TTL)—based games an art form, expertly squeezing as much power as possible out of only a few dozen chips inside coin-operated arcade games. But their venerable 1950s-era technology was rapidly becoming obsolete. By the mid-1970s, microprocessors were ubiquitous, relatively inexpensive, and promised vastly improved graphics over Atari's offerings. Worse, they also allowed for Atari's games to be instantly and relentlessly cloned by competitors.

Facing stiff competition in the coin-operated arcade market, Atari also saw its grip on the home market loosening. *Home Pong* (page 65), along with its sequels *Super Pong* and *Pong Doubles*, now had lots of competition in the world of home video games. Dozens of companies were flooding the market with clones, notably Coleco's Telstar, released in 1976, which used the General Instrument AY38500 microchip. But Atari's home division faced an even more existential problem: Consumers were tiring of *Pong* derivatives. Meanwhile, rumors were flying that Fairchild Semiconductor was preparing to release its Channel F, a microprocessor-powered home console featuring interchangeable game cartridges (page 77).

Nolan Bushnell, Atari's founder and CEO, knew that the future of video games lay in home consoles. Under his guidance, Atari had in 1973 purchased the Grass Valley, California–based think tank Cyan Engineering, and by 1975 had tasked it with developing a home console capable of running interchangeable games. The most immediate hurdle was finding a suf-ficiently powerful microprocessor. Chips such as the Motorola 6800 packed the horsepower but cost more than $100 each—economically unfeasible for what was supposed to be an affordable home console. One chip, however—the MOS Technology 6502—promised top-end processing power for one-sixth the price of its competitors. Using an innovative manufacturing process, MOS Technology managed to cram many more integrated circuits on each silicon wafer compared to rival chips, dramatically reducing the overall price. In late 1975, Atari struck a deal to purchase MOS Technology 6502 chips for $8 apiece. With the beating heart of Atari's home console secured, it was time to design the rest of the body.

By early 1976, the project was known as "Stella," named after the bicycle belonging to one of the engineers. To build Stella's internals, Atari tapped the legendary Silicon Valley designer Jay Miner, who set up a war room in Los Gatos, California. There his team fine-tuned the MOS chip and designed the sound chip, the cartridge slot, and the controllers. Yet work was still proceeding too slowly, for in the fall of 1976, Fairchild Semiconductor launched its Channel F system. Under immense pressure to bring its home console to market, Atari brought the entire Stella team to its Sunnyvale, California, headquarters and devoted nearly every remaining resource to the project.

Bushnell knew it wasn't enough. Atari had to have Stella in production soon or else it would be lost in the deluge of copycat consoles that would inevitably flood the market—the same fate that befell *Home Pong*. But with its sales dwindling, Atari lacked the cash flow to complete Stella. Nolan Bushnell needed to make a bold play. "In order to go into the consumer marketplace, we just needed much deeper pockets," he later said, "and that's why we decided to sell." Leveraging the blockbuster potential of Stella, Bushnell sold his company for $28 million to Warner Communications, who immediately dumped $100 million into the struggling home console. Bushnell stayed on as Chairman and CEO and did his best to preserve Atari's spirit, but steadily the entertainment behemoth would impose its buttoned-up corporate culture onto the famously countercultural game maker.

Perhaps symbolizing this new ethos, Stella was immediately renamed the Atari Video Computer System (VCS), a move meant to directly challenge the Channel F, which was released to consumers as the Video Entertainment System (VES). With the fresh infusion of Warner cash, Atari hired top engineering talent and the VCS quickly took form. The eventual prototype sported a 1.2 MHz processor, 128 bytes of RAM, custom video and audio chips, and two controller ports that could support eight-way joysticks, paddle controllers, and keypads. Reflecting the rushed nature of the project, the VCS would be notoriously difficult to program, with developers having to shoehorn unconventional code to harmonize hardware not meant to work in unison. Quirks that could not be engineered out of the system were instead integrated into games as features. One such trick, known as "flicker," allowed engineers to incorporate more moving objects than the hardware allowed for by having objects disappear between frames, a notable example being the four shimmering ghosts in the *Pac-Man* VCS port, who alternatingly appear every fourth frame.

Atari debuted the VCS at the 1977 Summer Consumer Electronics Show and officially launched the console in October following a

ATARI'S CX40 JOYSTICK

Few video game objects achieve the kind of icon status of the Atari VCS joystick. The square, black plastic controller remains instantly recognizable for a generation who played *Space Invaders*, *Pac-Man*, and *Pitfall!*. Originally designed by an engineer named Kevin McKinsey for a never-released dedicated *Tank!* home console, the controller was repurposed as the CX10 joystick and bundled with the Atari VCS in 1977. Following the launch, Atari implemented a series of redesigns to reduce costs, replacing the CX10 with the cheaper yet still capable CX40 joystick, which made the VCS accessible to the widest possible audience. Commenting on the growth of easy-to-play casual games for mobile devices more than thirty years after the debut of the Atari VCS, Nolan Bushnell explained, "In the beginning, all games were casual. A one-button joystick is something that easily resonates with everyone."

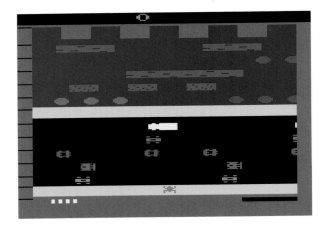

series of manufacturing delays stemming from faulty microchips and issues with the plastic molding. Atari also agreed to license the VCS to Sears, which marketed the console under its Tele-Games brand. The VCS retailed for a pricey $199 (nearly $800 in 2018 dollars) and came bundled with two joysticks, paddle controllers, and the game *Combat*, based on the coin-operated arcade games *Tank!* and *Jet Fighter*. Despite arriving in time for the 1977 holiday season, the VCS sold a modest 250,000 units, largely because the market was flooded with massively discounted *Pong* clones that had been rendered obsolete by the VCS and the VES.

Atari continued to lose money on the VCS, with fewer than six hundred thousand sold in 1978 compared to a production run of eight hundred thousand. After Atari required another cash infusion from its parent company to stay afloat, Bushnell abruptly resigned following a highly public disagreement with Warner. Sadly, he would not remain at the helm to see more pros-

perous times: With the Fairchild VES failing to gain traction and the sudden success of Atari's *Adventure* (1979), one of the first graphical adventure games, the public finally understood that Atari's home console was not just another way to play *Pong*. Realizing that gamers needed to be weaned onto the VCS with ports of familiar arcade hits, Atari licensed Taito's international juggernaut *Space Invaders*, which instantly increased sales of the VCS to more than two million units, helping Atari gross over $2 billion in 1980. Other popular games followed, including *Missile Command* (1981), *Asteroids* (1981), and *Frogger* (1982). In 1982, VCS sales reached a staggering ten million, largely on the coattails of its *Pac-Man* port, which sold seven million copies.

The VCS was eventually rebranded the 2600 after Atari released the more advanced 5200 in 1982, followed by the 7800 in 1986. Yet the venerable 2600 would soldier on, released in various forms (and by various parent companies as Atari swung in and out of bankruptcy) until

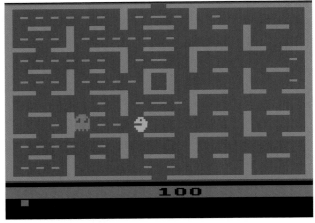

1992. The faux-wood-paneled console that was launched during the heyday of disco, alongside *Star Wars* and punk rock, would sell more than thirty million units over fifteen years, enduring as a budget console even as powerful competitors such as Sega and Nintendo released technologically superior systems. By today's standards, the 2600's graphics and gameplay were primitive. Planes looked like pixel blobs with wings, people looked like pixel blobs with legs, and racecars looked like pixel blobs with wheels. Yet despite the simple graphics, the games charmed America and sold, and sold, and sold.

In the long history of playthings, the Atari 2600's life was brief. But its impact was enormous. The Atari 2600, more than any other system, brought the video game into the home.

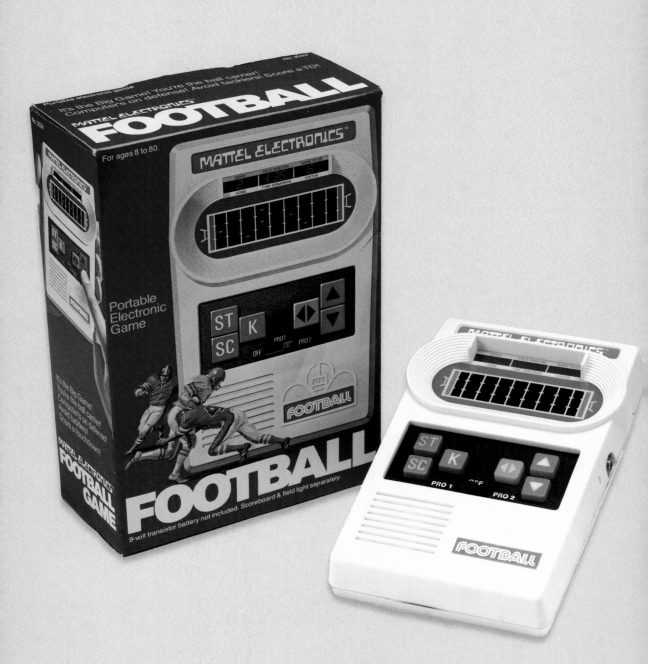

MATTEL
FOOTBALL

(1977)

Players dashed up, down, and sideways in this battle of LED dots that captivated players in the late 1970s. Avoid enough tacklers to score a touchdown, and the player earned a synthesized fanfare.

very spring, video game enthusiasts await one of the most highly anticipated events of the year: the unveiling of the next *Madden NFL* cover. Ever since EA's founder, Trip Hawkins, conceived the series with the legendary football coach and broadcaster John Madden, the Madden NFL series has become a cornerstone of the video game market, selling more than one-hundred million copies and generating over $4 billion in revenue. For NFL players, perhaps nothing better signifies superstar status than appearing on the cover of the latest *Madden NFL* game. But before football games featured razor-sharp graphics, 360-degree camera angles, crushing sound effects, and hyper-realistic gameplay, players had to rely on simple LED lights and the unparalleled processing power of the human imagination.

"It's the Big Game! The computer's on Defense! You're the ball carrier! Cut back! Speed Up! Avoid tacklers! Run for daylight! Score a Touchdown!" These are not taken from the box from the latest *Madden NFL* game, but from a 1977 ad for a Mattel Electronics handheld toy. At the time, handheld electronic games were still in their infancy. Depending on the definition of "electronic," some cite the first commercial handheld electronic game as Japanese toymaker Waco's 1972 *Electro Tic-Tac-Toe*, a simple two-player game that used tiny light bulbs to illuminate red or green squares on a tic-tac-toe board. While the box boasted that players could use their "tactical skill with enjoyment," the game featured no logic beyond battery-operated lights, so its claim as the first electronic handheld device is dubious at best.

It was not until George Klose, an engineer at Mattel—a toy company best known for Barbie dolls and Hot Wheels cars—decided to repurpose the internals of a calculator that the first true electronic handheld game was born. His creation, Mattel *Auto Race*, simulated movement with no actual moving parts; an LED display produced "blips" that raced one another on the screen. While microprocessors were available and cheap, it was difficult to find one that could be miniaturized into a handheld unit. Eventually, the chip manufacturer Rockwell International, which had pioneered the use of tiny microchips in calculators, supplied the hardware necessary to make *Auto Race*. Gameplay was simple but effective: the player's car, represented by a bright vertical dash blip, had to complete four laps to win while navigating three lanes and swerving around opponents. *Auto Race* even featured a gearshift lever, allowing players to accelerate and decelerate.

The company followed up *Auto Race* with Mattel *Football* in 1977. The two-player game action took place on a nine-panel LED display signifying the yard markers of a football field. Similar to *Auto Race,* players on the field appeared as illuminated hyphens, with the user-operated ball carrier rendered with a longer hyphen. The goal of the game was to navigate the runner through five computer-controlled defensive backs situated along the field and reach the end zone for a touchdown. Using directional arrow buttons, players zigged and zagged and juked to avoid being digitally tackled. A ᴋ button allowed a player's team to punt or kick a field goal on the fourth down, depending on the distance to the end zone. A second LED screen displayed the down, the yards remaining for a first down, and the field position. When a player either scored or turned the ball over on downs, the game was handed to the second player. Touchdowns and field goals yielded a quick electronic fanfare. Whichever player had scored the most points against the computer after four two-and-a-half minute quarters won the game. For more challenging gameplay, a second difficulty level "for real adventurers" featured defenses that reacted 50 percent faster.

Football ran on a single nine-volt battery and was sold exclusively by Sears for about $26. Mattel was still skeptical about the lasting power of electronic games and produced an initial run of just one hundred thousand copies. Nevertheless, within six months *Football* was a smash hit, and Mattel had to scramble to produce more units. By early 1978, sales of *Football* approached five hundred thousand *per week*. The company quickly ordered a sequel, *Football 2*, which allowed players to pass the ball among other more advanced features.

Football heralded the beginning of the handheld revolution. Kids could now bring the gridiron into the bedroom, the living room, or even the backseat of the car. With the availability of cheap microprocessors and LEDs, toys manufacturers had to inject inventiveness into their products beyond a new outfit for Barbie or a new Hot Wheels paintjob. Electronic games needed to dazzle and entertain, and they had to outdo each other every year. In 1978, Milton Bradley raised the bar with *Simon*, the famed color-and-sound matching game that sold millions of units and became immortalized in pop culture (page 103). These early handheld devices were technologically inferior compared to full-size arcade cabinets of the time, but the ability to hold an electronic game in your hand while tucked in bed or waiting in the doctor's office or during an endless car ride created a bond with video games that no smoky arcade could match.

"Self-contained!" boasted Mattel *Football*'s eight-page instruction manual. "Needs no TV set!!" As video games penetrated ever deeper into the household, they also found their way into the jacket pockets, school bags, purses, and the hands of millions of players eager for portable electronic play.

ZORK
the great underground empire, part 1

ZORK

(1977)

Players who descended into *Zork*'s Great Underground Empire discovered a realm of the imagination that they interacted with through amazingly lifelike word commands. Navigating the game's puzzles and obstacles required keeping careful records, though maps such as this one from the Zork Users Group certainly helped. Steve Meretzky, who helped design this map, donated it to The Strong.

YOU ARE STANDING IN AN OPEN FIELD WEST OF A WHITE HOUSE, WITH A BOARDED FRONT DOOR. THERE IS A SMALL MAILBOX HERE.

So begins *Zork*, one of the first interactive fiction computer games. It would sell more than a million copies across multiple platforms throughout the 1980s while employing the most powerful graphics chip available then or now: the human imagination. *Zork* was entirely text-based, with no graphical interface beyond glowing text on a computer screen.

Zork was inspired by *Colossal Cave Adventure* (typically shortened to *Adventure*), the first-ever text-based video game. Created in 1977 by Will Crowther at Stanford University and extended by Don Woods, *Adventure* was loosely based on the Mammoth Cave system in Kentucky and included elements of Tolkien high fantasy. Players sought lost treasure by typing in one- or two-word commands to navigate the cave and interact with objects. Designed to run on PDP-10 minicomputers, *Adventure* described such scenes as: YOU ARE IN A VALLEY IN THE FOREST BESIDE A STREAM TUMBLING ALONG A ROCKY BED and YOU ARE IN A MAZE OF TWISTY LITTLE PASSAGES, ALL ALIKE. Players moved around by typing phrases like "go south" or "go west." A wise decision led to treasure, while less-fortunate choices led to scenarios including YOU FELL INTO A PIT AND BROKE EVERY BONE IN YOUR BODY! NOW YOU'VE REALLY DONE IT! *Adventure* swept through Stanford and then to the Massachusetts Institute of Technology (MIT) over ARPAnet, a precursor to the modern internet that allowed research institutions to share computer systems. According to legend, so many engineers became obsessed with solving *Adventure* that the entire computer industry lost two weeks of productivity.

One of these engineers was Tim Anderson, a member of MIT's Dynamic Modelling Group. After solving *Adventure*'s final puzzle, Anderson along with his team—Marc Blank, Bruce Daniels, and Dave Lebling—looked for ways to improve the game. For one, they were frustrated with *Adventure*'s two-word command inputs. Instead of being limited to "attack monster," for instance, Anderson and his crew wanted to say, "attack monster with Elvish sword." If the game could recognize prepositions and conjunctions, an entirely new dynamic layer to the game could be created.

After a few all-night sessions, Anderson and Blank created a prototype map comprising four rooms. It wasn't very good—the game consisted of a band playing "Hail to the Chief" nearby a "chamber filled with deadlines"—but the technology was sound, and the team set to work on a second, more intricate version. They set their game world "in the ruins of an ancient empire lying far underground," with players "venturing into this dangerous land in search of wealth and adventure." Like *Adventure*, the goal of Anderson's game was to penetrate deep underground, retrieve the treasures, and return alive.

The four friends never intended to call the game "Zork." Unable to agree on an official title, they temporarily settled on a nonsense hacker phrase—*Zork!*—they used often in conversation. *Zork* was much more complex than *Adventure*, with multiple characters, including a thief, a cyclops, and a troll. Interestingly, Anderson and his team chose to write *Zork* in a rarely used language called MDL instead of the ubiquitous FORTRAN, in which *Adventure* and most other games were programmed. For this reason, *Zork* was only playable on certain computers and therefore did not extend much beyond MIT and a scattering of hackers over ARPAnet. Somehow, however, whispers of a killer new game on MIT's network spread virally, and soon computer users all across the country were finding ways to play it.

The game was crude, but beloved. Players overlooked some of the more obvious flaws, such as a "bottomless pit" only accessible from a house attic, but Anderson and his team diligently updated *Zork* when they had time, adding in rivers, boats, cars, and more maps including a coal mine maze and a notoriously difficult volcano puzzle. As the user base exploded (propelled partially by an unauthorized FORTRAN port), the team decided to finally give *Zork* a "proper" name. For a brief time, they called the game *Dungeon*—that is, until Tactical Studies Rules (TSR), publisher of the wildly successful *Dungeons & Dragons* tabletop game (page 61), threatened to sue. They quickly changed the name back.

In 1979, Anderson, Blank, and Lebling along with other members of their MIT team founded a software company called Infocom. Initially created to sell productivity software, Infocom eventually focused entirely on creating a commercial version of *Zork*. Eyeing home microcomputers such as the TRS-80 and the Apple II, which could fit on a desk and were relatively affordable in comparison to mainframes, Infocom knew they could make a lot of money with a successful game. The original *Zork* was too large to fit on a single disk, so they broke it up into three installments: *Zork I: The Great Underground Empire* (1980), *Zork II: The Wizard of Frobozz* (1981), and *Zork III: The Dungeon Master* (1982).

```
 West of House                                    Score: 0        Moves: 2
 ZORK is a registered trademark of Infocom, Inc.
 Revision 88 / Serial number 840726

 West of House
 You are standing in an open field west of a white house, with a boarded front
 door.
 There is a small mailbox here.

 > open the mailbox
 I don't know the word "

 >Open the mailbox
 Opening the small mailbox reveals a leaflet.

 >read the leaflet
 (Taken)
 "WELCOME TO ZORK!

 ZORK is a game of adventure, danger, and low cunning. In it you will explore
 some of the most amazing territory ever seen by mortals. No computer should be
 without one!"

 >_
```

The success of the Zork franchise helped establish Infocom as a powerhouse in text-based adventure games, releasing some forty titles in the 1980s, many of them *Zork* sequels and spin-offs. Infocom also revolutionized how games were sold: instead of only distributing *Zork* in specialty computer stores and mail-order catalogs, Infocom sold their games through bookstores and other mainstream retail outlets, enabling them to reach a much larger audience. The company developed such a solid reputation for storytelling that Douglas Adams refused to work with any other company to adapt his bestselling novel *The Hitchhiker's Guide to the Galaxy* into a computer game. Released in 1984, Infocom's version of Adams's novel became a mammoth hit.

Zork enjoyed a rabid fan base obsessed with solving puzzles and exploring imaginative worlds. Players who were stumped by a particular maze or riddle often wrote letters to Infocom seeking hints. In response, the company unveiled the *New Zork Times*, a monthly newsletter that published clues as well as teasers for upcoming games. Infocom even published hint books written in invisible ink so players could selectively unlock clues without spoiling other puzzles. Perhaps the biggest challenge for players was simply navigating the virtual environments that the game conjured up. Smart players quickly realized they needed to draw maps, and enterprising entrepreneurs such as the Zork Users Group sold lavishly illustrated maps (of which one can be seen in the collections of The Strong).

Today, Infocom is no more. After an ill-fated venture into productivity software that led to a flirtation with bankruptcy, Infocom was acquired by Activision and was eventually shuttered in 1989. Yet *Zork* remains popular to this day with a devoted fan base and many playable versions floating around the internet. *Zork* phrases have become popular memes, most notably: "It is pitch-black. You are likely to be eaten by a grue." A grue, of course, is a "sinister, lurking presence in the dark places of the Earth" with a debilitating fear of lantern light. *Zork* proved that you don't need killer graphics—or any graphics, for that matter—to make a great video game. Good writing and effective storytelling are just as important as the tech.

SIMON

(1978)

Four colors, four tones, and an easy-to-understand interface made *Simon* the hot Christmas gift of 1978. Creator Ralph Baer, who had earlier developed the first home video game system, donated this production model to The Strong.

It's just after midnight on May 15, 1978, and a thousand revelers are packed into the iconic New York disco Studio 54. The elite venue's famous disco ball twinkles as Diana Ross and Gloria Gaynor are piped through the massive sound system. Club drugs are passed openly among the crowd as New York's hippest celebrities crane their necks toward center stage. Yet they're not hoping to catch a glimpse of Mick Jagger or the Bee Gees. In fact, they're not looking at a person at all—they're here to see a plastic children's toy called *Simon*.

Simon's story begins two years earlier, when Atari released the arcade game *Touch Me*. It was a curious move from a company still riding high from its smash hit *Pong* (page 49), which had sparked America's obsession with video games. Unlike *Pong*, *Touch Me* was primitive even by standards of the time. While arcade game manufacturers were outdoing themselves with sleek cabinets adorned with ornate artwork, *Touch Me* was dressed in a wooden pedestal like something out of low-budget science-fiction movie. It had no graphics and just four large buttons. The gameplay was simple: Players observed a sequence of blinking electric lights and repeated the same sequence by pressing the buttons. The sequences became faster and longer until the player made a mistake. Unsurprisingly, *Touch Me* was a commercial flop; arcade patrons simply preferred the fast-paced action of video games over *Touch Me*'s cerebral memory exercises.

Yet one man saw potential in Atari's forgettable game: Ralph Baer. Baer got his start in the video game industry with his Brown Box (page 21), a prototype home video game console that he licensed to Magnavox, later released in 1973 as the Odyssey. When he spotted *Touch Me*, Baer observed, "Nice gameplay. Terrible execu-

tion. Visually boring. Miserable, rasping sounds." The problem with *Touch Me*, he reasoned, wasn't the gameplay; it was the design and the intended audience. Baer knew he could build a handheld version for a younger crowd who did not spend time in smoky bars.

He also had an axe to grind with Atari. In 1974, Baer, flanked by a team of Magnavox lawyers, successfully sued Atari for stealing his intellectual property. Atari's founder, Nolan Bushnell, had witnessed a demonstration of the Odyssey in early 1972, and one of the featured games was none other than table tennis. After returning home, he directed his star engineer, Al Alcorn, to focus his efforts on creating a coin-operated arcade version of table tennis, which would eventually become *Pong*. (For more information, see *Pong*, page 49; and the Odyssey, page 41). Despite the lawsuit, Atari continued to make millions of dollars off *Pong* and its multitude of sequels. Baer realized that creating a handheld version of *Touch Me* might not only be a marvelous electronic game, but also an opportunity for sweet revenge. He partnered with the legendary toy design firm Marvin Glass and Associates and set to work developing a prototype. Together with programmer Lenny Cope and Howard Morrison, a partner at Marvin Glass, Baer designed an eight-inch rectangular console powered by a low-cost Texas Instruments TMS 1000 microprocessor. Perhaps still vexed by Atari's success with *Pong*, Baer coyly dubbed his copycat product "Follow Me."

Like *Touch Me*, "Follow Me" featured four large buttons, each able to play a distinct note. While the *Touch Me* sound effects were grating on the ear, Baer found inspiration for the tones in "Follow Me" in the pages of his family encyclopedia, where he noted that a bugle would play four pleasant and harmonic notes. When pressed, the blue button played an E note; the yellow button a C#; the red button an A; and the green button another E note, one octave lower than the blue. While the coin-operated *Touch Me* had to be played standing in an arcade, "Follow Me" could be played in bed or on the couch.

Baer pitched his game to the Milton Bradley Company, one of the preeminent toy manufacturers of the time. The company immediately licensed "Follow Me," redesigned the case into a saucer, and renamed it *Simon*, a reference to the popular children's game "Simon Says." Milton Bradley then gave *Simon* the full Madison Avenue treatment, spending enormous sums of money on marketing and penning the catchy adver-poem: "Simon's a computer, Simon has a brain, you either do what Simon says or else go down the drain." *Simon* was aggressively priced at $24.95 and unveiled at Studio 54 in New York City, a four-foot model of the game suspended over the dance floor like an alien spacecraft. Adding to the hype, Steven Spielberg's *Close Encounters of the Third Kind*, released just months earlier, serendipitously featured humans playing a musical version of "Simon Says" with an alien ship that produced musical tones reminiscent of *Simon* the toy.

Simon instantly became a top seller and ruled the holiday season. The game became so popular that Milton Bradley could not meet demand, prompting enormous lines of anxious families hoping to get their hands on the hottest toy on the market. "More than a few youngsters are sure to be wearing long faces Christmas morning when they don't find this season's hit, a game called *Simon*, tucked under the tree," proclaimed the *Chicago Tribune* on December 20, 1978. "It's not Santa's fault. There just aren't enough to go around."

Simon was a goldmine for Milton Bradley (and later its parent company, Hasbro) and would spawn sequels such as *Pocket Simon* and *Super Simon*. The game remains popular to this day, and while the electronics and sound effects have been improved, the gameplay remains virtually identical to the original version. Hoping to cash in on the success of *Simon*, Atari resurrected *Touch Me* in 1978 and hastily put together an awkward handheld version. But the interface was not nearly as intuitive, and, ironically, the public largely saw it as a *Simon* knockoff.

Simon may not be a video game as we traditionally think of them, but it was an important electronic game whose interactivity and sophisticated hardware paved the way for handheld electronic games to revolutionize play. Ralph Baer, the man who had launched the home video game revolution, had now given a boost to the market for mobile electronic games. Baer gave this production Simon to The Strong museum along with all his personal papers documenting the toy's creation and even the Compton's encyclopedia—after all, it was while scanning the letter "B" that he found the idea to use a bugle for the notes.

SPACE INVADERS

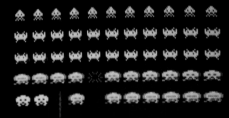

CREDIT 00

SPACE INVADERS

(1978)

A phalanx of pulsating aliens descended on desperate players in this video game, which launched a mania for arcade games in Japan and the United States. *Space Invaders'* progressively more challenging gameplay meant few could play for very long but players were tempted to see if they could do just a little bit better the next time. It joined the World Video Game Hall of Fame in 2016.

O uter space dominated the imagination in the 1970s. The United States had staged a series of moon landings and begun work on the Space Shuttle program. The American and Soviet governments were openly speculating about the possibility of space-based nuclear missiles and defense systems. The limitless expanse of space had also permeated pop culture: *Star Wars*, released in 1977, became a global phenomenon and raked in more than $700 million. Released later that year, Steven Spielberg's *Close Encounters of the Third Kind* hauled in almost $300 million. With the advent of cheap microprocessors, arcade game manufacturers were embroiled in their own space race: Which game would be the first to make millions off the public's obsession with the heavens?

The first commercial space-themed arcade video game was *Computer Space*, released by Nolan Bushnell and Nutting Associates in 1971 (page 29). By 1978, however, the arcade landscape had changed entirely. Atari's *Pong* (page 49) had been a smash hit, selling tens of thousands of units and almost singlehandedly introducing the world to video games. But as *Pong* knock-offs and sports game variants flooded the market, the restless arcade industry, armed with the latest technology, was ready for its next blockbuster release.

The industry's initial response to *Star Wars* would not come from Atari, but from the Japanese firm Taito. Taito was founded in 1953 as a vending machine distributor and was later the first company to distill and sell vodka in Japan. It later moved on to coin-operated jukeboxes, electromechanical arcade games, and, in 1973, video games. Like many manufacturers, Taito got its start by copying *Pong*; Taito's version, *Elepong*,

sold well and helped the company gain a foothold in Japan's burgeoning video arcade industry. Taito later released simple games based on sports like soccer, basketball, and hockey. In 1974, Taito, along with its U.S. distributor Midway, came out with *Gun Fight*. Unlike its previous releases—almost all derivatives of Atari sports games—*Gun Fight* was entirely unique. It was the world's first commercial arcade video game to use a microprocessor, which offered the best graphics and the smoothest gameplay on the market. *Gun Fight* also helped bring the concept of the "shooter" game to video arcade games, casting players as dueling Old West cowboys armed with revolvers.

In 1977, eyeing the success of *Star Wars*, Taito tasked its star engineer, Tomohiro Nishikado, with developing a space shooter. For inspiration, Nishikado looked to an earlier Taito mechanical coin-operated game called *Space Monsters* and—according to legend—a nightmare he had involving Japanese schoolchildren who were attacked by aliens while waiting for Santa Claus on Christmas Eve. The resourceful tots hastily cobbled together a cannon with spare automobile parts and blasted the aliens from the sky before they could invade Earth. This reminded Nishikado of Atari's 1976 hit *Breakout* (page 71), which featured a vertical playfield with a layer of bricks at the top of the screen that players smashed using a bouncing ball and a horizontally moving paddle.

Nishikado devised a game in which players controlled a laser cannon moving along a fixed horizontal axis at the bottom of the screen to defeat waves of aliens approaching from the top. After experimenting with various animations including tanks, planes, and battleships, he settled on squid-like alien imagery inspired by the 1953 film *The War of the Worlds*. The game, which took a year to develop, was powered by an Intel 8080 microprocessor and a Fujitsu MB14241 video shifter, an early precursor to today's discrete graphics chips. The gameplay was simple and addictive: Five rows of eleven aliens slowly advanced from side to side, dropping downward toward the player upon reaching either side of the screen. Players had to dodge projectiles and blast the aliens before they reached the bottom of the screen. When all the aliens were destroyed, a new wave of enemies appeared and the difficulty increased. He dubbed the game *Space Invaders*.

The game performed flawlessly except for a peculiar glitch that bedeviled Nishikado. The hardware used in *Space Invaders* was not sufficiently powerful to run the game at a constant speed; the more aliens there were on the screen, the slower they moved. As players blasted aliens, the remaining enemies descended faster and faster, making gameplay increasingly difficult. Instead of trying to redesign *Space Invaders* to run more stably, Nishikado decided to retain the quirk as a challenging gameplay dynamic. He then composed background sounds featuring heavy, pulsing bass notes reminiscent of a thumping heartbeat that sped up as the aliens grew closer, compounding the feverish gameplay.

Space Invaders could not be won. Instead, it popularized the use of a "difficulty curve" that increased the challenge level of the game as a player progressed. While other arcade games featured time limits or continued at the same difficulty level indefinitely, *Space Invaders* introduced audiences to an entirely new, endlessly more exciting mode of gameplay. Additionally, *Space Invaders* also introduced a "high score" that ticked higher the more aliens a player blasted and persisted indefinitely on the screen until it

was bested by another player (or the machine was turned off). This new feature encouraged arcade patrons to play again and again and again.

The game was so addictive, in fact, that stories circulated that Japan experienced spot shortages of one-hundred-yen coins. Entire arcades sprang up featuring only *Space Invaders* consoles, and by the end of 1978 Taito had installed more than one hundred thousand machines and grossed over $600 million in Japan alone. That same year, Taito licensed *Space Invaders* to Midway for distribution in the American market, where it sold sixty thousand units in just two years. By 1982, *Space Invaders* had generated $2 billion in quarters (approximately $5 billion today), easily surpassing global ticket sales for *Star Wars*. All told, *Space Invaders* raked in more than $6.6 billion (in 2017 dollars), making it the second-highest-grossing arcade game of all time after *Pac-Man* (page 131).

Space Invaders turned the nascent video game industry into a global juggernaut. The game spawned numerous sequels, including an extremely successful port to the Atari 2600 (page 86) that massively boosted sales of the home console. *Space Invaders* propelled an industry, heretofore largely dependent on rudimentary sports games and *Pong* clones, into one that valued fast-paced action, storytelling, and fantastical settings. When Shigeru Miyamoto, the legendary designer of *Donkey Kong*, *Super Mario Bros.*, and *The Legend of Zelda* among countless other classics, was asked what video game he believed revolutionized the industry, he instantly replied: "*Space Invaders*. Before I saw it, I was never particularly interested in video games and certainly never thought I would make video games."

ADVENTURELAND

(1978)

Before video games came in designer packages, *Adventureland* creator and founder of Adventure International Scott Adams used baby-bottle liners to package and sell his cassette-tape games. This rare artifact, part of the Scott Adams Adventure International Collection, is perhaps the earliest known example of an unopened independent computer game.

cott Adams was hooked. Rather, he was *obsessed*. He had been playing *Colossal Cave Adventure* (see page 98 for history and gameplay) for ten days in 1977 during early mornings and late evenings on a PDP-10 minicomputer at Stromberg Carlson, where he worked as a systems programmer. Adams played again and again and again, determined to acquire every treasure and achieve the coveted maximum score of 350 and the title of "Grand Master." Finally, in the wee hours of the night, he hit the magical number. "I had done it," Adams later wrote. "I was a *bona fide* adventurer!" He was hungry to play more text-based games that combined the interactivity of computers with the immersive storytelling of a novel. Moreover, he wanted to play them at home with the Tandy TRS-80 personal computer he had just purchased from Radio Shack.

This was the dawn of the home-computer revolution. The year 1977 had witnessed the introduction of the TRS-80 along with the Apple II and the Commodore PET (or Personal Electronic Transactor) personal computers. Previously, computers were multimillion-dollar machines reserved for large research institutions, but these modestly priced machines—each retailed for under $1,500 for the base model—brought computers into middle-class homes. This was possible because microchips offered the computing power of massive circuit boards on thumbnail-size silicon wafers. Thanks to low-cost, high-performance chips such as the MOS Technology 6502, which powered the Apple II (and later the Atari 2600 and the Nintendo NES), and the Zilog Z80, which powered the TRS-80, computers were coming to the masses.

Yet there was a dearth of software available for these machines to run, especially games. Adams realized that if he could create his own text-based game, he could sell it to ordinary computer users. The first problem was technical: home computers could still not quite match the power and storage capabilities of massive mainframes like those on which Adams had played *Colossal Cave Adventure*, so he spent several weeks developing a compression algorithm. Second, he had to come up with a compelling story; despite having thousands of science-fiction novels in his collection, he had never tried to write a story himself.

Due to technological limitations and a modest 120-word vocabulary, Adams's game only accepted two-word commands such as "go west" or "take lamp." The goal was to discover thirteen artifacts, including a statue of Paul Bunyan's blue ox, a golden fish, a dragon's egg, a diamond necklace, and a magic carpet. There was no plot in the traditional sense; players were given a list of treasures and were challenged to find them all—"without," as the opening screen promised, "leaving your armchair!"

Adams dubbed his game *Adventureland* and slaved away for months coding it in the BASIC computer language. (For more about BASIC, see pages 56–57.) He was so consumed by the game that his then-wife, Alexis, who was pregnant, began hiding the disks containing the game's source code to gain his attention. "Once she hid them in the oven," Adams recollected. "Boy did she get some attention that time!" Fortunately she did not turn on the oven, and the world's first commercial text-based game survived to hit store shelves.

Adams published *Adventureland* on loose cassette tapes painstakingly copied one by one on his TRS-80, and sold them without any product packaging. This was a time before software was marketed to consumers, so Adams had to hand sell his game to individual stores. One day an enterprising owner at a Chicago-area Radio Shack suggested to Adams that he could sell more games if *Adventureland* came in retail packaging. Adams knew he had to find a low-cost solution. Inspired by his infant daughter's baby bottles, the new father placed the cassette games into baby bottle liners and stapled a bi-folded business card at the top to seal them. Along with Ziploc bags, these bottle liners acted as the first retail packaging for computer games.

Adventureland sales steadily picked up, and Adams went on to found the company Adventure International with his wife. Despite her initial frustrations with her husband's hobby, Alexis had a knack for video game design and co-created the company's second game, *Pirate Adventure*. This game transported players to Pirate Island, where they must build a ship and sail it to Treasure Island in order to discover Long John Silver's lost treasures. Alexis later collaborated on and helped generate ideas for the company's *Voodoo Castle* (1979) and *Mystery Fun House* (1979) adventure games.

Later Adventure International packaging resembled book covers and featured a range of artwork, but the 1981 *Scott Adams Adventure*

Series Limited Gold Edition introduced an entirely new concept to computer games: the limited edition. These "limited gold edition" games came in a plastic clamshell case styled like a leather-bound book and included a certificate of authenticity signed by Adams. The series is perhaps the first example of a video game sold as a collectible.

The *Adventure* games were not the most advanced text-based games available. Infocom's *Zork*, released commercially in 1980, featured a more dramatic storyline and a larger vocabulary. (For more information about *Zork*, see page 97.) Nevertheless, Scott and Alexis Adams were pioneers in the commercial computer game industry. Before *Adventureland*, no one knew how to package or sell games for microcomputers. Scott Adams's donation to The Strong of more than 130 original games created by him and his company, printed source code, product catalogs, advertising flyers, photographs, comic books, magazines, and other materials demonstrate just how trailblazing Adventure International's efforts were to the computer game industry. Adams went from scrounging for baby bottle packaging to employing fifty people in 1984.

When asked how he achieved this without any sort of blueprint, Adams simply said: "As the business grew I learned as I went."

```
I am in a forest. Visible items:

Trees.

        Some obvious exits are: NORTH SOUTH EAST WEST
_____


A voice BOOOOMS out:

Welcome to Adventure number: 1 "ADVENTURELAND".
In this Adventure you're to find *TREASURES* & store them away.

To see how well you're doing say: "SCORE"
Remember you can always say "HELP"
    -------> Tell me what to do?
```

THE NEW FATHER PLACED THE CASSETTE
GAMES INTO BABY BOTTLE LINERS AND
STAPLED A BI-FOLDED BUSINESS CARD
AT THE TOP TO SEAL THEM. ALONG WITH
ZIPLOC BAGS, THESE BOTTLE LINERS ACTED
AS THE FIRST RETAIL PACKAGING FOR
COMPUTER GAMES.

SPEAK & SPELL

(1978)

English spelling has always bedeviled young learners. Texas Instruments harnessed the first mass-produced speech-synthesizer chip to create a toy that helped kids master tricky words such as *abscess, corsage,* and *laughter.* The toy was later immortalized in pop culture by helping a friendly alien phone home in Steven Spielberg's film *E.T. the Extra-Terrestrial.*

n 1866, inventor Halcyon Skinner filed a patent for an "Apparatus for Teaching Spelling." At the top of his invention sat an enclosed spool of paper that exposed one of many pictures, including animals and everyday household objects. Using the built-in keyboard, students spelled the names of the objects as they appeared in the window, while rotating letter wheels displayed each typed letter. The simple device could not communicate whether a student spelled a word correctly, but it was one of the very first toys specifically developed to teach children how to spell.

More than a century later, in 1976, engineer Paul Breedlove had a similar idea. His company, Texas Instruments (TI), pioneered efforts in the development of microchips that led to a new technology called "bubble memory," which allowed for data to be saved in a solid state with no moving parts. Instead of a spinning hard drive, bubble memory used a thin film of magnetic material to store tiny bits of data, similar to how calculators worked. Breedlove was tasked with finding a fast way to commercialize TI's latest innovation. Realizing that bubble memory could allow for a device to memorize and recite the spoken word, he visualized a toy that could help children learn new words.

Breedlove sketched out his idea for what he dubbed *Speak & Spell*. The toy would require using TI's solid-state memory to store full words just like TI calculators at the time stored numbers. Unlike tape recorders, there would be no moving parts. When a user punched in letters, *Speak & Spell* had to retrieve a word from its memory, process it with an integrated circuit, and then speak the word electronically. Intrigued by Breedlove's plan, TI authorized a $25,000 budget.

Breedlove enlisted the help of three engineers: Gene Frantz, responsible for case design, display, and overall operation; Larry Brantingham, charged with integrated circuit design; and Richard Wiggins, responsible for voice processing algorithms. As Wiggins said in an interview years later, "The challenge was that [*Speak & Spell*] had to be solid state (no pull strings!), cheap (meaning it used a low cost semiconductor technology), and the speech had to be good enough so that the user could understand the word out of context—a little bit harder than using a word in a sentence." TI threw more and more engineers onto the project as it gained traction.

The eventual product was programmed with hundreds of commonly misspelled words, from "beauty" to "scissors" to "shovel," and even included words that gave many adults pause, such as "abscess" and "bureau." *Speak & Spell* worked as its name implied: The game spoke a word out loud and kids spelled it using a built-in pushbutton keyboard. As they typed, the letters appeared on a vacuum fluorescent display (VFD) screen. Housed in a red plastic case, *Speak & Spell* commended the player after a correct answer ("That is correct"), while an incorrect answer prompted the machine to say, "Wrong, try again."

Speak & Spell was not the first talking toy. Other toys used pull strings—think Woody from *Toy Story*—to activate prerecorded tape players. TI's creation, however, was the first to employ a digital chip that could store hundreds of words. As for the voice of *Speak & Spell*, the company chose Robert Phillips, a radio DJ from Dallas with a crisp drawl. In addition to the standard spelling game, users could install cartridges into *Speak & Spell* that offered new games, special accents (such as British English), and new languages like Japanese and German. Games included the

TOYS THAT TEACH

The brain loves to learn through play, so it's not surprising that adults have long tried to create playthings that help children learn specific skills, including spelling. The English philosopher John Locke, in his *Some Thoughts Concerning Education* (1693), suggested parents paste letters on the side of wooden blocks to help children learn the sounds and ordering of letters.

Voila! The alphabet block.

The Strong museum's collections contain dozens of examples of spelling toys from the nineteenth and twentieth centuries, including McLoughlin Bros.'s *New Yankee Letter Blocks for Word Building* (1879) and Hood's *Spelling School* (1897). *Speak & Spell* was only the latest iteration in the age-old quest to help children decipher the phonetic confusion of the English language.

classic *Say It*, where players had to spell ten words "spoken" by the unit; *Mystery Word*, an electronic version of hangman; *Memory*, which tested letter recognition and visual memory; and *Same As*, which tested homophone recognition.

Retailing for $50, *Speak & Spell* was an immediate hit and soon became one of the best-selling toys of all time. The unit would see numerous redesigns as technology progressed, such as an updated vocabulary, a QWERTY keyboard (as opposed to an ABC keyboard), and a liquid crystal display (LCD). *Speak & Spell* was enshrined in pop culture after helping a friendly alien phone his home planet in the film *E.T. the Extra-Terrestrial*, and Depeche Mode even named their 1981 debut album after it. While *Speak & Spell* helped a generation of kids learn to spell,

more recently it has developed a cult following among hackers and musicians through a process known as circuit bending. By opening the toy's case, cross-wiring terminals, and adding additional resistors and switches, clever tinkerers can distort *Speak & Spell*'s voice or even turn it into a unique instrument—a technique employed live and in the studio by musical artists such as Beck, CocoRosie, and Eisbrecher.

Though not a video game in the traditional sense, *Speak & Spell* was one of the first products to embrace computer technology and wield it for an educational purpose. *Speak & Spell* embodied the hope that computers could make everyone's lives better, from friendly aliens desperate to phone home to children struggling with spelling.

ASTEROIDS

(1979)

Arcade cabinets are physical structures that focus the attention of the player. Atari developed this prototype *Asteroids* to test the game. The cabinet featured hand-drawn art, and the game's developers later signed it.

n the spring of 1978, Atari was the undisputed king of video games. After releasing *Pong* five years earlier, Atari's coin-operated division and its subsidiary, Kee Games, were pumping out game after game, from the multitude of *Pong* sequels to *Tank*, *Breakout*, and *Sprint 2*. In 1977, Atari had revenues of $40 million, much of which was plowed into marketing its fledgling home console, the Atari 2600 (page 86). While the company knew that home video games were the future, it was still very much dependent on its blue-chip arcade cabinets. And until 1978, no company could touch Atari's supremacy.

Then came Taito's *Space Invaders*, which introduced several revolutionary features—most notably the difficulty curve and the progressive high score—that made the game endlessly replayable. (For more information about *Space Invaders,* see page 107.) Atari's cherished tenet was to create products that were easy to learn and difficult to master, but the American juggernaut had just been schooled at its own game by a Japanese upstart best known for creating jukeboxes and vodka.

Atari was eager to reclaim its throne. One possibility was to create a *Space Invaders* clone, a tactic used by other firms such as Sega and Nintendo. But as Atari engineer Ed Logg would later write in his notebook about the November 1979 Amusement and Music Operators Association show, "The show had many copies and variations of *Space Invaders*. I thought very few of them were any good." Atari was determined to create something completely original. With these marching orders, senior Atari executive Lyle Rains summoned Logg into his office. Logg had built a successful career at the Control Data Corporation before joining Atari's coin-operated arcade division. Eager to make a name for himself, he had designed *Super Breakout*, a successful update to Atari's hit game *Breakout*. Rains was impressed by Logg's ability to retain the original spirit of *Breakout* while adding new and exciting features—an ability he hoped could be harnessed to create Atari's next blockbuster.

Space Invaders allowed players to move their cannon left and right, but Rains wanted to move his cannon upward and downward and even off the screen. He pitched his idea to Logg and the two immediately thought of Nolan Bushnell and Ted Dabney's 1971 creation *Computer Space*, the first mass-produced arcade video game. (For more information about *Computer Space*, see page 29.) Rains described his new idea to Logg as a "little flying ship as in *Computer Space*; big rocks becoming little rocks; fly and shoot till they all go away."

Rains and Logg dubbed their idea *Asteroids*, then turned to designing it. Much had changed since 1971, with new microprocessors allowing for sophisticated graphics and vastly superior gameplay. One option was to develop *Asteroids* with raster graphics, which used thousands of tiny pixels to generate images; this was the same technology that powered nearly all arcade games up until then. Although visually pleasing, raster graphics were imprecise and cartoon-like, giving images a distorted quality—think of the famous pixelated aliens from *Space Invaders*. The second option was vector graphics, a relatively new technology that used electronic beams to project thin glowing lines and shapes on a monitor. Unlike raster graphics, vector images were completely smooth and distinct. Logg insisted that this technology, while unconventional, would enable players to pilot their ships with much better precision.

With the help of engineer Howard Delman, Rains and Logg procured vector hardware from the Atari team behind *Lunar Lander*, a game released in August 1979 in which players piloted a lunar-landing module on the moon. The physics of *Asteroids* were based on *Spacewar!*, the famed space-combat game created in 1962 at MIT. The *Asteroids* gameplay was quite simple: Players controlled a triangular ship, dodging and blasting floating asteroids on the screen. Each time an asteroid was hit, it broke up into smaller, faster asteroids that were more difficult to avoid. A "hyperspace" button—also inspired by *Spacewar!*—enabled players in dire situations to disappear and reappear at a random location, at the risk of landing on top of an asteroid. *Asteroids* also featured wraparound screen edges, allowing objects that drifted off one edge to reappear at the opposite side. After players cleared the screen, a new level started with a more difficult wave of asteroids.

The game was an immediate hit with Atari employees, who begged Logg to leave the office so they could play the prototype. In late summer, Logg and Colette Weil from Atari's marketing team brought an *Asteroids* cabinet to an arcade in Sacramento, California, to gauge consumer interest. One man walked over, put in his money, and died three times within twenty seconds. But instead of leaving out of frustration, he put another quarter in. "I thought, okay, if he's dying three times and still putting in another quarter, he must think it's his fault, not that the game has got it in for him," Logg recollected. "He died again, almost instantly. He put in quarter after quarter after quarter." Although the field test reports from Logg's notebook detail that many players said they liked *Space Invaders* better than *Asteroids* because it was "easier to play," *Asteroids* outperformed *Space Invaders*, *Starhawk*, and Atari's own *Lunar Lander* where it counted most: in the cash box.

Players were captivated by the crisp gameplay and the throbbing, heartbeat-like sound effects that intensified as the asteroids became faster and more dangerous. In addition, an ingenious feature allowed players to add their initials

ASTEROIDS HIGH SCORE

On April 5, 2010, a man named John McAllister broke a twenty-seven-year-old record that few believed could be bested: the *Asteroids* high score. The official mark of 41,336,440 was set by fifteen-year-old Scott Safran in 1982, who dodged and blasted asteroids for three straight days to achieve the feat. Playing with a friend's original *Asteroids* cabinet, McAllister also stayed up for three delirious days, nearly losing out on the record after a last-minute bathroom break depleted all but two of his remaining lives. But he rallied, finally logging his now-record 41,338,740th point at 10:18 P.M. Pacific time.

McAllister punched in "E-L-F" next to his high score, and then the freshly minted arcade legend went to bed.

to their saved high score, seducing them into playing again and again to become the *Asteroids* king or queen of their local arcade.

Asteroids became an instant classic, displacing *Space Invaders* as the bestselling arcade game and reasserting, at least for the moment, Atari's dominance in the industry. The company sold more than seventy thousand units, earning an estimated $150 million in sales while generating $500 million in quarters for arcade operators. Demand was so high for *Asteroids* that Atari ordered the *Lunar Lander* division to cease production and make *Asteroids* cabinets instead—causing hundreds of *Asteroids* games

to be shipped in *Lunar Lander* cabinets. According to legend, arcade operators had to jury-rig extra-large coin boxes on the *Asteroid* cabinets to keep pace with frenzied demand.

Asteroids harnessed the best elements of existing arcade games, invented a slew of new features, and combined them all into one ultimate package. It was fast, furious, and thoroughly addicting. As Atari's Howard Delman later reflected, "*Asteroids* is a classic man-against-machine game. It was simple to learn, obvious what you had to do, and you could improve quickly, but however good you got, the game was always one step ahead."

Asteroids designer Ed Logg organized his game design notes, sketches, company memorandums, correspondence, focus group summaries, field test reports, and other documentation into this black vinyl binder. This is part of The Strong's massive Atari Coin-Op Divisions Collection, a one-of-a-kind assemblage of materials, that provides us with insight into how Atari created their bestselling coin-operated video game of all time.

MARKET RESEARCH

In the early 1970s, Atari hired Carol Kantor to their marketing team. Having worked in the market research department at the Clorox Company, she brought to the young video game company techniques used to study and better understand consumer behavior. Kantor pioneered video game market research, and along with Colette Weil (hired in 1977), Mary Takatsuno (later Fujihara), and Linda Benzler (later Adam) they conducted focus groups, field observations, player surveys—and even recorded telemetry data from "coin drops."

Logg's *Asteroids* notebook includes pages of focus groups, field tests, and player surveys conducted by Weil (then Atari's Director of Market Research) and her team. Using these methods, they blazed a trail for future Game User Researchers, whose work has become indispensable to video game developers.

RALPH BAER'S
LIGHT ANTI-TANK WEAPON

(1979)

The military continually enlists the latest technology, so top brass readily responded to Ralph Baer's development of a modified light anti-tank weapon that could blast simulated Russian tanks.

Consider popular images of warfare today: pilots driving drones remotely with joysticks, point-of-view body cameras on soldiers, generals hunched around a laptop at a conference table monitoring a battle thousands of miles away. Why does modern warfare seem so much like a video game?

Military strategy and gaming have been inextricably linked for as long as humans have waged war. From the invention of chess in ancient India, to nineteenth century kriegspiel—a system of wargames invented by a lieutenant in the Prussian army in 1812—to Cold War–era simulations of nuclear war, games have not only helped military leaders learn to think strategically, they have had a profound effect on how we think about the art of war. Traditionally, war games have reproduced the bird's-eye view of the commanding officer, not the infantryman. But with electronic games, for the first time it became possible to simulate not just what it felt like to be a general conducting large-scale strategy, but also what it felt like to be an individual soldier in theater.

One crucial step in this journey took place in a lab at a defense contractor in Nashua, New Hampshire. Ralph Baer, inventor of the pioneering video game console the Brown Box (page 21) and the electronic game *Simon* (page 103), had been experimenting with the technology behind so-called light guns—plastic model guns with light sensors that could register whether a player had "hit" a virtual target. So when Al Nunes, a Sanders Associates employee and a former U.S. field engineer, strode into his lab at Sanders on Canal Street in Nashua clutching a dangerous-looking four-foot cylinder of steel, Baer was ready for him.

Nunes wanted to know if Baer was able to create a first-person shooter simulation that, instead of white dots on a black screen, could show real stock footage of Russian tanks rolling over the countryside. And instead of a plastic gun, could Baer use the object Nunes had brought him: an actual decommissioned M72A2 Light Anti-tank Weapon? "Of course," recalled Baer. The result, a Cold War–era simulation of what a gunner might see on the ground while facing Russian tanks, not only helped reproduce the experience of being an individual soldier, it represents the increasingly close—and sometimes uneasy—relationship between the video game industry and the military.

The Light Anti-tank Weapon (LAW) was outfitted with a small light-sensing optical scope, while footage of Russian tanks were projected onto a screen. Baer had figured out how to encode each of the video's 250 television scan lines with location information. When a soldier pointed the optical scope of the LAW at the screen, an Apple II computer not only knew which of the 250 horizontal lines he was pointing at, but also how far along that line he was. And if that point corresponded with where the image of the tank was at that moment, the system registered a "hit"—and displayed a primitive "explosion" where the tank used to be.

The military loved it. In his memoir, Baer recalled a trip to the Pentagon with Al Nunes and their colleague George Mitchell, their unwieldy but sophisticated demo in tow: "We spent the day rolling a large cart loaded with our equipment all over the infinitely long hallways of that monstrous collection of concentric-ring buildings." Word quickly spread throughout the Pentagon, and Baer, Mitchell, and Nunes ended their day nervously watching a two-star general demonstrate the LAW to the undersecretary of the army, Dr. Walter LaBerge. "The gear worked flawlessly," Baer later recalled.

Many of the earliest video game pioneers, however, were wary of their inventions being used for destruction rather than for entertainment. In 1981, for example, army officials noticed the release of an Atari arcade title called *Battlezone*, a vector-based game that simulated fantasy tank warfare (UFOs and an exploding volcano were involved). The army contacted Atari and wanted to know if it could build a similar product for military training purposes. After all, every time a soldier pulled a trigger expending a live round, it cost tax payers thousands of dollars. Many of Atari's notoriously countercultural employees were vehemently opposed, not least of all the original programmer of *Battlezone* itself, Ed Rotberg. In the end, Atari created a *Battlezone* redux called the "Bradley Trainer," named after the army's new Bradley Fighting Vehicle. But after Atari manufactured two prototypes for the army to test, the game never made it into full production.

As the 1990s saw the explosive popularity of first-person shooters, army officials realized that video games could also be a very effective recruiting tool for manning an all-volunteer army of digital natives. Published by the U.S. Army in 2002, and powered by Epic Games' Unreal Engine, *America's Army* was part entertainment, part recruiting tool, and part marketing device for the army. At a time when few Americans served in the military, *America's Army* appealed to a crucial demographic. A teenager wondering if military service was right for him or her could spend hours lost in the game, learning about military operations while battling other potential recruits, active soldiers, veterans, or even players interested in America's military from across the globe.

Not only did the game prove to be enormously successful—over thirteen million people have registered an *America's Army* account—its simulations were so realistic that there have been reports of soldiers not otherwise trained as medics drawing on the in-game training they'd received as teenagers to save actual lives in the field. *America's Army* and other military-funded games such as *Full Spectrum Warrior*—which began as a training tool for the military, became an Xbox and PlayStation 2 game, and was also used therapeutically to treat soldiers returning from Iraq and Afghanistan with post-traumatic stress disorder—proved that video games not only allowed the army to communicate with a new generation of gamers, but, if harnessed properly, had the potential to train, entertain, and heal them.

Did Ralph Baer foresee, standing in the Pentagon in 1979, firing a decommissioned M72A2 Light Anti-tank Weapon at a projection screen amid a tangle of wires, that the technology he was pioneering would one day inspire video game–based recruitment? Possibly not. But with warfare itself increasingly resembling electronic games, the link between virtual war and actual war may only be getting stronger.

PAC-MAN

(1980)

When a video game becomes a Halloween costume, you know it's a phenomenon. Pac-Man fever gripped America in 1980 as players dropped in billions of quarters in their quest to devour dots and gobble ghosts. The Strong inducted the game into the inaugural class of the World Video Game Hall of Fame.

n his book *Free to Learn*, psychologist Peter Gray notes that young mammals of nearly all species share a universal joy of chase games. A young Labrador bounds away from her brother and then bounds back, just as a human toddler shrieks with joy as her father pursues her down the hallway. Freeze tag is a staple of playgrounds everywhere, while eighty thousand football fans roar with anticipation as a defensive back sprints toward a scrambling quarterback. "In nightmares and in real life, nothing is more terrifying than being chased by a predator or monster," Gray writes. "But in play, nothing is more delightful." Not surprisingly, some of the earliest and most popular video games centered on chase. For more than forty years, electronic games have provided players with the opportunity to experiment with the virtual dangers of chase play, and no game better embodies this instinct than *Pac-Man*.

According to legend, the bestselling arcade game of all time began with a pizza, when twenty-four-year-old Toru Iwatani removed a slice and became transfixed by the remaining mouth-shaped pie. At the time, in 1978, Iwatani was working for the Japanese corporation Namco, a leading arcade game manufacturer. Founded in 1955, Namco initially operated kiddie rides on the roof of a department store in the city of Yokohama, Japan, before focusing on coin-operated amusements. In 1974, struggling for revenue, Namco made a last-ditch effort to revitalize its business by purchasing Atari's Japanese division for $500,000, allowing it to exclusively distribute Atari games in Japan. With a stable cash flow Namco could finally focus on its own games, later releasing modestly successful titles such as *Gee Bee* (1978) and *Galaxian* (1979),

but the company was still seeking that elusive blockbuster hit.

As Iwatani stared at this peculiar mouth-shaped pizza, he thought of the Japanese onomatopoeic slang phrase *pakku*, used to describe the sound a mouth makes as it repeatedly opens and closes. What if, he reasoned, a simple arcade game could be based around eating? Until then, most blockbuster arcade games involved blasting things like aliens and asteroids with weapons. "In the late 1970s, there were a lot of games in arcades which featured killing aliens or other enemies that mostly appealed to boys to play," Iwatani explained in an interview with *Time* magazine in 2015. "The image of arcades was that they were darkly lit and their restrooms were dirty." While plenty of women certainly enjoyed playing *Space Invaders* (page 107) and *Asteroids* (page 121), the stereotype of arcades as grimy, raucous boys' clubs was not entirely untrue. Iwatani wanted to create a game that was popular with everyone and could help attract more female players.

Iwatani's original design called for an animated pizza running around a maze eating everything it came across. Due to technological limitations, his team settled for a plain yellow wedge with a chomping mouth, dubbed *Puckman*, derived from the Japanese word *pakku* (which sounds like "puck-u"), meaning to *munch* in English. (When the game was eventually introduced to the American market, the name was changed to *Pac-Man*; U.S. licenser Midway foresaw that not-so-clever vandals could easily change the *P* in *Puckman* to an *F*.) Like all great arcade games, the object was simple. Players used a joystick to direct Pac-Man around a maze, eating dots, while avoiding four ghost enemies: Blinky, Pinky,

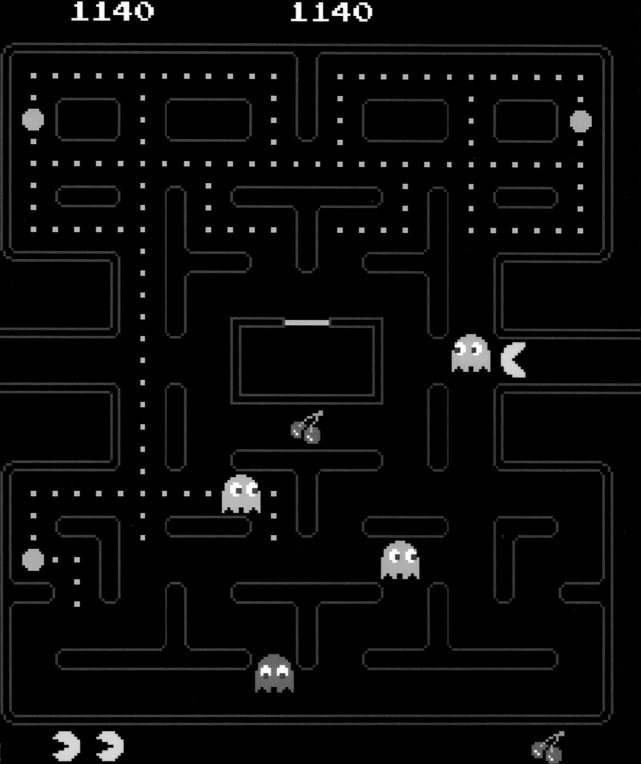

Inky, and Clyde (originally named Akabei, Pinky, Aosuke, and Guzuta in Japan), each with their own strengths and weaknesses. Unlike *Space Invaders*, where a monolithic wave of aliens slowly and predictably descended toward the player, the ghosts in *Pac-Man* gave chase with seemingly random and unpredictable movements—adding to the frenzied nature of the gameplay. If a ghost touched Pac-Man, the player lost a life. Once Pac-Man ate all the dots, the game restarted with a newer, more difficult level.

Like *Space Invaders* and *Asteroids* before it, there was no time limit for *Pac-Man*; a player continued until she ran out of lives—and the longer she played, the harder the game became. This difficulty curve compounded the sense of "chase" that made gameplay so feverish and entertaining. But *Pac-Man* also introduced a novel feature that turned the tables on the chase dynamic: if a player ate one of four special large dots, the ghosts turned blue for several seconds and Pac-Man could eat them. For a short time, the hunters became the hunted.

After more than a year of development—an eternity in the arcade industry at the time—Namco released *Pac-Man* to the Japanese market. The game sold modestly, but *Space Invaders* remained king; many arcades had been built solely to house *Space Invaders* cabinets and operators were not ready to give up their cash cow quite yet. Moreover, sales were cannibalized by Namco's successful game *Galaxian*, released around the same time, which was designed to compete with Taito's *Space Invaders*. Undeterred, Namco cast its gaze to the United States, teaming up with the distributor Midway to produce a version for the American market. Midway made several distinct modifications: It changed the name *Puckman* to *Pac-Man*, tweaked the

cabinet artwork by changing the color scheme from white to yellow and giving Pac-Man feet and eyes, and slightly increased the difficulty level.

In an arcade environment saturated with alien shooters, Atari sports games, and clones of alien shooters and Atari sports games, American audiences were eager for something fresh. Iwatani was correct in his belief that a new audience of gamers were ready to spend their quarters if only companies stopped pandering exclusively to young men. In October of 1980, when Midway released *Pac-Man* to America, Pacmania officially began. *Pac-Man* swiftly outpaced Atari's *Asteroids* to become the bestselling arcade game, grossing more than $1 billion in quarters in less than a year. As the American obsession with *Pac-Man* intensified, the sluggish worldwide market finally let loose. Within eighteen months of its release, over three hundred fifty thousand cabinets had been sold, and over four hundred thousand were sold by 1982.

Perhaps the biggest reason for its success was its appeal to the other half of the population. The statistics paint a stunning portrait: according to one study, while 95 percent of *Defender* players—a 1981 scrolling shooter game by Williams Electronics in which players must defeat waves of aliens—were male, 60 percent of *Pac-Man* players were female. *Pac-Man* was also the first game to generate a merchandising frenzy that reached far beyond the arcade. *Pong* may have been a groundbreaking game, but no companies made *Pong*-branded ping-pong paddles. The aliens in *Space Invaders* did not have unique personalities or names like Blinky, Pinky, Inky, and Clyde. The wedge-shaped ship in *Asteroids* was not a loveable cartoon character with an insatiable appetite. *Pac-Man* became the first game with universal name recognition, even among people who had never stepped foot inside an arcade. By the mid-1980s, the world's favorite dot-gobbler was plastered on lunchboxes, T-shirts, cereal and pasta boxes, and every possible plastic product that toy manufacturers could think of. A *Pac-Man* animated TV series produced by Hanna-Barbera aired from 1982 to 1983. Costumes featuring Pac-Man and his iconic orange, red, pink, and blue pursuers were routinely among the most popular during Halloween.

Pac-Man was the first game to truly break free of the cultural constraints of the arcade. A video game did not have to be edgy or violent or feature aliens to be successful. Nor did it have to be dependent on the weekly allowances of thirteen-year-old boys to gain a following. With a pizza-shaped wedge and four blundering ghosts as its official mascots, the high-flying video game industry was finally in the driver's seat of American pop culture.

MISSILE COMMAND

(1980)

Dark, dystopic dreams haunted *Missile Command* creator Dave Theurer while he was making this game about defending cities against nuclear missile attack.

Dave Theurer awoke to the sound of an earth-shattering crash. *A hydrogen bomb vaporizing San Francisco. Nuclear war had begun. It was the end.* These thoughts raced through Theurer's half-asleep mind as sweat poured down his face. The seconds ticked agonizingly by as he waited for the high-pressure nuclear shockwave to crush his house. But it never came, nor did the fiery inferno or the mushroom cloud. Finally, he remembered where he was. The earth-shattering crash was not a Russian nuclear-tipped intercontinental ballistic missile (ICBM), but a plane taking off from nearby Moffett Field in Mountain View, California. This was not the first nightmare he'd had about nuclear war. A few days earlier he dreamed he was hiking in the mountains over the Bay Area when suddenly missile streaks appeared, heading right for him. He had these dreams almost nightly, ever since he began working on a game called *Missile Command*.

The election of former actor and strident anticommunist Ronald Reagan to the presidency in 1980 signaled a more aggressive approach to U.S. Cold War foreign policy. Under Reagan the U.S. launched the biggest peacetime arms buildup in American history. Although the threat of nuclear war may not have felt as omnipresent as in the 1960s, rising tensions with the Soviet Union and the March 1979 meltdown of a nuclear reactor at Three Mile Island, Pennsylvania, had many Americans anxious about all things nuclear. In 1980, Theurer was working at Atari as a game designer. He had recently finished a game called *Four Player Soccer*, a sequel to the 1978 smash hit *Atari Football*, and he was searching for a new project. One day he received a call from his boss, Steve Calfee. "Make me a game that looks like this," Calfee said when Theurer entered his office, tossing him

a magazine clipping. The story was about space satellites and included a picture of a radar screen, which had caught the eye of Gene Lipkin, Atari's president of coin-operated games. Calfee envisioned a game where the player must defend his or her cities from enemy missiles appearing from the top of the screen. When the player's cities were destroyed, the game was over. The rest of the game mechanics were left up to Theurer.

He agreed to work on the game, which would be called *Missile Command*, under one condition: players had to be *defending* their cities, not attacking enemy ones. "Realizing that the bombs would kill all of the people in the targeted city, I did not want to put the player in the position of being a genocidal maniac," Theurer said in an interview with *Polygon* in 2013. The Atari ethos was generally heavily rooted in counterculture, and the idea of creating a "bomb them back to the Stone Age" arcade game during the midst of the Cold War was anathema to the engineers. But a game where players *defended* cities was far more noble, albeit with a Sophie's Choice–like twist: as the game became more difficult, players would have to decide which cities to protect and which to sacrifice.

Missile Command was not the first game to play with the prospect of nuclear war. In 1946, the Long Island, New York–based International Mutoscope Corporation released *Atomic Bomber*, an electromechanical arcade game in which players assumed the role of a bombardier in a B-29 aircraft. Just a year earlier, the United States ended World War II by dropping atomic bombs on Hiroshima and Nagasaki. "Timely . . . and profitable!" the game's sales literature boasted. "The Atomic-Age is the country's leading topic of conversation. The ATOMIC BOMBER will be your leading profit item . . . Now, at last, you can give the public an outlet for their 'Atomic Thinking.'" Despite the devastating potential of atomic weapons, the public did not yet understand the possibility that such weapons could destroy the world. It was not until the Cold War arms race that people finally understood how the fate of the world rested in the hands of a very select group of individuals.

Theurer initially planned for the cities in *Missile Command* to represent six cities in Atari's home state of California: San Francisco, San Luis Obispo, Eureka, Los Angeles, Santa Barbara, and San Diego. But he later realized the game might resonate more with players if they visualized the cities as Boston, New York, and Philadelphia, or Houston, Dallas, and Austin, so Atari removed the geographic identifiers and left the rest up to the imagination.

Using a trackball in gameplay, a player moved a crosshair across the sky and used one of three buttons to launch countermeasures from three respective artillery batteries. When a countermeasure exploded, its fireball lingered for several seconds and destroyed any enemy missiles that entered it. Players were tasked with defending six cities, any of which could be destroyed by a single missile. A level was cleared when all enemy missiles were either destroyed or reached their targets, and points were rewarded for the number of cities and countermeasures remaining. At the start of the subsequent mission, a player's artillery batteries were replenished but destroyed cities remained ruined, though they could be occasionally rebuilt when players reached a certain score. A player lost when all his or her cities were destroyed.

Missile Command embodied the nightmare scenario of the Cold War. Indeed, players could not win the game but could only delay the inevitable. Instead of the typical "Game Over" screen, the game greeted players with a blood red mushroom cloud over which the ominous words "The End" flashed wildly. Theurer suggested that his repeated nightmares of nuclear Armageddon likely influenced the game's foreboding conclusion. Theurer worked tirelessly on *Missile Command*, often for days straight without any sleep. At one point due to exhaustion, he even needed a friend to work his keyboard because he had forgotten how to type. What few nights he did sleep were filled with visions of exploding ICBMs and annihilated cities. Yet the mental toll paid off in commercial success: when *Missile Command* hit arcades nationwide it was an immediate hit, becoming one of Atari's bestselling coin-operated games. In 1982, Atari ported the game to its 2600 home console, where it became the system's fourth most popular cartridge, selling more than 2.5 million copies. Dave Theurer, meanwhile, would go on to design another iconic Atari product, *Tempest*, as well as the innovative 3-D game *I, Robot*. Yet nightmares of nuclear holocaust would still occasionally haunt him.

Atari's mission for its games was to always promote fun. But *Missile Command*'s "fun" symbolized the paralyzing fear that nothing could be done to end nuclear war once it had begun. In *Missile Command*, players could never turn the tables and target the enemies themselves, only their offensive weapons. And yet there was unmistakable enjoyment in assuming humanity's last stand, blasting away as inevitable doom drew ever closer.

"That was the whole point of the game," explained Theurer, "to show that if there was ever a nuclear war, you'd never win."

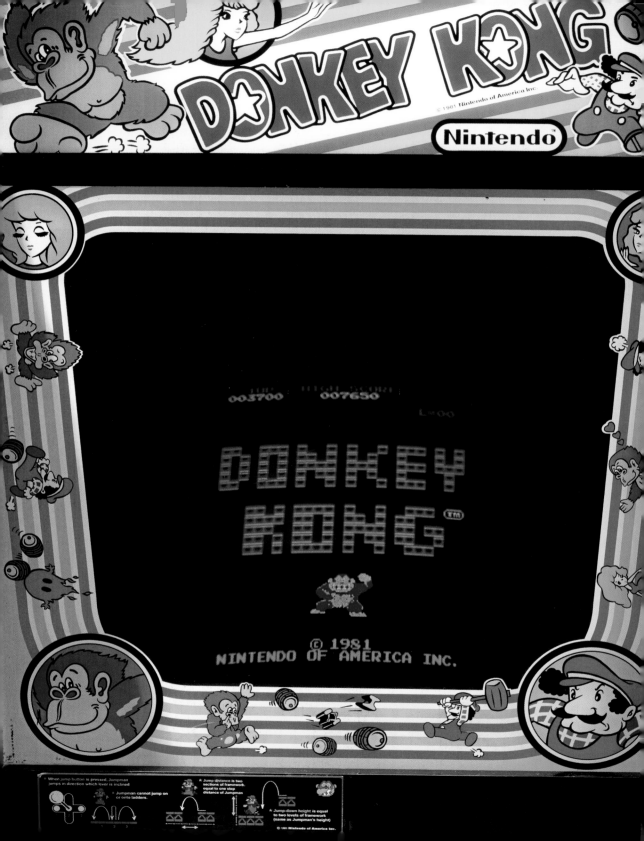

DONKEY KONG

(1981)

Donkey Kong not only charmed players but also introduced two key figures in the history of video games. One was Shigeru Miyamoto, the game's designer who has gone on to become the most important game developer in history. The other was "Jumpman," the game's mustachioed hero who soon became known as a plucky plumber named Mario. *Donkey Kong* entered The Strong's World Video Game Hall of Fame in 2017.

Trivia time: When did Mario first appear in a video game?

You might say, "In *Super Mario Bros.* for the Nintendo NES." After all, the game is named after him!

But Mario first appeared four years earlier in the 1981 arcade game *Donkey Kong*, which took arcades by storm and launched the career of the most accomplished game developer in history. *Donkey Kong* set new standards in story development for arcade games and charmed players with its jaunty audio and appealing graphics.

Yet *Donkey Kong* was never supposed to happen. For most of its storied existence, Nintendo (founded in 1889) was a playing-card company that later dabbled in electromechanical amusements such as love testers (page 25). During the 1970s, Nintendo ventured into the video game industry after securing a licensing deal from Magnavox to distribute the Odyssey home console, and subsequently released its own home gaming system, the Color TV-Game, in 1975. That same year, the company tested the coin-operated arcade waters with various sports and shooting games. Eyeing its rival Taito, which was making a killing in America with *Space Invaders* (page 107), Nintendo established its American headquarters in 1980.

Nintendo's president, Hiroshi Yamauchi, designated his son-in-law, Minoru Arakawa, to head up the American division. Arakawa ordered three thousand units of *Radar Scope*, a shooter game that Nintendo had released in Japan to modest success, hoping Americans would be captivated by the game's innovative three-dimensional third-person gameplay. Unfortunately, *Radar Scope* sold barely a thousand units, partly because arcade operators hated the game's dis-

tinctive high-pitched chirping sound effects. This meant two thousand cabinets were sitting in mothballs in Nintendo's warehouse. The fledgling division stood to lose an enormous amount of money unless the cabinets could be refashioned into something sellable.

Nintendo decided to put a young game designer named Shigeru Miyamoto in charge of finding something, anything, that could be put in the *Radar Scope* cabinets and sold to American arcades. Miyamoto had graduated several years earlier with a degree in industrial design and initially wanted to produce comics, known in Japan as manga. Dating back to the nineteenth century, manga was popular among all age groups and depicted everything from comedy to romance to horror stories. However, upon playing *Space Invaders* in 1978, Miyamoto was suddenly inspired to design video games. Through a mutual friend, he secured an interview with Nintendo in 1977 and was subsequently hired into their planning department. He went on to create the artwork for *Sheriff*, one of Nintendo's first coin-operated arcade games, and later helped develop *Radar Scope*. Trained as an industrial designer, Miyamoto was not an engineer in the traditional sense. Rather, he conceptualized games and passed along the design to engineers. Needing a fresh, innovative product to save the Nintendo of America division, the twenty-nine-year-old Miyamoto was handed complete creative control to quickly design a new game for the old *Radar Scope* cabinets. It would be his first time designing a game from scratch.

Miyamoto never forgot his love for manga and envisioned his arcade game resembling a live-action comic book featuring discrete characters with individual personalities. At the time,

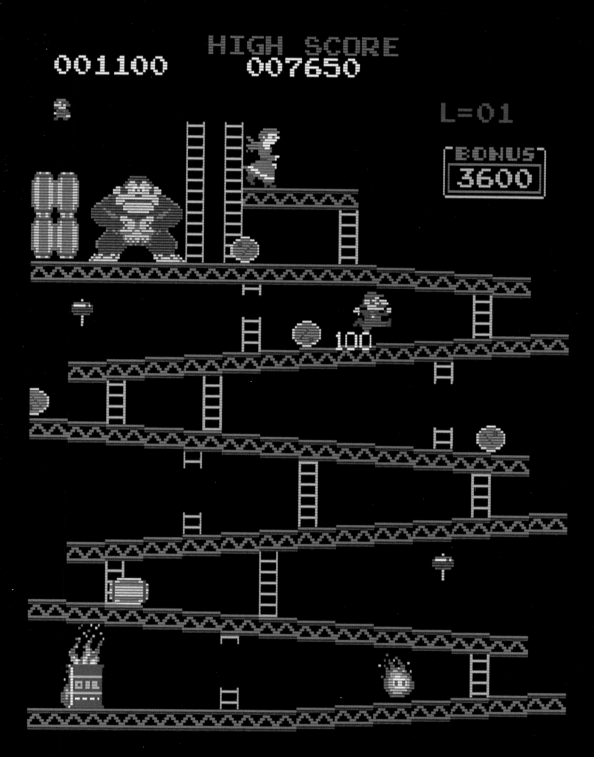

the vast majority of games were shooters or racing games that lacked any sort of imaginative story. (*Pac-Man*, with its loveable dot gobbler and goofy ghosts, was probably the closest to having original characters, but there was no story involved.) Miyamoto initially began work with a boy-saves-girl theme involving Popeye, but Nintendo was unable to secure the rights to the famous cartoon character. Likely inspired by a Popeye cartoon set in a construction site, he decided to adapt his idea to *King Kong*, with a lovestruck gorilla stealing a pretty girl (later named "Pauline").

And who was the hero destined to save Pauline from the clutches of the evil gorilla? Miyamoto sketched out a plucky, mustachioed man who raced across girders, jumped over hazards, climbed ladders, and leaped along moving platforms, desperate to reach his beloved. Meanwhile, the gorilla would toss barrels to impede the hero as he climbed upward through various construction sites. Miyamoto initially called the hero Jumpman, but he would later be renamed Mario after Mario Segale, the owner of Nintendo's warehouse, who, according to legend, was constantly hounding Arakawa for overdue rent payments. Insisting that the storyline be explained to players, Miyamoto began the game with a cutscene of the ape scrambling up scaffolding while clutching a screaming Pauline, then stomping his feet to cause metal girders to fall away into an obstacle course. Just as Mario reached Pauline at the end of each level, the ape would escape with her, setting up the next, more difficult, level. While simplistic, this story-driven approach was revolutionary for the time, enticing players not just to attain a high score, but to progress farther in the narrative.

Miyamoto fed his conceptual drawings to the software developer Ikegami Tsushinki, who oversaw the engineering team. Upon seeing the game, Yamauchi and Arakawa immediately realized they had a potential blockbuster on their hands. The game was fresh and addicting, and its bold, vibrant graphics brought to life a world of girders, ladders, and barrels. Miyamoto dubbed his creation *Donkey Kong*, a mashup of King Kong and Miyamoto's misinterpretation of the English word "Donkey," believing it to mean "stupid."

Nintendo of America hastily refashioned the existing *Radar Scope* cabinets, and *Donkey Kong* went on sale in July 1981. It was an instant hit. Nintendo sold its initial two thousand cabinets almost immediately and ordered thousands more. By October, Nintendo of America was selling four thousand *Donkey Kong* cabinets per month, and by June 1982, had sold sixty thousand, earning Nintendo hundreds of millions of dollars. *Donkey Kong* became Nintendo's most profitable arcade game ever, selling approximately one hundred thirty thousand cabinets in the United States and Japan, ranking it only after *Pac-Man* and *Space Invaders* in lists of the bestselling arcade games of all time.

And it was Mario, of course, who would continue to make Nintendo's fortune. Mario's telltale outfit and mustache were easily discernible on the machine's primitive graphics, the chief reason he was brought back in 1985 to star in *Super Mario Bros.* for the Nintendo Entertainment System (page 182). Meanwhile, *Donkey Kong* spawned numerous sequels, many of which allow players to control Donkey Kong himself (or his offspring, as in the case of *Donkey Kong Jr.*). And, of course, *Donkey Kong* launched the storied career of Shigeru Miyamoto, who would go on to create some of the most beloved video game characters of all time.

Just as Mario saved Pauline, *Donkey Kong* would save Nintendo's fortunes and transform the former playing card company into a video game juggernaut. To this day, Nintendo's empire remains glued to the very same characters who pioneered a new generation of story-driven games so many years ago.

UTOPIA

(1981)

Designer Don Daglow's groundbreaking world-building simulation challenged players to guide the development of an island nation by gathering resources, battling pirates, and building a civilization. The Strong cares for the Don Daglow Papers.

The great author and humanist Sir Thomas More coined the term "utopia" in the early sixteenth century, a combination of the Greek words *ou* ("no") and *topos* ("place"). In his 1516 book of the same name, More describes a fictional island in the South Atlantic Ocean where citizens live in total peace and harmony, men and women are equally educated, and all property is communal. The book depicts a society that is perfect in every way, but is also, as the title suggests, impossible to achieve. Since More's book, "utopia" has come to describe fanciful ideas that are impossible to achieve. Yet in 1981, more than five hundred years after More published his book, Mattel Electronics built an actual utopia.

The story of *Utopia* the game—the ancestor to today's real-time strategy games—begins in the late 1970s with a junior high school teacher named Don Daglow. It was a turbulent time for his school district, and fears of losing his job consumed him as he drove home one day. Suddenly an advertisement crackled on the radio: "Are you interested in the exciting world of video games? Would you like to have a career in creating the future of this new exciting entertainment media?" Daglow had some experience coding games; while at Pomona College, he had produced various games for mainframe computers, such as an interactive baseball simulator, a *Star Trek* game, and a *D&D*–style role-playing game called *Dungeon*. Anxious for a new career, Daglow called the number at the end of the advertisement.

He was eventually set up with the video game division of Mattel Electronics, which was hard at work on its Intellivision home console. The Intellivision was a sophisticated machine featuring a 16-bit General Instrument processor, a sound chip that could output three distinct sound

channels, and two twelve-button keypad controllers. When the console launched in 1980, Mattel hired the famed writer and literary editor George Plimpton to help promote the system. "Mr. Intellivision," as he became known, routinely showcased Mattel's system against the Atari 2600 and highlighted the Intellivision's superior graphical capabilities and sophisticated games. Mattel released the Intellivision with a thin library of games, so the company established an in-house development team in 1980 to rapidly develop titles for the console. A newly hired Daglow became part of the original five-person development team known as the "Blue Sky Rangers."

The former social studies teacher completed his first project, an educational game called *Geography Challenge*, in a matter of months. Noting how most releases involved sports or ports of popular arcade games, he decided for his next project to focus on a strategy simulation. As a teacher, he had occasionally used a board game called *Diplomacy* in his history class. Set in Europe just before the outbreak of World War I, players in *Diplomacy* control major powers, form and betray alliances, manage resources, and conquer territory. Daglow had created his own variation in which he taped out the borders of countries on the floor of the school cafeteria and challenged students to run fictional countries. He envisioned harnessing the spirit of these simulations and reimagining them in what would become *Utopia*.

Daglow worked on *Utopia* full time for six months, learning how to blend real-time gameplay and strategy elements into a medium that generally lacked intellectual titles. He was aided by the complex nature of the Intellivision's controllers. Notoriously difficult to use in other games, the telephone-shaped controllers sported fourteen separate buttons and a circular control dial. This made them unwieldy for traditional sports and shooter games, but the intricate design was perfect for a game like *Utopia*, which required players to juggle numerous tasks at the same time.

Utopia was designed for two players, each controlling a separate island. (In the single-player mode, the second island was ignored and a player attempted to set a high score.) Using the control dial, players took turns moving a rectangular cursor around to construct buildings such as factories, schools, hospitals, and forts. Other expenditures included boats, support to insurgents on the opposing island, and feeding a fickle citizenry who must remain happy at all times—otherwise, rebels could burn buildings and decrease a player's score. Spending gold wisely was the key to success in *Utopia*: too much spent on the military and citizens became unruly, while too many people-pleasing infrastructure projects meant being overrun by pirates, rebels, and enemy armies. The game lasted as many as fifty rounds (depending on user configuration), with each round lasting up to 120 seconds. The winner had the most points at the end of the game—and, thus, came closest to building a true utopia by improving the well-being of his or her people.

In an era of alien-blasting shooters, *Utopia* was a refreshingly cerebral game. Thanks to randomly generated weather patterns and natural disasters, no two games were alike. The sheer number of variables, the simple but remarkably detailed graphics and sound effects, and the limitless paths to victory made for an endlessly replayable game, with or without a human opponent. Only the Intellivision was capable of running a game like *Utopia*, which required greater processing power than the Atari 2600 had and a

multi-button keypad that allowed players to efficiently manage resources against a ticking clock. The game was extremely well-received by critics and players alike, selling nearly two hundred fifty thousand copies and helping to prop up Mattel's struggling console. *Utopia*'s deep and challenging gameplay foreshadowed later bestsellers such as *SimCity* and *Sid Meier's Civilization*.

Released in 1981, *Utopia* also represents the very best of the video game industry before it imploded two years later under the weight of its own excesses. Don Daglow's game perfectly combined strategy and action, while demonstrating the wondrous ability of video games to entertain and educate all at once. But just like the mirage that was Utopia itself, the video game industry believed its double-digit growth would continue forever. Thomas More wrote in *Utopia* that "anticipated spears wound less," but few in the industry could anticipate the spears of market saturation and consumer indifference that would soon be relentlessly hurled at them. Even Mattel's Intellivision business, which employed 1,800 people at its peak with revenues of hundreds of millions of dollars, crashed back to Earth and was sold off for pennies on the dollar in 1984.

Don Daglow, however, would survive the crash and go on to produce bestselling titles for Electronic Arts such as *Earl Weaver Baseball* (1987). In 1988, he formed his own company, Stormfront Studios, and later produced the first graphical massively multiplayer online role-playing game, *Neverwinter Nights* (1991). Just like the countless pathways to victory in *Utopia*, the former schoolteacher's career is a testament that success can be found in the most unlikely places. "Our dreams pick us," Daglow said in a 2016 interview. "I thought I was going to be a playwright."

RIVER RAID

(1982)

Pioneering female designer Carol Shaw created the bestselling game *River Raid* for the Atari 2600, in which players strafed ships, helicopters, and planes. Carol donated this game and a copy of the source code to The Strong as part of its Women in Games initiative.

You are piloting a B1 StratoWing Assault Jet deep behind enemy lines, your mission to swoop down low, just feet above the treacherous River of No Return, and blast away bridges to halt the enemy's advances. Everything is standing in your way, from choppers and tankers to impossibly narrow canyons that require pinpoint navigation. The odds are stacked against you, but deep down you have what it takes to become a true River Raider. "To learn to fly successful missions, you'll need the sensitivity, touch and sharpshooting skills of a precision jet pilot," states the manual for Activision's *River Raid* for the Atari 2600. "But that takes time and practice." *River Raid*, created by Carol Shaw—the first widely recognized female video game designer and programmer—is a masterpiece of game design and one of the most popular and critically acclaimed titles for the Atari home console.

As the daughter of a mechanical engineer, Shaw became interested in electronics at an early age. She learned BASIC programming in high school and went on to earn a bachelor's degree in electrical engineering and computer science at the University of California, Berkeley, in 1977, and a master's degree in computer science the following year. While earning her master's, she interviewed for a job at Atari Inc., which hired her as a microprocessor software engineer. Her first task was to design a polo-themed video game that would be released as a tie-in to Ralph Lauren's Polo cologne. The idea eventually fell through, but Shaw's 1978 game *Polo*, nevertheless, became one of the first documented video games designed and programmed by a woman. *Polo* was later released in the 1996 CD-ROM compilation *Stella Gets a New Brain*.

Shaw worked at Atari for the next two years,

where she designed and programmed games such as *3-D Tic-Tac-Toe* (1979) and *Video Checkers* (1980) for the Atari 2600, and a calculator program for the Atari 800 computer (1979). She also worked on an *Othello* variant (1978) and on the 2600 port of *Super Breakout* (1981). After leaving Atari in 1980, Shaw spent sixteen months at Tandem Computers, where she used her knowledge of the 68000 assembly language to help program their line of computers that were designed to continue operation even with multiple hardware faults and failures. Shaw missed the fast-paced world of game design, however, and received an invitation to return to the video game world—this time with Activision.

Before Activision opened its doors in 1979, the only games for a video game console were made by the manufacturer; there were no third-party developers. This scheme proved lucrative for Atari and other console makers, but many programmers believed they were not given sufficient credit or compensation for games that sold well. In May 1979, Atari programmers David Crane, Alan Miller, and Bob Whitehead met with Atari's CEO, Ray Kassar, to demand royalties and prominent credit on game boxes. Kassar allegedly scoffed and compared programmers to "towel designers." Soon after, the programmers— whose games made up nearly half of the company's sales at the time—left Atari to found Activision, a third-party, independent game developer and publisher that sought to promote its game designers in much the same way as a record album would promote its artists. Early Activision titles include Larry Kaplan's *Kaboom!* (1981) and David Crane's *Pitfall!* (1982), with the latter selling some four million copies. And for each game it produced, Activision devoted a page of the manual to prominently showcase the game's designer.

Activision's devotion to its designers made Shaw feel at home with the publisher. Although much of her previous work focused on video game adaptations of board games, Shaw decided to begin designing an action game. Inspired by Stern's side-scrolling shooter arcade game *Scramble*, she initially wanted to create a space shooter. But her boss, Alan Miller, noted that these kinds of games were extremely common and suggested she try something more unique. She came up with an idea for a vertical scrolling game where a high-speed jet hugs a river bank to avoid enemy radar and blast away bridges. The only problem was that Atari 2600 cartridges were generally limited to 4KB of memory—precious little space to store the amount of river terrain needed. However, Shaw was able to navigate memory limits by developing an ingenious approach in which objects and terrain were generated by an algorithm, not stored in memory. This meant players could experience a near limitless amount of twisting rivers and treacherous terrain, depending on how long they could stay alive.

River Raid was born. Players took control of a jet that could strafe left and right, decelerate and accelerate to avoid the riverbank, and attack enemies, which included tankers, helicopters, jets, and bridges. Another novel feature was the fuel indicator at the bottom of the screen, which depleted and caused the jet to crash unless players filled up at fuel depots. Players scored points for destroying enemies, with every ten thousand points granting a new life. For players who scored fifteen thousand points, Activision invited them to mail in a photograph of their high score in return for a River Raiders patch and a letter of congratulations. And, as the

manual promised, players who scored a million points were invited to "please send us a photo. Such an achievement will certainly rank you as one of the world's greatest video game competitors!"

The *River Raid* manual also bridged the gap between designer and player by prominently featuring a photograph of Carol Shaw, along with a signed note from her, offering hints and tricks to succeed at the game. "By knowing the river, pinpointing areas with the highest concentration of enemy, *and* the most fuel depots, you'll have a much better chance of surviving," she advised before signing her name and adding: "And, please, do drop me a note and let me know how you're doing. I'd really like to hear from you!"

River Raid was a massive hit for Activision, selling more than a million units for the Atari 2600. It was later ported to the Atari 5200, ColecoVision, and the Intellivision consoles. *River Raid* won numerous awards for its technological achievements and level design, including Best Action Videogame in the 1984 Arkie Awards from *Electronic Games* magazine.

Get an incredible score on an Activision game? The company encouraged players to take photographs of their success and send a copy to the company to receive awards, like this *River Raid* patch donated to The Strong by Carol Shaw.

E.T.
THE EXTRA-TERRESTRIAL

(1982)

Atari's *E.T. the Extra-Terrestrial* did not cause the video game market crash of 1983, but in its wake the reeling company dumped truckloads of its unsold products into an Alamogordo, New Mexico, landfill. The town of Alamogordo donated to The Strong this mud-caked cartridge excavated from the dumpsite in 2014.

Some call *E.T. the Extra-Terrestrial* for the Atari 2600 the game that single-handedly killed the video game industry. Others are more generous, merely judging it the worst game of all time. Neither of these claims are true. But one thing is: in the span of a year, the most powerful game company of its day saw its fortunes quite literally buried in a New Mexico landfill.

In the early months of 1982, Atari was a goose that laid golden, cartridge-sized eggs. "Have you played Atari today?" asked its commercials of the time, and for millions of kids growing up in the 1970s and early '80s, the answer was a resounding yes. Atari's coin-operated division was holding strong despite fierce competition from Japanese imports like *Donkey Kong* and *Pac-Man*, but most important, the home console on which Atari had staked its entire business—the VCS (2600)—was finally a mammoth bestseller. After a slow start, consumers were bringing video games into their homes at an unprecedented pace. With the help of several key ports, notably *Space Invaders*, *Missile Command*, and *Asteroids*, sales of the VCS reached ten million units in 1982. By then, Atari controlled a staggering 80 percent of the video game market and was inhaling more than $2 billion in annual revenue, accounting for nearly 70 percent of Warner's operating profit.

In 1982, Warner and Atari began negotiating with Universal Pictures to create a video game based on the summer's hit film, *E.T. the Extra-Terrestrial*, directed by Steven Spielberg. The movie was an instant blockbuster, quickly surpassing *Star Wars* to become the highest grossing film of all time. *E.T.* was the rare film that was popular with all age groups, and Warner hoped that an *E.T.* video game would have similar

cross-generational appeal. The only problem was securing a license, and Universal was demanding a king's ransom. Eager to have an *E.T.*–branded game in stores before the 1982 holiday season, Warner agreed to shell out a reported $21 million to acquire the rights to *E.T.* (Just seven years earlier, Nolan Bushnell, Atari's founder, had sold his entire company to Warner for just $28 million.)

When the contract was inked at the end of July, Atari had to scramble to find someone on staff to design and program the game. To produce enough copies for the holiday season, *E.T.* had to be completed by September 1. Atari's CEO, Ray Kassar, was understandably anxious: games usually took upward of a year to create, a process that involved teams of coders, debugging, and extensive testing with focus groups. Atari needed to make good on its twenty-one-million-dollar gamble in just over a month. Even Kassar's own engineers told him the deadline was impossible. Suppressing the desperation in his voice, Kassar dialed up a designer named Howard Warshaw.

Warshaw was fresh off creating a well-received video game adaptation of another Spielberg film, *Raiders of the Lost Ark*. When Kassar asked if he could produce an *E.T.* game in five weeks (and after Kassar reportedly offered him $200,000 and a free Hawaiian vacation as compensation), Warshaw replied, "Sure. I'll do it." He had two days to think of an idea before flying to Los Angeles to meet with Spielberg, and came up with a theme involving E.T. "phoning home," as he famously did in the film. Players would control the friendly alien as he hunted down various pieces of electronics that were necessary to communicate with his spaceship, all while battling nefarious scientists and FBI agents. Spielberg, however, was unimpressed,

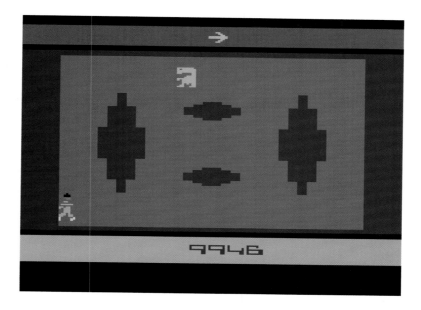

and asked Warshaw if he could design a simpler game similar to Namco's *Pac-Man*. Warshaw bristled at the idea, believing such gameplay would be derivative and fail to capture the film's tenderness.

Going against Spielberg's vision, Warshaw proceeded with his original idea. He installed a game-development system in his home so he could work on *E.T.* throughout the night. After slaving away for five weeks, he managed to put together a playable game despite the crushing time constraint and the intrinsic difficulty of making a video game featuring a nonviolent extraterrestrial. *E.T.* tasked players with guiding the pixelated alien from a top-down perspective, finding pieces of an interplanetary phone scattered around various landscapes depicting scenes from the film. E.T.'s energy level depleted as he moved, requiring players to occasionally restore it by collecting Reese's Pieces candy. When E.T. found all three components of his phone, he raced against the clock to meet his spaceship before it blasted off. Atari did not have time

to conduct the rigorous testing to which their games were normally subjected. The company needed something, anything, *E.T.*–branded to sell for Christmas, and it began printing copies of the game almost immediately after Warshaw delivered the source code. Atari knew it had to sell an inordinate amount of copies to recoup its licensing fee, and so it ordered a wildly optimistic five million copies of the game.

E.T. was a massive commercial failure. Despite selling approximately 1.5 million units—quite an achievement for the day—the proceeds were dwarfed by the game's massive production costs and licensing fees. *E.T.* also suffered from poor reviews. Many players found the game too difficult and demanded a refund, while glitches were rampant due to the lack of thorough testing. The game was repetitive, too, with players frequently falling into and extricating themselves from pits and other hazards. Readers of the computer magazine *Softline* named *E.T.* the second-worst Atari game of 1983, after *Congo Bongo*.

But *E.T.* is best known for symbolizing—others go so far as to say *causing*—the video game crash of 1983, the industry-wide recession that saw revenues plummet by many hundreds of millions of dollars. The once-booming electronic gaming industry imploded as stores returned unsold stock to game companies. The few consumers who were buying games plucked old titles for pennies on the dollar from bargain bins. Several game companies went bankrupt immediately, including US Games and Games by Apollo, while others limped along before succumbing to the inevitable.

Even Atari could not avoid financial ruin. In December 1982, Atari announced that instead of the 50 percent year-over sales increase it had earlier promised, it expected a modest 10 to 15 percent increase—a drop largely due to sales that failed to match the overproduction of *E.T.* and *Pac-Man*, the latter of which sold an impressive seven million copies but left another several million languishing on shelves. Atari's stock crashed the following day, and Ray Kassar was later accused of insider trading after he sold thousands of Atari shares just prior to releasing the poor sales figures. Atari collapsed, teetering in and out of bankruptcy as it was repeatedly bought and sold by a parade of parent companies.

In a display of remarkable hubris, Atari had insisted its distributors place massive orders at the end of 1981, which meant a tidal wave of unsold stock returned to Atari's warehouses after Christmas 1982. Combined with the unsold *Pac-Man* and *E.T.* cartridges, the company had millions of pounds of useless plastic it needed to dispose of. Unable to find buyers, Atari finally dumped fourteen trucks' worth of merchandise into a landfill in Alamogordo, New Mexico. As the *New York Times* reported at the time, "Guards kept reporters and spectators away from the area as workers poured concrete over the dumped merchandise." The "Atari video game burial," as it became known, became the subject of rampant conspiracy theories and urban legends, some fueled by the location's close proximity to Roswell, New Mexico. While Roswell's history of covering up aliens may be dubious, a 2014 excavation revealed the Alamogordo landfill did indeed represent the final resting place of several hundred thousand copies of *E.T. the Extra-Terrestrial*, *Pac-Man*, *Missile Command*, *Adventure*, and other games and products. Some of those cartridges dug up in Alamogordo, including *E.T.*, are now in the collections of The Strong museum.

E.T. did not cause the video game crash of 1983, but it encapsulated an out-of-control industry collapsing under its own excesses. The crash of the home video game market was precipitated by several factors, chief among them a saturation of the home video game console market. While gamers today have their pick of perhaps a half-dozen premier consoles, there were dozens of dueling game machines (some even used adapters to play a competing console's games) to choose from during the early 1980s. Too many software companies produced too many games, glutting warehouses and retailers with more titles than could be sold. And as *E.T.* proved, many of these games were poorly developed and rushed to market. Compounding the problem, companies like Atari recklessly gambled their survival on a handful of releases, doling out exorbitant licensing fees and ordering enormous production runs. The price of home computers had also become so low that consumers could have a fully functional PC for the price of an Atari, sapping demand for single-purpose game machines.

For his part, Warshaw acknowledged *E.T.*'s shortcomings but remained proud of his effort. "Yeah, it's got some problems," he admitted to *A.V. Club* in 2005. "If I'd had another week or two to work on it, it may well have been a much better game. But for a five-week effort, which is what it was—about thirty-five days that I had to work on it, including the design—it's a hell of a game."

ONE-ON-ONE:

DR. J VS. LARRY BIRD

(1983)

Sports games from the 1970s and early 1980s were mostly generic. Electronic Arts not only brought fast-paced basketball to computer screens, but it also injected personality with superstar athletes such as Julius "Dr. J" Erving and Larry Bird.

n May 1983, Julius Erving and Larry Bird, two of the NBA's biggest stars, faced off for a much-publicized one-on-one matchup. Erving, nicknamed "Dr. J," played small forward for the Philadelphia 76ers and had popularized a theatrical style of above-the-rim play, transforming the slam dunk from a rarely used trick into a display of power and intimidation. Bird, on the other hand, possessed the unrivaled skill of anticipation, able to reduce the chaotic game of basketball into a slow-motion chess match. A power forward for the Celtics, Bird was also among the most efficient shooters of his day, displaying a machinelike penchant for point scoring rivaled only by his aptitude for trash talk. The 76ers and Celtics squared off in the Eastern Conference Finals in 1980, 1981, and 1982, and Dr. J vs. Larry Bird became one of the biggest rivalries in sports. Their storied one-one-one matchup in 1983, however, took place not on the floor of an arena, but in a video game.

The tale of their electronic rivalry began ten years earlier with an entrepreneur named Trip Hawkins, who had not yet graduated college and was already a failed businessman. Hawkins had convinced his father to lend him five thousand dollars to create *Accu-Stat Football*, a board game that simulated NFL matchups. It sold poorly, and Hawkins abandoned the project before he graduated Harvard University in 1976 with a degree he designed himself in Strategy and Applied Game Theory. Realizing that the future of sports gaming lay in microprocessors, not dice, he attended Stanford Business School and found a job at a scrappy upstart called Apple Computer. An acolyte of Steve Jobs, he quickly grasped the limitless potential of personal computers, especially for gaming.

By 1982, when he was a marketing director at Apple (and after making a small fortune following the company's public offering), Hawkins had watched with dismay as countless video game consoles flooded the market, all with a range of hastily cobbled-together games. He even viewed the Atari 2600, which had seen massive success with its impressive catalog, as a passing fad that would be swiftly outdated. "I considered the 2600 a toy, played for amusement, destined to be an electronic hula hoop that was dead in a few years," he told *Vice Sports* in 2017. Personal computers like the Apple II, on the other hand, were increasingly affordable and able to perform far more tasks than playing video games.

In early 1982, Hawkins met with Sequoia Capital to discuss his idea for a next-generation video game company called Amazin' Software. His mission was to elevate a video game industry that he saw as too dependent on shoddy, quickly developed titles that lacked artistry. The Sequoia executives were supportive and encouraged him to leave his job at Apple. Hawkins agreed, and by December he had invested $200,000 of his own money in addition to a $2 million infusion from Sequoia Capital. Hawkins's company, which he renamed Electronic Arts (EA) to reflect his aesthetic vision, would treat games like carefully crafted musical albums. He even called his engineers "software artists," believing the beauty of art was universal, whether it was crafted with oil, acrylic, a microphone, or digitized ones and zeroes. For this reason, Hawkins managed to attract talented game programmers who previously had toiled without any recognition.

Inspired by "The Catch," the famed fifty-eight-yard touchdown pass from Joe Montana to Dwight Clark that won the 1981 NFC title game for the San Francisco 49ers, Hawkins first tried to create a simple football game. But computers were not sufficiently powerful to animate twenty-two players at a time, and EA quickly abandoned the project. Instead, Hawkins realized that a one-on-one basketball game could free up precious computing resources while reflecting a style of play often found in real life.

Yet he needed this game to embody the ethos of the fledgling company, one that prided artistry, class, and a healthy dose of attitude. For a one-on-one game, nameless, faceless, blocky players wouldn't cut it. It needed to feature recognizable stars, and Hawkins immediately thought of his favorite NBA player, Julius Erving. Dr. J was the embodiment of the NBA's flashier new image. Acrobatic, outspoken, and tough, Erving's sky-walking persona would be the perfect face for not just EA's first sports game, but for EA itself. Hawkins signed him for $25,000, 2.5 percent of royalties, and a small stake in the company. Dr. J would become the first African-American to star in a video game.

But against whom would Dr. J face off? Hawkins needed not just a real-life rival, but one with a dramatically different stature and playing style to showcase the technical abilities of the game. Larry Bird was the obvious choice. The lanky three-point-chucking forward was the perfect foil to the basket-driving Dr. J. Both were household names, and their rivalry was among the most storied in sports. Hawkins signed Bird to similar terms, and EA photographers staged a photoshoot featuring Erving and Bird grimacing in street clothes in front of a graffiti-covered wall.

EA's first sports game, *One-on-One: Dr. J vs. Larry Bird*, was born. While many computer games of the day sported little packaging be-

yond a stapled plastic Ziploc bag, EA dressed their game in an eight-inch cardboard vinyl-record-style package with a gritty photograph of a shirtless Erving and a sitting Bird positioned in front of a graffiti-covered brick wall. It was a unique presentation that forever changed how video games were presented to the public. Nowadays we take for granted cover art and package design, from majestic *Madden NFL* superstars to the stylistic, cartoon-paneled box art from the Grand Theft Auto series, but while many video games featured box art, EA's slick graphics and unique rock album–like packaging looked like nothing else the video game industry had previously produced. Reflecting EA's commitment to its designers, the subtitle read "By Eric Hammond, Larry Bird & Julius Erving," prominently featuring the name of *One-on-One*'s lead programmer before the stars of the game themselves. Hawkins wanted consumers to flock to individual developer's releases like they flocked to the latest Michael Jackson album. Every box featured the following message:

We're an association of electronic artists who share a common goal. We want to fulfill the potential of personal computing. That's a tall order. But with enough imagination and enthusiasm we believe there's a good chance for success. Our products, like this game, are evidence of our intent.

One-on-One was released in May 1983, just as much of the video game world was crashing down. With companies hemorrhaging cash and hurtling toward bankruptcy as consumers rejected generic, poorly constructed releases, EA debuted its masterpiece for the Apple II personal computer. Players assumed the role of either Erving or Bird and could play against another human or the computer. On offense, players could shoot or spin toward the basket, and on defense they could attempt to steal or block a shot. An especially acrobatic dunk could shatter the backboard, prompting a disgruntled janitor to sweep up the shards. The game featured shot-clock violations, instant replays, realistic sound effects including crowd noise, hacking fouls for over-aggressive defense, and countless other features that made *One-on-One* a truly immersive experience.

One-on-One solidified EA's position as a serious player in the gaming industry. The game retailed for $40 and reached number two on *Softalk* magazine's bestseller list, ultimately selling millions of copies over its lifetime. EA would continue to use its celebrity-driven marketing approach to launch many of the most successful game franchises of all time, including *FIFA*, *Tiger Woods Golf*, and *Madden NFL*. Hawkins and his team of software artists had picked up the pieces of the shattered video game industry and refashioned them into a new model that would redefine the gaming experience.

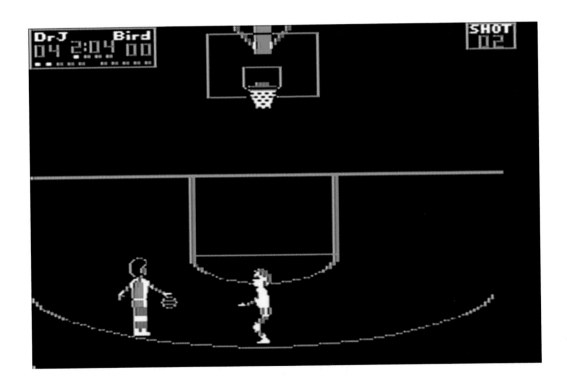

AN ESPECIALLY ACROBATIC DUNK COULD
SHATTER THE BACKBOARD, PROMPTING
A DISGRUNTLED JANITOR TO SWEEP
UP THE SHARDS.

PINBALL
CONSTRUCTION
SET

(1983)

Designer Bill Budge's revolutionary construction game allowed players without any knowledge of programming to become game creators by offering a toolbox of electronic flippers, thumper bumpers, slingshots, and sound effects to create their own video pinball games.

For those who experienced the thrill of the Nintendo Entertainment System (NES) when it was first released in 1985, few games were as rip-roaring as *Excitebike* (1984), which let players race virtual dirt bikes up and down 8-bit hills. But the feature that made the game endlessly replayable was the design mode, which allowed users to create and race on their own tracks. By adding daunting hills and well-placed speed bumps and mud puddles to trip up opponents, you were no longer merely playing the game; you were actively taking part in *creating* it. This sort of customization is now standard in many games—the wildly popular *Minecraft* (page 291), for instance, allows players to build entire worlds—but the concept was entirely new during the age of linear

arcade games. *Excitebike*, however, was not the first game to introduce players to this innovation. A year earlier, programmer Bill Budge released *Pinball Construction Set*, which empowered players to customize content and design aspects of their gameplay experience.

Budge began his career working at Apple as a software engineer. In his spare time, he coded games for the Apple II, many of them knockoffs of popular arcade games like *Asteroids* and *Pong*. Later, he met a traveling electronics salesman who agreed to sell Budge's games to computer stores. With a steady cash flow, Budge left his job at Apple and devoted himself to his next project, a pinball game called *Raster Blaster*. Released in 1981 through his company BudgeCo and playable on the Apple II, the game was lauded for

Much like the typewriter John Steinbeck used to write his 1939 novel *The Grapes of Wrath* or the camera Orson Welles used to film his 1941 movie *Citizen Kane*, this is the Apple II computer on which computer game pioneer Bill Budge programmed his iconic game *Pinball Construction Set*. He donated it to The Strong.

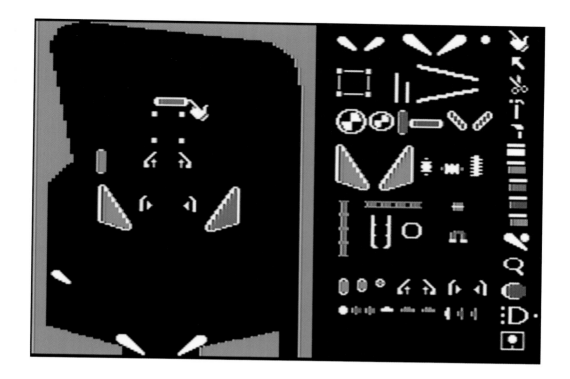

its smooth graphics and visual accuracy. It was even voted *Softalk* magazine's Most Popular Program of 1981.

Budge moved on to his next, more formidable challenge: a pinball construction game. While working at Apple, Budge had been struck by a project called Lisa, a desktop computer that would become one of the very first PCs to offer a graphical user interface. (The Lisa was released in 1983, but was quickly overshadowed when Apple introduced the Macintosh the following year.) Budge was captivated by primitive Lisa programs that allowed users to draw pixels, use a magnifying glass, and create polygons. What if he could design a game for the Apple II that combined similar construction abilities with his passion for pinball? He envisioned a game with the thrills of *Raster Blaster* but with a creative layer

allowing players to move around bumpers, flippers, and sling shots to create their own game.

Budge dubbed his project *Pinball Construction Set*. Development proved challenging; the Apple II had very limited memory and graphics capabilities, and he had to squeeze every last ounce of horsepower out of the processor. Furthermore, the Apple II did not have a mouse, so Budge had to adapt two separate joysticks to control horizontal and vertical movement of the cursor. To make the program realistic, he purchased a 1976 Gottlieb *Target Alpha* pinball machine and stripped it down, being sure to match the virtual flippers, bumpers, drains, and kickouts to their electromechanical counterparts. Budge, who said he did not actually enjoy playing video games and pinball all that much, later described the process of having to play pinball continually for many months straight as "sheer torture."

Despite his apathy toward pinball, he created a beautifully designed construction game—a dazzling blank pinball playing surface with access to a toolbox containing dozens of color, sound effect, and component combinations. All these choices provided a would-be game designer with millions of pinball possibilities. Instead of writing a game program or following a set of text-based instructions, a player only needed to use her joystick to drag and drop icons of flippers, thumper bumpers, and slingshots onto an empty playing surface. Players could also modify the game's gravity and stretch or compress an object's shape in order to affect how the ball traveled across the table. Such seemingly endless options led many players to compose a new pinball game, save it on a floppy disk, and challenge their friends to top their creations.

Budge was overwhelmed by the work of programming, marketing, and distributing the game himself and quickly realized he was not cut out for the entrepreneurial lifestyle. Throughout the process he was repeatedly pestered by his former Apple coworker Trip Hawkins, who had started a software company and wanted to publish Budge's titles. The company, Electronic Arts (EA), was founded on the premise that video games were an art form, and that their designers were rock stars. EA packaged their games like vinyl records, featuring exotic cover artwork and the prominently displayed names of the individual game designers. Hawkins promised Budge that he could retain his autonomy while letting EA handle the unpleasant work of packaging and distributing the games. "Trip was really pushing, and I was kind of stubborn," Budge told *Wired* in 2011. "I didn't totally

trust anybody else." Eventually Budge agreed to join EA, partly swayed by the company's ability to rapidly port *Pinball Construction Set* to other platforms, such as the Commodore 64 and the IBM PC.

Budge blended in well at EA and even appeared in an infamous advertisement sporting studded wrist cuffs next to his fellow bohemian software artists. The title of the article appearing alongside the photo asked: "Can a Computer Make You Cry?" Budge's *Pinball Construction Set* sold more than three hundred thousand copies, and established the foundation for an entire game genre. Developers later produced dozens of construction games including *Music Construction Set* (1984), which was the first EA title to sell one million copies; *Racing Destruction Set* (1985); *Wargame Construction Set* (1986); and one of the first role-playing video game construction sets, *The Bard's Tale Construction Set* (1991). All of these games provided users with the ability to create aspects and versions of games they might have previously purchased. In April 1984, an *InfoWorld* magazine cover story even called the "computer erector set movement" begun by Budge "software's missing link."

By enabling casual gamers with no programming experience to customize games, Bill Budge democratized game design and directed the way for future game designers. Ultimately, Budge and his *Pinball Construction Set* paved the way for such popular user-customizable games as *LittleBigPlanet* (2008), *ModNation Racers* (2010), and *Super Mario Maker* (2015). Budge donated the Apple II computer on which he designed *Pinball Construction Set* to The Strong, where it has been displayed in the museum's *eGameRevolution* exhibit.

SUCH SEEMINGLY ENDLESS OPTIONS
LED MANY PLAYERS TO COMPOSE A NEW
PINBALL GAME, SAVE IT ON A FLOPPY DISK,
AND CHALLENGE THEIR FRIENDS TO
TOP THEIR CREATIONS.

✡ the orbs

1. Daventry —
   - A small bird can accompany him-giving him "secret advice" every now + then (the good guy?)
      (Birds are messengers of the gods.?)
   1st. - Outside castle
         Hags who become gift-bestowing maiden; maiden who becomes hag-really witch.
   9/14/17/34 - tournament grounds   Sold sunlight? (is this the stuff you're
   #503 2353 - town (look at "The Village" under The Handbook of Folklore. gathering? The "essence" of
                                                      congealed   the sun? cosmic essence
                  - Harbor area   + look under The "fisher folk"

                  - Brendan's house

                  - River
                                sells charms or spells.
   3 witches with only one   collect secrets? (May want Runes) Black Annis?   Unicorn?
   eye between them — - Enchanted Forest (witch fairies (hill?)(or evil witch)(Fairy Queen.)
   can get →   flies,weeds,frogs,toadstools   Boar?   owl   Green Man
   lost.   - Swampy area   Hecuba

                  - At least one large lake (something in lake?) (Sword?)

                  - Dwarves area (underground?)(in forest?)(magic metalworkers)(fix sword-iron boots?)

                  - mushroom area? (Floored with thick moss.)

                  - meadowy area

                  - A church or monastery

                  - lagoon
                  - seals/selkies
                  - Bay
                  - some elves or fairies or good + working with "God" to fix things.
   (white doe) - Deer (lured into forest by it. See Fairy hill. Fairy has "problem" -
   white stag? - Bees (secret wisdom) need to solve it). She'll then help you. (Lunar).
   ∫ - swan(s)
   ₹ - Crane (s) (3?) (Celtic Goddesses.) (Bestow beauty + charm)? (Could turn into Fairies.
                                                               maiden (s).)(skins.
                  - "Can't see" the fairy hill (unless have mask piece? because it's magic.) or

                  - "Perilous" Bed idea — but with something else?

                  - Black knight to fight? Near enchanted castle or tower?

                  - magic tapestry?

                  - Sword (broken? magic? in lake?)(Inscription on it?)

                  - Fairy gold. Vanishes if touched by human hands. (Dwarves may want this material"

                      or — the fairy gold alway vanishes when he leaves the Enchanted Forest or something

                      Can you understand fairy language?

                  - Dryads - nymphs of forests + trees. (Talking tree?)

                  - Naiads - nymphs of rivers + streams. (or Nixies.) (Female "seducers" - drown you.
   #1 maybe   seven
   an hole - Hydra - nine-headed water snake monster. Head grows back after cutting it off.
   lump creature   or Naga - kind of same thing.   get central head

KING'S QUEST

(1984)

While at home caring for a young child, Roberta Williams fell in love with how computer games opened new worlds to explore. Soon she mapped out scripts and scenarios for graphic adventures like *King's Quest,* which is part of The Strong's Ken and Roberta Williams Collection.

n 1979, Roberta Williams and her husband, Ken, purchased an Apple II computer. Ken worked at IBM and used the computer to develop a compiler (a program that translates one code language into another) for the FORTRAN language. When Ken wasn't programming with the computer, Roberta used it to play. Almost immediately she became obsessed with *Colossal Cave Adventure*—the granddaddy of text-based games and the inspiration for *Zork* (page 97), *Adventureland* (page 111), and many other similar titles. Based on the Mammoth Cave system in Kentucky, *Colossal Cave Adventure* tasked players with exploring a vast underground lair rumored to be filled with treasure. The game's storytelling and interactive capabilities captivated Roberta. After playing every text-based adventure game she could find, including Scott Adams's *Adventureland* and Softape's *Journey,* she asked her husband a simple question: Why don't we design our own game?

Roberta was not a computer programmer; a mother who stayed home to raise her children, she joked that she "didn't even know how to plug a computer in." But Roberta was a skilled artist, and with Ken's programming expertise they began sketching out ideas. Roberta eventually came up with *Mystery House*, a game she based on the Agatha Christie novel *And Then There Were None* in which a killer lures ten people to an island and then methodically hunts them down. Unlike other text-based games, *Mystery House* included simple digital pictures accompanying each room a player entered; in fact, *Mystery House* was the first computer adventure game to feature graphics. Otherwise, gameplay was similar to most text-based adventure games: the program provided players with a brief description of their surroundings before prompting the player for a command. Set in an abandoned Victorian house, players had to navigate seventy rooms while interacting with common household objects to find jewels, all while unraveling a harrowing murder plot. Released through the Williams' company, On-Line Systems, the game sold for around $25, and despite being available only via mail order and in Los Angeles–area computer stores, it sold more than ten thousand copies—a huge hit for the time.

By 1983, Roberta and Ken Williams had renamed their company Sierra On-Line (reflecting their new headquarters near the Sierra Nevada mountains) and had released six games, notably *The Wizard and the Princess* (1980), the first computer adventure game with full color graphics; and *The Dark Crystal* (1983), based on the Jim Henson fantasy film of the same name. Roberta and Ken also began hiring programmers to expand their portfolio of games, not all of which involved serious gameplay. In 1981, for instance, they released *Softporn Adventure*, a comedic text-based adventure in which players helped a down-on-his-luck playboy acquire items to win the affections of women. (*Softporn Adventure* would later inspire the notorious Leisure Suit Larry series, published by Sierra from 1987 to 2009.) Not all of Sierra's releases were hits: Housed on six double-sided floppy disks, the sprawling *Time Zone* (1982) invited players to travel through time to solve puzzles and meet historical figures. The game did not sell well, largely due to its high $99.95 price tag, and it is among the rarest of Sierra games to find today.

In 1982, Sierra partnered with IBM, which sought launch titles for its upcoming home computer, the PCjr. Featuring color graphics and a sophisticated sound system, the PCjr was IBM's first attempt to break into the nascent home computer market. IBM was looking for games featuring a compelling storyline and a graphics engine that could showcase the technical abilities of the PCjr. Eager for a more challenging project, Roberta drafted a story based on her childhood love of fairy tales, especially Andrew Lang's Fairy books. The eventual game, *King's Quest*, would tell the story of a young knight named Sir Graham, who must seek out three legendary treasures to save the kingdom of Daventry from ruin.

In addition to an absorbing story, *King's Quest* had graphics that were leaps and bounds better than any other in the genre. Previously, most games presented a static picture accompanied by a text description. But *King's Quest* was the first adventure game to integrate animated graphics. Players could move Graham around the game using arrow keys while entering traditional text commands to interact with people and objects. Typing "open door," for instance, portrayed an animated Graham opening a castle door and entering a richly detailed castle, while "get fiddle" instructed our hero to pick up an instrument stashed in a dark corner of a room.

Despite its groundbreaking gameplay, *King's Quest* was almost lost to the sands of time. The IBM PCjr failed miserably due to its high price, a woefully uncomfortable keyboard, and a lack of expandability among many other problems. (The popular computer columnist Steven Levy wrote in 1984 that "The machine has the smell of death about it.") As an exclusive launch title for a computer that the *Chicago Tribune* later compared to the Ford Edsel and New Coke, Sierra suddenly had to find a new medium for its masterpiece. Fortunately, Sierra retained rights to *King's Quest* and managed to port it to the Tandy, Apple II, Amiga, Atari ST, and Commodore personal computers, where the company found a large and

loyal fan base that catapulted the game into a blockbuster franchise for Sierra with numerous sequels.

While *King's Quest* is widely considered a groundbreaking early graphical adventure game, Roberta Williams occupies another place in history. In an industry dominated by men and punctuated by larger-than-life alpha males, Roberta Williams is a testament to how some of the very best video games come from the heart, not coding prowess. Her very first game, *Mystery House*, took place in a setting with which she was well accustomed as a stay-at-home mother: the home. For all the fabled Silicon Valley companies that emerged from grimy garages, Sierra was born at the kitchen table from the wildly creative mind of a mother who had countless domestic responsibilities in addition to her career as a game developer. As video game historian Laine Nooney writes, "One can be a better mother from a kitchen table, even if what is 'made' there may not be a meal. Thus, perhaps Roberta did not come to the table so much as the table came to her, as an object with agency within a broader condensation of domestic, architectural, and gendered expectations for behaviour and orientation."

Roberta Williams created games like *King's Quest* that were smart, compelling, and fun. And in an era when game designers increasingly relied on graphics at the expense of storytelling, Roberta's games always featured memorable characters and plots in addition to immersive visuals. The fan mail she received testified to their power. As one adoring fan who, like Roberta herself, was a wife and a latecomer to computers, wrote: "Please continue to create forever. . . . Thanks for everything, especially giving me an opportunity to say how much I love you."

ТЕТРИС™

(TETRIS)

Now Compatible With **IBM PS/1**™

BEST
- Entertainment
- Action/Strategy
- Original Game Achievement
- Critic's Choice: Best Consumer Software

SOFTWARE PUBLISHERS ASSOCIATION

Certified **OVER 250,000 SOLD** SOFTWARE PUBLISHERS ASSOCIATION

IBM PC or Tandy 1000
- 256K RAM
- Hercules, CGA, EGA, or Tandy 1000 16-color
- 5¼" & 3½" disks enclosed
- Joystick optional

RAM-resident version included

The Soviet Challenge

Spectrum HoloByte™

TETRIS

(1984)

First written for a mainframe computer, *Tetris* became a hit when it was ported to personal computers, arcade games, and handhelds. Players loved the brain-bending challenge of sorting the four-square shapes into neat rows. *Tetris* entered the World Video Game Hall of Fame in 2015.

etris might seem like a simple game: rotate and move falling shapes in order to complete solid horizontal lines that then disappear. But like all great video games, the challenge becomes apparent with time. The pieces vary in shape and, as the game continues, they fall ever faster, stacking on top of one another and forcing the player to try to fit them in before the lines fill to the top. What begins as a simple brick-laying game quickly escalates into a heart-pounding race against the clock. And yet, the history of *Tetris* is as complex as the game is simple. It's a tale of intrigue, deception, handshake deals, and the Soviet Union's last stand.

In 1984, Alexey Pajitnov was working as a software engineer for the Dorodnitsyn Computing Center at the Soviet Academy of Sciences. The son of two writers, Pajitnov grew up in an intellectual family who disdained the Soviet system but knew better than to publicly challenge it. As a boy, he loved puzzles and logic games. Later, studying mathematics in college, he also developed a fascination with computers. Working at the Computing Center at age twenty-eight, Pajitnov found that like the rest of the country, the research center was rudderless and constricted. Ostensibly there to research artificial intelligence and voice recognition, Pajitnov was unable to get much done due to severe overcrowding and bureaucracy, and so he began tinkering with game design on an Electronika 60, a clone of the American PDP-11 minicomputer.

While walking by a toy shop one day, Pajitnov spied something in the window. It was a pentomino puzzle, a popular toy in which players needed to place twelve shapes composed of five squares each into a rectangle. Pentomino puzzles were a staple of his childhood, and he suddenly realized he could recreate them on a computer screen. By definition, pentomino shapes are each composed of five smaller squares, but instead, Pajitnov used four-square shapes—tetrominoes—to create a game called *Genetic Engineering* in which players used the shapes to build larger ones. But Pajitnov felt the game was dull, and he quickly developed a new idea, one involving tetromino shapes tumbling downward like a waterfall. Players would have to fight a war against gravity, rotating and cramming geometric shapes together to keep a pile from growing too high.

Pajitnov called his idea "Tetris," a combination of "tetromino" and "tennis," his favorite sport. Fighting for precious hours at his Electronika mainframe computer, Pajitnov drew the game's graphics using spaces and brackets. This being 1970s-era technology, there were no sound effects and gameplay was extremely choppy. In spite of the neon-green shapes and a flickering interface barely sustained by a wheezing microcomputer, Pajitnov's creation was thoroughly addicting. In the ensuing weeks, *Tetris* fever consumed the Dorodnitsyn Computing Center. "Everybody who touched this game couldn't stop playing it," Pajitnov later recalled.

Tetris was quickly ported into various programming languages, most notably by an engineer named Vadim Gerasimov, who created a version for Turbo Pascal featuring color graphics and smoother gameplay. This and countless other ports spread like wildfire behind the Iron Curtain, draining productivity at every university and research center it encountered as engineers jury-rigged their machines to run it. The game's whirlwind tour of the Eastern Bloc during the mid-1980s is the earliest example of the *Tetris* Effect, a phrase coined by psychologists to explain what occurs when individuals devote so much attention to something that it begins to affect their thought patterns and invade their dreams.

But *Tetris* remained unknown to westerners until 1986, when a man named Robert Stein wandered into the Institute of Computer Science in Budapest, Hungary. Hungary was unique among Eastern Bloc countries as it permitted a small degree of private enterprise. This, in addition to its proximity to Vienna, meant that a steady stream of legal and illegal electronics regularly flowed in and out of Budapest. Devices that were nonexistent throughout most of the Soviet Union, such as Commodore 64 computers, were relatively common in Hungary. Stein was originally from Hungary, eventually fleeing to Britain after the failed 1956 revolution. He found work at an electronics distributor specializing in Commodore products, and later starting his own company called Andromeda Software. Much of his business came from importing low-cost games from places like the Institute of Computer Science in Hungary. It was there, in 1986, that he spied *Tetris* for the first time.

Stein couldn't stop playing. He wanted to buy the rights immediately, but the Hungarians insisted he had to speak to the game's original creator, Alexey Pajitnov, back in Moscow. Pajitnov expressed interest via telegram, and, believing the licensing process would be painless, Stein began shopping *Tetris* to Western publishers. Reception was lukewarm initially, but he eventually secured a deal with the British publisher Mirrorsoft, an operation funded by the newspaper tycoon Robert Maxwell, and then with the American publisher Spectrum HoloByte. Having licensed *Tetris* to two publishers, Stein now had to *actually* secure the rights to the game—a task that quickly became a crash course in Cold War–era international relations. Over in Moscow,

Pajitnov's employer, the Dorodnitsyn Computing Center, caught wind of his deal and immediately claimed ownership of the game. After various poorly translated telegrams and a failed meeting with Pajitnov and Soviet bureaucrats in Moscow, Stein finally lied to Mirrorsoft and Spectrum Holo-Byte, claiming he had secured the rights to *Tetris* and they were free to publish. (Fortunately for Stein, his gambit paid off and Pajitnov eventually agreed to a deal in May 1988.) Thanks to thawing Cold War tensions and a brilliant marketing campaign that spotlighted *Tetris*'s exotic origins, the game was a wild success following its 1987 release. Available on many popular home PC systems, *Tetris* sold one hundred thousand copies its first year in America, and one hundred fifty thousand the following year.

But *Tetris* mania would not arrive until the world's preeminent game company, Nintendo, threw its weight behind the peculiar falling block game. That story begins with a man named Henk Rogers, a successful Dutch-born game importer who had made a name for himself bringing Western titles to Japan. For years Rogers had attempted to gain access to the booming Famicom/NES market, but Nintendo's famously ironclad licensing terms prevented many third-party games from getting a piece of the action. In the mid-1980s, after reading that Nintendo's president, Hiroshi Yamauchi, was an enthusiast of the ancient Chinese strategy game *Go*, Rogers wrote him a letter in which he claimed—falsely—to have the rights to the most technologically advanced *Go* game available. Surprisingly, Yamauchi invited him to Kyoto, and the two hammered out a deal over Scotch and several rounds of *Go*. Rogers then hastily secured the rights to a passable, if unremarkable, computerized version of *Go* from a tiny British firm. The eventual Nintendo port sold a respectable one hundred fifty thousand copies for the Famicom, but most important, it gave Rogers's company, Bullet-Proof Software, a foothold in the elite sphere of developers allowed to publish games for Nintendo.

At the Consumer Electronics Show in January 1988—a mecca for game importers—Rogers came across the Spectrum HoloByte display and, like so many others, became addicted to fitting together *Tetris*'s waterfall of tetromino shapes. He knew immediately the game would be a perfect match for Nintendo. By May, he had successfully brokered a deal between Spectrum HoloByte and Nintendo to produce *Tetris* for the Famicom. The only problem, as Rogers soon realized, was that *Tetris*'s other publisher,

Mirrorsoft, had already licensed the game to an Atari affiliate called Tengen. After countless made-and-broken handshake deals and shouting matches, Rogers finally managed to engineer a deal straight from the mind of Rube Goldberg: Stein's company Andromeda would license *Tetris* rights to Mirrorsoft, who would license *Tetris* to Tengen, who would in turn license *Tetris* to Rogers's company Bullet-Proof, who would finally produce a *Tetris* game for Nintendo.

The deal was a tremendous success. The NES version of *Tetris* (1989) sold an astounding one hundred thirty thousand copies in its first month and sales would eventually reach two million. A game that began life deep inside the cold, concrete walls of a Moscow research center had finally conquered the world. But *Tetris* wasn't

done, for in 1989, Nintendo was putting the final touches on its handheld Game Boy system, which would soon revolutionize the video game industry. Nintendo decided that the simple yet addicting *Tetris* would be the perfect companion with which to bundle their new handheld unit. After another whirlwind of backroom negotiations involving Rogers, Stein, Pajitnov, and a parade of Soviet bureaucrats, Bullet-Proof secured the handheld rights to *Tetris*. Because Pajitnov was in the Soviet Union he could not reap the profits, but with Rogers's help he eventually emigrated to the United States in 1991 and continued his career in game development.

As Rogers would later say, "*Tetris* made Game Boy and Game Boy made *Tetris*." *Tetris* would eventually sell some thirty-five million copies for various versions of Nintendo's iconic handheld system. *Tetris* for Game Boy quickly became one of the most beloved games of all time and ultimately built the market for puzzle and casual games. It remains the most ported game of all time, with over 170 million copies sold for more than sixty-five different platforms. *Tetris*'s success demonstrates that the best video games don't just mimic previous video games—they draw inspiration from other sources. A quarter century after its creation, *Tetris* is proof positive that the best sources for innovative games, from America to Japan to the farthest reaches of Russia, are the play and life experiences that most move and fascinate us.

NINTENDO ENTERTAINMENT SYSTEM

(1985)

In 1985, the Nintendo Entertainment System resuscitated the ailing home video game market. This modified console, donated by Nintendo of America, reveals the relatively inexpensive but powerful internal hardware like the custom PPU (picture processing unit) chip inside the bestselling console.

n late 1985, the American video game industry seemed ruined. After years of double-digit growth, too many consoles and too many poorly designed games had oversaturated the market. The carnage began slowly, with retailers returning unsold stock to game companies. The trickle became a tidal wave, and soon entire companies were crumbling under their own excesses. With each console offering a large range of titles, and with third-party developers such as Activision piling on countless more, consumers stopped spending on new releases and turned to the bargain bin. Revenues, which had reached the billions by 1983, plummeted to barely $100 million by 1985. Video game companies went bankrupt and even the king of electronic gaming itself, Atari, hemorrhaged $500 million following the crash and was eventually sold off by its parent company, Warner Communications. With increasing competition from personal computers such as the Apple II, the future for game consoles seemed bleak. That is, until Nintendo revived the market with its Nintendo Entertainment System (NES) console late in 1985.

The famous NES was actually launched two years prior in Japan as the Family Computer, or Famicom. The Famicom wasn't Nintendo's first foray into the console market; in 1977, it released the Color TV-Game for the Japanese market, a dedicated console that could play simple sports and racing games but lacked interchangeable cartridges. The Famicom's story begins in 1980, when Nintendo eyed the Atari 2600's dominance in the home console market and began secretly developing its own interchangeable cartridge-based system, one that was cheaper and more powerful than its competitors. Nintendo's presi-dent Hiroshi Yamauchi tapped the head of the company's hardware-focused Research & Development 2 (R&D2) team, Masayuki Uemura, to spearhead the project. Uemura seemed the natural choice as he'd worked on Nintendo's *Home Pong* (the color TV game series) and *Breakout* (Block Kuzushi) clones.

To keep costs on the new console project down, Uemura opted for an older but tried-and-true microchip called the MOS 6502. Variants of this affordable chip had powered other legendary machines such as the Atari 2600, the Commodore 64, and the Apple II. However, to generate the cutting-edge graphics his bosses demanded, Uemura had to pair the MOS 6502 with a custom graphics chip, known as a picture processing unit (PPU), which could pump out more colors, more sprites (moveable player graphics), and more memory. This meant bigger, faster, more colorful games. Most outside companies refused to produce a PPU at Nintendo's asking price, but eventually the semiconductor manufacturer Ricoh agreed to produce three million chips over two years—an astoundingly high order that guaranteed Nintendo's console would be either a wild success or a massive bust.

To Nintendo's relief, the Famicom sold well in the Japanese market. Retailing for ¥14,800 (approximately $65 in 1983), the console was less than half the cost of its competitors while delivering vastly superior graphics. It was sold alongside three cartridges based on ports of Nintendo arcade games: *Donkey Kong*, *Donkey Kong Jr.*, and *Popeye*. Nintendo firmly marketed the Famicom toward children and families. It featured bright red plastic, smooth corners, a traditional top-loading cartridge system, and two simple, permanently wired controllers that could be neatly stowed in cutaways along the console's sides. Thanks to an effective marketing campaign, the Famicom sold half a million units within six months. Yet Nintendo was soon faced with its first crisis: complaints poured in that the Famicom intermittently froze during gameplay. Nintendo eventually narrowed the problem down to a faulty circuit and subsequently ordered a massive recall just before the holiday shopping season. Defective units were repaired with new motherboards, and although Nintendo spent millions of dollars to address the issue, the company earned a measure of goodwill with its customers that continues to this day.

Armed with a successful console, Nintendo expanded its game offerings, pouring massive resources into its own line of games including *Excitebike* (1984) and the future juggernaut series *Super Mario Bros.* (1985) and *The Legend of Zelda* (1986). Believing that the flood of third-party games had caused the video game crash, Nintendo imposed strict licensing restrictions on outside developers. Following these rules, many third-party game companies found success with the Famicom, notably Hudson

Soft's port of *Lode Runner* (1984) and Namco's *Tower of Druaga* (1984).

Nintendo was ready to introduce its console to the American market. In 1983, it negotiated with Atari to release the Famicom in America as the "Nintendo Enhanced Video System," but Atari bailed out because of mounting losses as a result of the crash. Forced to plod alone into the wreckage of the American video game market, Nintendo repurposed the Famicom into the Ad-

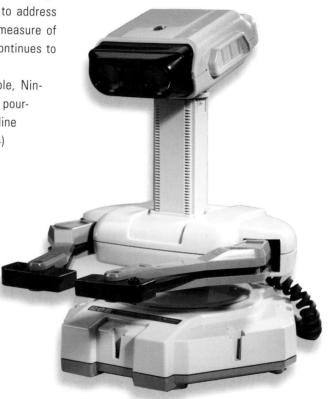

Facing reluctant retailers who had little interest in yet another video game console and latching on to a craze for robots in the toy industry, Nintendo devised eye-catching accessories like this R.O.B. (Robotic Operating Buddy) to bundle with the NES.

vanced Video System (AVS), a console-computer hybrid complete with a keyboard, cassette data recorder, and many other advanced peripherals. When Nintendo showcased the AVS at the 1984 Consumer Electronics Show in Las Vegas, however, attendees were skeptical of the console's ability to succeed. Retailers did not place any orders, and the press speculated that Nintendo was setting itself up for failure. "This could be a miscalculation on Nintendo's part," the magazine *Electronic Games* later suggested.

Nintendo realized it would have to abandon the hybrid approach and release the AVS solely as a video game console, just as it had in Japan. Careful to avoid appearing like just another video game system in a market saturated with clones and derivatives, Nintendo did away with the AVS's bells and whistles and positioned its console—now called the "Nintendo Entertainment System" (NES)—squarely in the toy market. To distinguish the NES from other consoles, Nintendo called its cartridges "paks," added a Robotic Operating Buddy (R.O.B.), a light gun "Zapper," and engineered a front-loading cartridge chamber that kept games hidden from view. (This also made the NES more prone to breakdown, although Nintendo addressed this flaw by building a highly regarded repair network.) Nintendo also continued to ensure that third-party developers could not flood the market with poorly built games by installing a lockout chip that prevented unauthorized games from running on the NES. As Nintendo president Yamauchi later said, "Atari collapsed because they gave too much freedom to third-party developers and the market was swamped with rubbish games."

Nintendo initiated a limited test launch on October 18, 1985, in the New York City market,

releasing the NES with a modest production run of one hundred thousand units alongside a catalog of seventeen games including *Duck Hunt*, *10-Yard Fight*, *Baseball*, *Kung Fu*, and *Wild Gunman*. Nintendo sold most of its stock, and after experimenting with various other test markets, launched the NES nationwide in September 1986, with a multimillion-dollar marketing budget. The console sold more than a million units that year, and Nintendo raked in over $300 million. (By comparison, according to some estimates the entire video game industry only made $100 million in 1985.) Leading the charge was *Super Mario Bros.*, which became available in the U.S. starting in early 1986 and took the American market by storm. (For more about *Super Mario Bros.*, see page 189.)

The NES rapidly became a mammoth hit, eventually selling some sixty million units during its long and storied production history while immortalizing countless game characters including Mario, Link, and Samus Aran. Why did the NES succeed in such a desolate market? Many credit Nintendo's strict licensing terms that limited most third-party companies to five yearly releases, with Nintendo controlling all cartridge manufacturing. With game producers having to conform to Nintendo's standards of quality and their family-friendly image, the company had complete control over distribution and was able to avoid the deluge of poor-quality games that doomed Atari and so many other game companies.

But most important, Nintendo embraced a generous customer service operation by instituting a massive repair network and a free hotline. It also launched the *Nintendo Fun Club*, a free newsletter that offered tips, tricks, and video game news. The newsletter was later replaced by *Nintendo Power* magazine, which enjoyed a circulation of nearly four hundred seventy-five thousand at its height. In an industry hamstrung by the stench of Atari's demise, Nintendo proved that electronic games were not a passing fad, and that with good engineering, high-quality games, and an unwavering devotion to customer service, video games would never lose their grip on the steering wheel of pop culture.

SUPER MARIO BROS.

(1985)

As the face of the bestselling video game franchise of all time, Mario forged an 8-bit empire. It takes only a brief screenshot or a few bars of music for people all over the world to recognize Nintendo's iconic plumber. It is no surprise that The Strong inducted the game in the inaugural class of the World Video Game Hall of Fame.

Before he changed his occupation, Mario was a carpenter known as "Jumpman." In the arcade game *Donkey Kong* (page 141), he was tasked with saving his girlfriend, Pauline, from the clutches of an evil gorilla. *Donkey Kong* was a massive hit for Nintendo, selling more than one hundred thirty-two thousand units and launching the career of the legendary designer Shigeru Miyamoto. According to legend, Mario earned his permanent designation after Mario Segale, the Italian-American landlord who owned Nintendo of America's warehouse, disrupted a staff meeting to demand an overdue rent payment.

Mario's second appearance came in Nintendo's 1982 sequel *Donkey Kong Jr.*—only this time, the tables had turned. Mario, having successfully rescued Pauline, captured Donkey Kong and placed him in a cage as punishment. It was up to the great ape's namesake, Donkey Kong Jr., to rescue his father and defeat the erstwhile hero Mario. Players controlled the young gorilla as he climbed vines, chains, and ropes while dodging Mario's obstacles, which included birdlike creatures called "Nitpickers" and anthropomorphic bear traps known as "Snapjaws."

Despite this star turn for Donkey Kong and his offspring, Miyamoto had always intended for his pudgy everyman to be the star. For this reason he designed Mario with distinctive features that stood out in 8-bit graphics and remained constant from game to game, from the red shirt and blue overalls to the iconic mustache and bulbous nose. In 1983, Nintendo released an arcade cabinet called *Mario Bros.* Once again designed by Miyamoto, *Mario Bros.* cast players as Mario and his younger brother, Luigi, as they defeated slimy creatures dwelling in the sewers of New York City—a change of scenery that reflected Mario's

occupation change. After a colleague suggested that Mario resembled a plumber more than a carpenter, Miyamoto designed the turtle-and-crab-infested netherworld through which Mario and his brother would navigate. Like in *Donkey Kong*, Mario could only run and jump; the plumber was only able to jump on and kill enemies who were lying on their backs. *Mario Bros.* was modestly successful despite being released during the depths of the video game crash, and various versions were ported to the Apple II, the Atari 2600, and other consoles. Miyamoto, however, had already turned his gaze to a far grander idea, one that would see Mario leave the grimy New York sewers for the picturesque Mushroom Kingdom.

Nintendo tasked Miyamoto, now their star game designer, with creating a Mario game exclusively for the Famicom. Once again, Mario would have to save a young woman—this time a beautiful princess named Peach—from the clutches of an evil creature. But instead of battling an ape, Mario would have to defeat an enormous, spiked turtle-dragon named Bowser. Interestingly, early designs for the *Mario Bros.* sequel included specifications for rifles, beam guns, and rockets, but Miyamoto eventually decided to preserve and enhance the "jump" as the core game mechanic. Unlike the original game, Mario would now be able to jump on turtles, or "Koopa Troopas," and invading, sentient mushrooms called Goombas.

Another addition was the "power-up" mushroom, which turned Mario into a stronger, supersized version, and the fire flower, which enabled Mario to chuck fireballs at his enemies. These power-ups were nearly always hidden in blocks throughout the game, many of them featuring the famous *?* symbol. Each level also contained special gold coins, and players could earn extra lives for each hundred coins collected. Similarly, catching a green mushroom meant a "1UP" life. While many players chose to play through the game in its entirety, others could take advantage of hidden warp zones containing pipes that allowed them to skip levels. There was also a two-player feature, allowing gamers to take turns playing Mario or his younger brother, Luigi.

Miyamoto dubbed his new, far more elaborate sequel *Super Mario Bros.* While *Mario Bros.* featured a static, underground setting that only slightly changed between levels, *Super Mario Bros.* consisted of eight beautifully drawn worlds, each comprising four stages. The final stage of each world brought players to a smoldering, lava-filled castle where Mario would fight Bowser or one of his decoys. Miyamoto also hid countless secrets in each world, including beanstalks and pipes that brought Mario to realms full of gold coins. Miyamoto became so obsessed with perfecting *Super Mario Bros.* that he put development of another future blockbuster—*The Legend of Zelda* (page 193)—on hold.

One cannot understate the importance of *Super Mario Bros.* to Nintendo and the history of video games. The game was a massive success for the NES soon after it launched in 1985. Nintendo even bundled the game with some NES console packages. *Super Mario Bros.* eventually became the bestselling home video game of all time until 2006, when it was surpassed in sales by Nintendo's *Wii Sports* (also bundled with the Nintendo Wii). The popularity of *Super Mario Bros.* led to a myriad of sequels and spiritual successors, many of which Nintendo still publishes today. Although these games feature updated graphics and controls, most still follow the basic premise laid out in 1985, with the iconic plumber jumping from platform to platform, fighting the same enemies and using the same power-ups on his quest to rescue Princess Peach. Non-platform games such as the racer *Super Mario Kart* (1992), the educational *Mario's Time Machine* (1993), and the role-playing game *Paper Mario* (2001), have cemented the franchise's popularity with gamers of all ages and tastes. Additionally, Mario's adventures spawned a television series titled *The Super Mario Bros. Super Show!* (1989) and the live-action *Super Mario Bros.* film starring Bob Hoskins, John Leguizamo, and Dennis Hopper (1993).

Mario himself became not only Nintendo's official mascot, but also the face of the video game industry as a whole. In the 1990s, a survey discovered more children recognized Mario than Mickey Mouse. In 2003, he became the first video game character honored with a figure in the Hollywood Wax Museum. As the most well-known video game character of all time, Mario is instantly recognizable even by those who have never picked up a gaming controller. To this day the plucky, mustachioed plumber remains the backbone of Nintendo's empire.

THE LEGEND OF ZELDA

(1986)

A year after the Nintendo Entertainment System debuted in America, Nintendo released *The Legend of Zelda*. The gold-colored packaging of this cartridge fit the fantastic theme of the role-playing game that earned admission into the second class of the World Video Game Hall of Fame.

An evil wizard has captured a beautiful princess and is on the verge of conquering the land of Hyrule. The only thing standing in his way is a tunic-clad adventurer named Link. The story of *The Legend of Zelda* is in many ways an ancient one. From Arthurian legends to Spaghetti Westerns, the silent hero who trudges alone through dangerous lands has long been a recurring theme. *The Legend of Zelda* shares a common plot with its equally famous cousin, *Super Mario Bros.*, and the two games were even developed simultaneously by the same developer, Shigeru Miyamoto. And yet *Mario* and *Zelda* could not be any more different. At the opening screen, Mario could only progress in one direction: left to right. The heroic Link, however, could venture left, right, up, or down into a dark, dark cave . . .

As a boy growing up in post-war Japan,

Shigeru Miyamoto often wandered the beautiful, haunting landscape surrounding his home in Sonobe, venturing into thick forests, hidden lakes, and dark caves with the help of a lantern. Miyamoto would later channel these memories to create a "miniature garden" for players to experience their own virtual adventures filled with wonder and excitement. More inspiration came from the small rooms and sliding doors of his family home, a common trait of traditional Japanese architecture. The mazelike floorplan would one day define the famously twisting, labyrinthine dungeons of *The Legend of Zelda*.

Miyamoto had long planned to create a video game based on his whimsical childhood memories. Yet instead of featuring linear gameplay in which action took place in a strict sequence, the designer envisioned this game to be open-ended. Players would be provided a basic goal—defeat the evil wizard and save the princess—but the rest was up to them. As for the name of the game, Miyamoto was inspired by the late American artist, writer, and socialite Zelda Fitzgerald, wife of F. Scott Fitzgerald. "She was a famous and beautiful woman from all accounts," Miyamoto later explained, "and I liked the sound of her name. So I took the liberty of using her name for the very first *Zelda* title." Exploration and problem-solving would be just as important as battling enemies and defeating dungeon bosses. Instead of competing for a high score, players would simply attempt to complete the game—which, given *Zelda*'s complexity, could take days or weeks. Such a game could never succeed in crowded arcades, where the

In 2012, Nicholas Bell made this shield, inspired by the one used by Link, the hero of Nintendo's long-running *The Legend of Zelda* series, for use during Halloween.

length of coin-operated gameplay was measured in minutes and seconds. Miyamoto also wanted *Zelda* to be difficult, leaving players with a sense of accomplishment when they finished it.

Miyamoto finally had the chance to fulfill his vision in 1984, on the heels of Nintendo's successful launch of its Family Computer (Famicom) console. Nintendo's brand-new game system sold briskly in Japan and was set to be released in the United States as the Nintendo Entertainment System (NES). A company that prided itself on thinking ahead, Nintendo wanted Miyamoto's grand adventure game to be a lead title for its new peripheral, the Famicom Disk System, which used floppy disks known as "disk cards" for data storage instead of traditional cartridges. Released in 1986, the Disk System connected to the original Famicom using a special RAM adaptor, allowing for larger, more sophisticated games while introducing rewritable memory, which enabled players to save their progress. With the ability to save and resume play at a later time, games could be far more complex.

In *Zelda*, players assumed the role of a young boy named Link who embarked on a quest to obtain the legendary Triforce—a triangular item that contained the essence and power of the goddesses who created his world—and save Princess Zelda from the machinations of the malevolent Ganon. (The famous three-triangles-within-a-triangle Triforce is actually a familiar design in Japan, one that dates back to the Hōjō clan, a powerful family that dominated Japanese politics in the twelfth and thirteen centuries.) Upon beginning the game, players were given a cursory explanation of the daunting task ahead of them before the black screen peeled away like stage curtains to reveal a top-down view of Link

in a forest clearing with four possible ways to trek—one of which is into a dark cave. Link is unarmed, but if the intrepid adventurer descends into the cave he meets an old man who presents him with a sword and declares, "It's dangerous to go alone! Take this." (The old man and his prophetic line have since become a viral internet meme, with countless variations depicting him offering everything from kittens to Kleenex boxes in place of the sword.)

Early designs of *Zelda* had Link beginning the game with a sword; some at Nintendo were worried players would forgo the cave altogether and plod to the first dungeon without a means of defending themselves. But Miyamoto resisted this nod toward traditional linear gameplay, maintaining that players should find their own way. Exploration and puzzle-solving were the ethos of *The Legend of Zelda*, and so too was community. Stumped players would have to trade secrets with their friends or read the *Nintendo Fun Club* newsletter for hints. Players would have to figure out for themselves which dungeons to tackle first, which items were necessary for which boss, and whether they should stock up on bombs and arrows at the shop. Like the twisting dungeons that composed it, Hyrule itself was a maze, with late-game areas only accessible with certain items. Miyamoto still imbued *Zelda* with a degree of linear progression, but like a densely covered forest path, it was up to the players to uncover it. Throughout all the puzzles and action, composer Koji Kondo's beautiful, haunting melodies were omnipresent— staying with players even long after they turned off the game.

Mario and *Zelda* were created simultaneously; at times development of the two games was so close that rejected ideas for one title were repurposed into the other, although progress for *Zelda* was delayed repeatedly as Miyamoto obsessed over *Mario*'s finishing touches. Nintendo finally released *Mario* to the Japanese market in September 1985 for the Famicom, while *Zelda* was released in February 1986 for the Famicom Disk System. Nintendo released the American version of *The Legend of Zelda* in August 1987 for the NES console.

Nintendo had to squeeze every ounce of memory out of its traditional game-pak cartridges to handle *Zelda*. At a significant cost, Nintendo managed to install a battery-powered RAM chip inside each one, allowing players to save their progress. Hoping to distinguish *Zelda* from other games, Nintendo included a cutaway in the packaging to reveal the unique, gold-colored cartridge. *The Legend of Zelda* was a massive bestseller, selling some 6.5 million copies. The franchise currently consists of nineteen core games that have collectively sold nearly 75 million copies. The Zelda franchise is one of the few to claim the honor of having more than one game receive a perfect score from the Japanese video game magazine *Famitsu* (*Ocarina of Time*, *The Wind Waker*, and *Skyward Sword*). The franchise also inspired a thirteen-episode animated television series that aired in 1989 and a set of graphic novels. The late comedian Robin Williams even named his daughter, Zelda Rae, after the series' eponymous princess.

While elements of the Zelda games remained constant, a hallmark of the series is Nintendo's devotion to introducing new features, from the notoriously difficult side-scrolling gameplay in *The Adventure of Link* (1987) to the alternate dimensions of *A Link to the Past* (1991) to *Ocarina of Time*'s time traveling (1998) to the limitless, convention-shattering *Breath of the Wild* (2017). Nearly thirty years after its release, *The Legend of Zelda* spawned a game series that ranks among the most iconic, daring, and beloved of all time.

LINK IS UNARMED, BUT IF THE INTREPID ADVENTURER DESCENDS INTO THE CAVE HE MEETS AN OLD MAN WHO PRESENTS HIM WITH A SWORD AND DECLARES, "IT'S DANGEROUS TO GO ALONE! TAKE THIS."

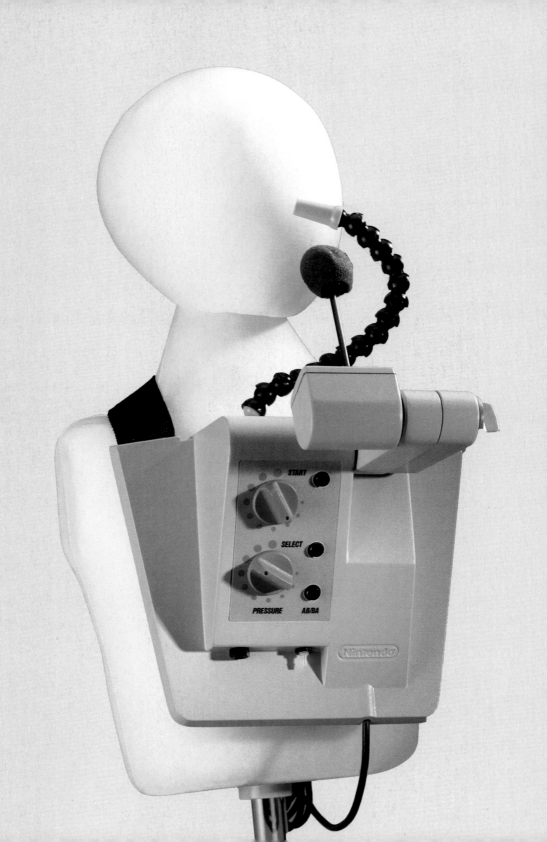

NES
HANDS FREE
CONTROLLER

(1989)

Nintendo worked with the Seattle Children's Hospital and eight-year-old Todd Stabelfeldt, who suffered from paralysis, to develop this Hands Free controller to make the company's games more accessible for people of various physical abilities. The company donated this controller for the NES to The Strong.

During the 1980s, with its runaway bestselling NES console, Nintendo introduced players to a mustachioed plumber named Mario who traveled to the Mushroom Kingdom to battle Koopa Troopas, confront the evil Bowser, and save Princess Peach. In *The Legend of Zelda*, players were transported to the overwhelmed kingdom of Hyrule, where a silent, tunic-clad adventurer named Link ventured through dark dungeons to defeat Ganon, the Prince of Darkness, and save Princess Zelda. These games and countless others engrossed players in wonderful new worlds as effectively as any fantasy novel could.

But some were shut out from these magical worlds. Quashing a Koopa Troopa, shooting Link's bow, defeating space pirates—these all required interacting with a controller. The famous rectangular Nintendo gamepad was a marvel of simplistic engineering, but for those who lacked the use of their hands, it represented a barrier greater than any dungeon boss. Nintendo, which famously encouraged its players to write in with questions and comments, was struck by letters from quadriplegic children who longed to experience the thrill of video games. The company prided itself on making games accessible to everyone, and so it teamed up with the Seattle Children's Hospital to develop a special hands-free controller. Nintendo's research-and-development team recruited eight-year-old Todd Stabelfeldt, who earlier that year became paralyzed from the neck down after an accidental gunshot, to help design the device.

The project took several years to complete due to the complexity of operating a game without fingers. The NES controller may seem rudimentary by today's standards, but controlling Mario is not a simple feat. The directional pad must be moved left, right, up, or down, and to defeat his enemies Mario must be able to jump diagonally or fall just so. Likewise, the A and B buttons are often pressed in rapid succession or held for long periods of time (such as to make Mario sprint).

Working with Stabelfeldt, Nintendo engineers created a sturdy device that was strapped to a user's chest. Players could operate the directional pad with their chin, fully allowing for all the complex movements available on the traditional controller. The A and B buttons were controlled by slightly "puffing" or "sipping" on a tube, while the START and SELECT buttons were activated by puffing or sipping harder. A set of controls allowed a helper to dial in the sensitivity of the tube to compensate for players with weaker or stronger lungs.

"Now everyone can play with power!" the NES Hands Free manual stated proudly, a twist on Nintendo's famous slogan "Now you're playing with power!" In a press release, Peter Main, Nintendo of America's vice president of marketing, said, "Individuals who are unable to use the current controllers, while not a huge portion of the user population, are nevertheless some of the people who can derive the greatest benefits from video game play; and it is important to us that they are able to have the option of using and enjoying the Nintendo Entertainment System." The National Spinal Cord Injury Association endorsed Nintendo's product, agreeing that "People with physical limitations throughout the country can now enjoy the therapeutic and entertainment value of video game play."

A smiling photo of Todd Stabelfeldt, who was so instrumental in designing the NES Hands Free, was prominently featured on the cover of the

NES Hands Free manual as well as in Nintendo's marketing material. He even toured the country modeling the device and giving live demos. Stabelfeldt continued to develop devices for the physically disabled, launching his own charitable foundation and starting his own database company. The "Quadfather," as he is affectionately known, continues to help Apple and other tech giants make their devices as accessible as possible.

Nintendo's commitment to players of all abilities helped spark a movement by game manufacturers to make sure virtual worlds are open and accessible to players who have faced many challenges in experiencing their own.

Jordan Mechner adapted filmmaking rotoscoping techniques to transform early computer game animations from herky-jerky movements to fluid actions for the characters in his seminal game, *Prince of Persia.* He filmed his brother running, jumping, and sword-fighting, then scanned the images into his computer to imbue his virtual characters with grace. These photos and other materials documenting his career are part of The Strong's Jordan Mechner Collection.

PRINCE OF

PERSIA

(1989)

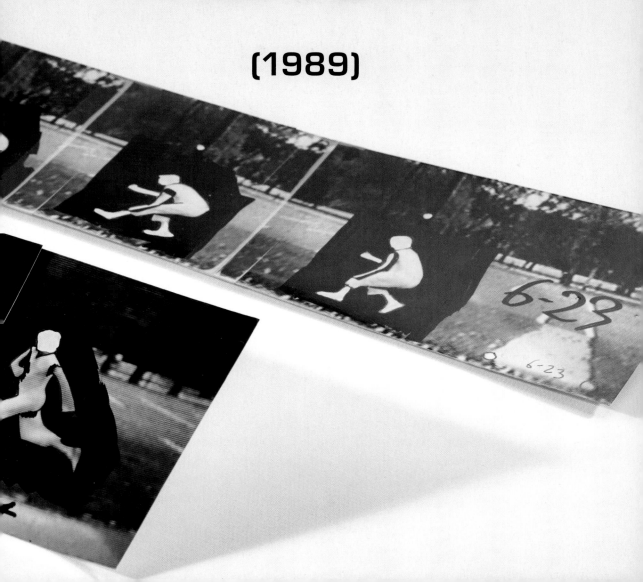

A century ago, two brothers from Brooklyn named Max and Dave Fleischer developed a device that allowed animators to capture live-action events frame by frame. They tested their system on the roof of Max's apartment building, where Dave, wearing a black clown suit, danced in front of a white sheet. Max captured the movements on film and projected them onto a glass plate that he then used to trace out pictures of individual movements. The result was *rotoscoping*, an animation technique that Max patented in 1915 that could produce amazingly lifelike movements. Seventy years later, Jordan Mechner, another New Yorker, used the same technique to revolutionize computer graphics when he filmed his brother running, jumping, and climbing. Using rotoscoping, Mechner was able to produce fluid, lifelike movements never before seen in a video game.

Mechner began his pioneering work while still an undergraduate at Yale University in the early 1980s. He had a passion for animation, but he was a poor artist who struggled to draw his own cartoons. With the popularity of the Apple II and other personal computers, Mechner gladly traded the pen for the keyboard and learned how to create animations for video games. Yet he was quickly dissatisfied with the stilted movement of characters in computer games; unlike in his favorite cartoons, video game characters were static and lurched across the screen awkwardly. Mechner wanted them to sway and dance and glide, just like in real life.

He began researching the technique of rotoscoping, which he had learned about in his history of cinema class. In 1983, he began experimenting by filming his karate instructor performing a variety of martial arts moves. Then he traced im-ages from the film and used a VersaWriter graphics digitizer tablet to copy the images onto the computer. On March 19, 1983, Mechner finished a test of this to see if it would work in a game he was developing, and in his diary, he recorded his excitement: "When I saw that sketch little figure walk across the screen, looking just like [his karate instructor] Dennis, all I could say was 'ALL RIGHT!'" Jordan's game *Karateka* (1984), a Japanese-themed karate game, became a best-selling title for the Apple II, with half a million copies sold. The game sent players on a martial arts–fueled adventure in feudal Japan to save a princess from an evil warlord. *Karateka* included several novel features, including fluid animations and a regenerative health system, and with it Mechner had established himself as a premier video game designer even before he had graduated from college.

Thrilled with *Karateka*, Mechner's publisher, Brøderbund Software, urged him to come up with another idea after he graduated from college. Yet the twenty-one-year-old dithered, at times preferring to move to Hollywood to make a go of it as a screenwriter. "In the time it'll take me to do a new game, I could write three screenplays," Mechner wrote in his journal. But as the months passed, he rekindled his love for video games. "A strange thing happened," he journaled on August 28, 1985. "I started getting images in my head of the characters: The Sultan. The Princess. The Boy. I saw the scenes in my mind as if it were a Disney movie."

Believing the exotic, Eastern setting was the driving force behind *Karateka*, he decided to feature the beautiful desert sands of the Middle East for his next idea. Mechner envisioned his new game as a combination of Brøderbund's 1983 puzzle-oriented platform game *Lode Runner* and Steven Spielberg's 1981 adventure film *Raiders of the Lost Ark*. This game would feature a protagonist named the Prince who must descend into colossal underground lairs filled with treasure, puzzles, and booby traps. To survive, the Prince relied on his superhuman acrobatic skills requiring complex key inputs to bypass sword-wielding enemies, spike traps, deep pits, and guillotines.

For this Arabian fantasy of a hero who rescues the princess from the evil clutches of the sinister Grand Vizier Jaffar, Mechner sought to create even more lifelike actions by perfecting the rotoscoping techniques he had used to make *Karateka*. First, he videotaped his younger brother, clothed all in white, running, jumping, and climbing. Then he took prints of individual frames and highlighted the body shapes so they would be easier to trace and digitize. Once they were computerized, he combined these individual frames to produce lifelike movement, and the result was a game that pushed computer animation to new levels of realism and sophistication. Players could run, jump, and dodge attacks with a level of fluidity never seen in any game, while health indicators for the Prince and his enemies made combat a gritty, exhilarating flurry of parries and slashes. He dubbed the game *Prince of Persia*.

Prince of Persia was warmly received. Charles Ardai of *Computer Gaming World* called it "a tremendous achievement" that "captures the feel of those great old adventure films." Even so, *Prince of Persia* was initially a commercial slow starter. It was released for the aging Apple IIe computer, but many gamers had already moved on to more sophisticated computers running Microsoft's Windows operating system. *Prince of Persia* sold just seven thousand units on the Apple II and

IBM PC platforms at first, and despite a hasty port to Windows, the game remained a failure, selling barely ten thousand copies in 1990. At that point Brøderbund and Mechner had moved on, believing their Arabian adventure to be a masterpiece, but a failed one. Then something curious happened: Brøderbund ported *Prince of Persia* to the new Apple Macintosh. In conjunction with a flurry of other ports in domestic and foreign markets, including for the Super NES, the Game Boy, and the Sega Genesis, the game was suddenly a bestseller three years after its initial release. *Prince of Persia* would eventually sell more than two million copies throughout the 1990s in various formats, spawning many sequels and even a movie, *Prince of Persia: The Sands of Time*, in 2010.

In many ways, the story of *Prince of Persia* is not unlike the story of electronic gaming itself: youth, engineering brilliance, and some dumb luck. For years, Jordan Mechner refused to define himself as a game developer, unsure of the future of the industry and holding out hope that he could make it as a Hollywood screenwriter. But like the vast Arabian desert, the limitless possibilities of game design always drew him back. When he moved to the Bay Area to begin work on what would become *Prince of Persia*, the young designer, like the Prince himself, was overwhelmed by the daunting tasks ahead of him. "I have to rent a car. I have to drive it," Mechner complained in a journal entry dated September 10, 1986. "I have to *move in*. I have to *buy* a car. I have to buy insurance. I've never done *any* of this stuff before . . . and now I have to do it all at once." And finally, almost as an afterthought, he added, "On top of this—or rather, at the bottom of it—I have to make a computer game. It's gonna be fun."

JOHN MADDEN FOOTBALL

(1990)

John Madden was a larger-than-life personality who loaned his name to Electronic Arts for its bestselling football series. This prototype cartridge was developed as part of the launch of the game for the Sega Genesis. Note the word CONFIDENTIAL blazoned across the front.

O n an overcast day in 1984, Electronic Arts CEO Trip Hawkins sat across from the legendary NFL coach-turned TV broadcaster John Madden. Loud, large, and brash, Madden had coached the Oakland Raiders to a Super Bowl win in 1977 and was now enjoying a highly successful role as a color commentator. Madden's jocular and flamboyant delivery made him an immediate hit with football viewers, routinely punctuating his play calling with cries of "Boom!" "Bang!" and "Doink!" while making an art form out of the telestrator, a device that allowed him to superimpose diagrams onscreen. Madden and Hawkins sat talking about video games in the dining car of an Oakland-bound Amtrak train snaking its way through the Rocky Mountains. (Madden was famously fearful of flying and only traveled via train and bus.)

Hawkins founded Electronic Arts (EA) in 1982 with the goal of elevating video games into an art form. EA promoted its games like music albums, spending lavishly on cover artwork and prominently featuring the names of game designers and programmers. The company also pioneered the use of celebrity promotion, notably with its blockbuster 1983 basketball title, *One-on-One: Dr. J vs. Larry Bird* (page 161). Hawkins disdained sports games with generic, blocky gameplay and believed that featuring actual sports figures brought EA's titles an unrivaled element of realism. *One-on-One* was a hit, but Hawkins's dream was to create a football game for his preferred platform, the Apple II computer. America's favorite broadcaster would be the perfect man to endorse it. "I picked John because I wanted a design partner that could help us make the game authentic but also have

selling-power from his name on the cover," Hawkins later said.

Madden, laying back in his seat and puffing a cigar, at first seemed enthusiastic about the idea. Although the legendary football coach trusted computers about as much as he trusted airplanes, he relished the idea of lending his face and expertise to a football simulation. Hawkins promised to make *John Madden Football* as realistic as possible, the only difference being that it would feature seven players on a side instead of the traditional eleven. The reason was technical: the Apple II simply lacked the memory and processing power to reliably display twenty-two moving figures. But Madden refused to lend his image to a seven-on-seven game. "If it was going to be me and going to be pro football, it had to have twenty-two guys on the screen," he told ESPN decades later. "If we couldn't have that, we couldn't have a game."

Madden signed on with EA, but only under the condition that it could produce a bona fide football simulation featuring a full contingent of players. Hawkins's team spent the next several years squeezing every last ounce of power from the Apple II. Hawkins also placed an emphasis on individual player skill ratings such as speed, strength, and agility to make in-game player battles on the field more dynamic. Madden, who once specialized in coaching linebackers, insisted that the game feature realistic blocking schemes and other highly complex elements. As the months became years, the Madden project became known internally as "Trip's Folly." While most EA games took less than a year and a half to produce, *John Madden Football* required more than three years of full-time work. At one point EA even hired an outside developer, Bethesda

Softworks, to complete the game, but the partnership broke down.

But EA stuck with the project and eventually managed to build a stable game on the aging Apple II platform. EA did not secure a license with the NFL—San Francisco's star quarterback was, for instance, listed as "Joe Idaho" instead of "Joe Montana"—but the team worked diligently to provide numeric skill rankings to differentiate players. At long last, EA released *John Madden Football* in June 1988. The game was advanced for its time and included many customizable features such as weather conditions, player fatigue, injuries, and penalty frequency. *John Madden Football* sold modestly, but Hawkins knew he had discovered a model for future success. By releasing a new *Madden* game every year, EA could create a near constant source of revenue.

Hawkins loved the Apple II, but EA's games had finally outgrown the venerable platform. For years he had believed home systems like the Nintendo NES to be passing fads, but by the late 1980s he grudgingly conceded that the future of video games lay not in home computers, but in the $2 billion console market. Hawkins toyed with the idea of partnering with Nintendo, but the company imposed strict rules on third-party game makers, expecting a say in everything from content creation to profit sharing. Instead, for the next *Madden* installment, Hawkins eyed the upcoming Sega Genesis platform, which promised vastly superior graphics and a control scheme ideally suited to sports games.

Hawkins hatched a risky plan to create a next-generation *Madden* game for the Sega Genesis without having to pay traditional licensing fees, which were as high as $10 per cartridge. Secretly he assembled a team to pick apart the Genesis and find a way to get EA's games to run on it. At the same time, he began public negotiations with Sega, biding his time until he could spring the reverse-engineered *Madden* on the Japanese company's executives and strong-arm them into licensing it at a wildly reduced rate. Somehow, the gambit worked. Sega, anxious to chip away at Nintendo's market share with a killer game, agreed to a $2 per cartridge license fee, and in December 1990, EA released *John Madden Football* for Sega Genesis.

The 1990 reboot redefined modern sports video games. Previous games, including the 1988 *John Madden Football*, emphasized statistical modeling over play-by-play action. The 1990 version transformed the virtual gridiron into a thrilling game that thrived on individual confrontations between players. It also fully brought video games into the mainstream. While *Pac-Man*, *Space Invaders*, and *Super Mario Bros.* were certainly played by gamers of all stripes, *John Madden Football* for the Sega Genesis became a staple of dorm rooms nationwide, its hypercompetitive gameplay proving to be the ultimate antidote for electronic gaming's "geeky" reputation. "Before *Madden*, jocks did not play video games," Rich Hilleman, who produced the game for EA, later said. "Somebody playing games was more likely to get made fun of on ESPN than get featured on there."

The game, and its consecutive annual releases at the beginning of each football season, has created a pop-cultural phenomenon that has generated more than $4 billion in revenue and changed not only gaming but the broadcasting of professional football. ESPN's "skycam" technology, for instance, which uses a wire-mounted system to suspend the camera over the field, provides broadcasters with a camera angle almost identical to the top-down, behind-the-quarterback perspective established by *Madden* games. Meanwhile, players fortunate enough to grace the cover of the next *Madden* game are celebrated as having reached a new level of stardom.

The 1990 version of *John Madden Football* sold approximately four hundred thousand copies for the Sega Genesis, and the game franchise has sold more than one hundred million copies since. In 2004, the NFL even honored the series by inducting it into the Pro Football Hall of Fame in Canton, Ohio. Because American football is little understood in Europe and Asia, the game has enjoyed much less popularity outside North America, but its emphasis on action and EA's approach to annual reboots has modeled the path to success for franchises in other sports such as soccer, hockey, baseball, and basketball.

John Madden, whose demands for realism shaped the franchise into the juggernaut it is today, even concedes that playing his namesake game changed the way he views football. "I used to say, 'Damn it, you can't go for it on fourth down all the time,'" he admitted. "But nobody in video games wants to give up the ball."

JOHN MADDEN FOOTBALL FOR THE SEGA GENESIS BECAME A STAPLE OF DORM ROOMS NATIONWIDE, ITS HYPERCOMPETITIVE GAMEPLAY PROVING TO BE THE ULTIMATE ANTIDOTE FOR ELECTRONIC GAMING'S "GEEKY" REPUTATION.

STREET FIGHTER II

(1991)

Capcom's *Street Fighter II* revitalized the arcade video game industry in the 1990s by transforming arcades, pizzerias, and living rooms into virtual arenas. Millions of eager players waited in lines to trade digital kicks, punches, and special attacks. The Strong inducted the fighting game into the World Video Game Hall of Fame in 2017.

n 1984, Yoshiki Okamoto was fired from his job at the video game conglomerate Konami for refusing to help code a driving game the company was working on; he instead built a shooter game called *Time Pilot*, and was even demanding a raise. Around six years later, he was working at another game firm, Capcom, when he hurled a pencil at his boss's face during an argument. But Capcom did not fire Okamoto and even tolerated his other outlandish behavior, which included sleeping under his desk and pranking coworkers. For Okamoto would soon produce the most important arcade game of the 1990s: *Street Fighter II: The World Warrior*. If *Space Invaders* (1978) and *Pac-Man* (1980) defined the arcade experience of the late 1970s and early 1980s, no game had more of an impact on the video arcade in the 1990s than *Street Fighter II*.

When Capcom took a chance in hiring the mercurial Okamoto in 1984, the company was still a relative newcomer to the video game industry. Founded five years earlier in Japan, Capcom (a clipped compound of Capsule Computers) began life building coin-operated arcade games, including the electromechanical *Little League* (1983), the vertically scrolling space shooter *Vulgus* (1984), and the aerial World War II shooter *1942* (1984), with many of its most popular titles designed by Okamoto. By 1985, Capcom's rivals Data East and Konami had released popular martial-arts games *Karate Champ* and *Yie Ar Kung-Fu*, respectively, and Capcom was eager to jump into what was fast becoming a blockbuster genre. Okamoto tasked two designers, Takashi Nishiyama and Hiroshi Matsumoto, with developing Capcom's own martial arts game.

Their answer was *Street Fighter*, released to arcades in 1987. Cosmetically, *Street Fighter* resembled *Yie Ar Kung-Fu*, casting very similar characters and featuring identical health bars at the top of the screen. But *Street Fighter* offered much better graphics and more frenzied gameplay. Players assumed the role of a young karate master named Ryu who competes in an international tournament to prove his worth. In single-player mode, gamers fought ten opponents from five countries, while the two-player mode cast a second player as Ryu's arch-nemesis, Ken. *Street Fighter* was a commercial success for Capcom, earning rave reviews while becoming a staple of arcades, especially in the United States. According to legend, *Street Fighter* led to an epidemic of sprained and dislocated fingers due to players mashing its six-button fight controls for hours at a time.

Capcom developed a sequel two years later called *Street Fighter '89*, but it barely resembled the original. *Street Fighter* had emphasized complex, combination-based fighting that, like martial arts itself, rewarded precision and patience. Using six buttons, players could perform three types of punch or kick attacks along with three special attacks that required linking precise button combinations. *Street Fighter '89*, on the other hand, was a traditional beat-'em-up game with a joystick and one button for attacking and one button for jumping. In fact, *Street Fighter '89* was so different from the original that it was renamed *Final Fight* at the insistence of arcade operators. The game was successful in its own right, spawning several sequels and ports, but devotees of the original *Street Fighter* were clamoring for a bona fide sequel.

Okamoto went to work. Some executives insisted that *Street Fighter II* shift to the simple two-button design from *Final Fight*, but Okamoto retained the six-button scheme because he did not want to make yet another brawler game. *Street Fighter* worked because it was complicated, it was difficult to learn, and at its heart it was a cerebral chess match packaged as a fighting game. Okamoto brought back Ryu and several of his enemies from the original game, including his former-trainer-turned-nemesis Ken and "M. Bison," an evil boss who bore a striking resemblance to the boxer Mike Tyson. (Fearing a lawsuit, Capcom changed his name to "Balrog" for the American market.)

The key difference in *Street Fighter II* was that gamers could now play as one of eight characters, such as the sumo wrestler Edmond Honda, a Russian brawler named Vodka Gobalsky (later changed to Zangief), and the featherweight speedster Chun-Li. Each character was given an extensive backstory, an adoring crowd, and dozens of distinct moves and combination attacks. Choosing Zangief meant delivering lurching but immensely powerful grappling attacks, while choosing Guile, the vengeful United States Air Force veteran, meant learning the difficult but overpowering Sonic Boom attack. Each character boasted signature moves that, to the delight of arcade operators worldwide, would require countless hours and quarters to master.

By studying these complex moves, the best players could rout a novice opponent with dizzying speed. In the dimly lit arcades of the 1990s, head-to-head face-offs between highly skilled opponents often drew massive crowds of onlookers witnessing a torrent of button mashing. Before access to online gaming, many of these skilled fighters even traveled like conquering heroes from one town to another to face local champions. These fierce official and unofficial arcade competitions and tournaments became a training ground for a generation of gamers and future eSports athletes.

Street Fighter II: The World Warrior was an astounding commercial success. Capcom sold more than sixty thousand original cabinets and a staggering one hundred forty thousand cabinets and game conversion kits of the company's "Champion Edition," making it one of the top-selling arcade games ever. Numerous sequels across many video game platforms followed. *Street Fighter II* defied the previously accepted wisdom that a game should be easy to play but difficult to master. *Street Fighter II* was difficult to learn, but its steep learning curve encouraged competition among players and reinvigorated the arcade industry in the 1990s.

Street Fighter II paved the way for future franchises including *Mortal Kombat* (page 223), *Tekken*, *King of Fighters*, and *Virtua Fighter*. Yet the game's influence also transferred from the arcade to the home. Console makers competed fiercely for the right to sell home versions of popular arcade titles, and Nintendo's exclusive agreement to sell *Street Fighter II* for its Super Nintendo Entertainment System (SNES) encouraged countless gamers to purchase an SNES just to play the game. *Street Fighter II* also invaded Japanese and American popular culture, spawning a line of Hasbro G.I. Joe action figures, two live-action Hollywood films, and numerous comic books, anime films, and animated television series and films.

In many ways, the motley cast of characters in *Street Fighter II* reflected the eccentric team behind the game's creation. As Yoko Shimomura, the famed Japanese composer who created *Street Fighter II*'s exhilarating soundtrack, later said: "I think the crazy personalities of the staff showed in the gameplay. Because all these unique people got together and everybody had something they wanted to do . . . And because of that, I think it turned out to be something unique."

SONIC THE HEDGEHOG

(1991)

Sega needed a mascot to compete with Nintendo's iconic Mario. The answer? A blue, speedy hedgehog named Sonic. *Sonic the Hedgehog* earned such success that it joined the World Video Game Hall of Fame in 2016.

For American brands, few events are more important than the annual Macy's Thanksgiving Day Parade. Like a football player officially attaining superstar status by appearing on a *Madden NFL* cover, a company can proclaim itself a pop-culture heavyweight with a fifteen-thousand-cubic-foot balloon snaking its way along Manhattan's Sixth Avenue. In many ways, a float heralds not just the arrival of a hot brand, but the enduring clout of a new form of entertainment. Mickey Mouse solidified his role—and that of cartoons at large—as a fixture of American cinema with a Macy's Parade appearance in 1934. Superman soared into the sky in 1939, helping make comic books a staple in every kid's desk drawer, while a spinach-munching Popeye loomed over Radio City Music Hall in 1957. Yet when video games finally earned their long-overdue appearance, parade-goers did not gaze up at Mario or Pac-Man. They were staring at a sixty-four-foot balloon of Sonic the Hedgehog.

During the early 1980s, as Atari muscled its 2600 console to the vanguard of the home console wars, Sega was enjoying a comfortable existence as a leading arcade game manufacturer, hauling in more than $200 million between 1981 and 1982. Sega had begun life in 1940 as Standard Games, a Hawaii-based company building coin-operated amusement machines for military bases. The company set up shop in Japan after the U.S. government banned slot machines in its territories, eventually changing its names to Sega Enterprises in the mid-1960s. Now focusing mainly on arcade games, in 1966, Sega released an electromechanical submarine simulator called *Periscope*, the first arcade game to cost twenty-five cents to play.

By 1983, Sega had released many bestselling arcade games including *Head On* (1979), *Turbo* (1981), *Astro Blaster* (1981), and *Zaxxon* (1982), and it had successfully licensed many of its titles to home console such as the Atari 2600 and the ColecoVision. Yet Sega's fortunes, like the rest of the industry's, turned with the video game crash of 1983, and its revenues plunged by more than $60 million. In a last-ditch attempt to jumpstart the home console market, Sega hastily developed its SG-1000 console, releasing it in 1983 to scant sales. As Chris Kohler wrote for *Wired*, "Few have heard of it, even fewer have played it, and the games weren't that great anyway."

The SG-1000 was swiftly crushed by Nintendo's NES console, and Sega changed hands several times until it was bought by the Japanese conglomerate CSK in 1984. It continued to develop a second console, the Sega Master System, releasing it in 1985 to the Japanese market and to the American market the following year. Although it was technologically superior to the NES, the Master System nevertheless failed to make a dent in Nintendo's market share, largely due to its shortage of quality games and a lack of recognizable characters. Sega had introduced the world to its first mascot, a would-be Mario named Alex Kidd, in the 1986 platform game *Alex Kidd in Miracle World*. Kidd boasted a red-and-yellow jumpsuit, large ears, monkey-like facial features, and Bruce Lee–inspired martial arts moves. *Alex Kidd in Miracle World* was critically acclaimed and sold well overseas, but the boy-monkey was poorly received in America, and Sega quickly began seeking ideas for a hipper mascot who could carry the banner for its brand-new 16-bit console, the Genesis.

Like the Master System before it, the Genesis was not selling well after its 1989 release in the U.S. Despite its impressive hardware, the Genesis still lagged far behind Nintendo's venerable console. Salvation arrived with the 1990 release of Electronic Arts' *John Madden Football* (page 207) for the Genesis, but Sega's fortunes continued to plummet after Nintendo released its Super Nintendo Entertainment System (SNES) to the American market in 1991. If it had any hope of surviving, Sega needed a flagship game franchise.

Sega handed its in-house development studio, known as AM8, the daunting task of creating a blockbuster game featuring an unforgettable new character who could overtake Mario's brand recognition. Soliciting ideas from a company-wide competition, initial concepts ranged from goofy old men to kangaroos to rabbits with muscular, prehensile ears. Hoping to distinguish its mascot from the pudgy, lovable Mario, Sega turned to increasingly edgier designs with animals that boasted speed, aggression, and a healthy dose of attitude. Finally, designer Naoto Ōshima submitted his idea for a hedgehog named "Mr. Needlemouse" who sported fangs, a human girlfriend named Madonna, and his own rock band featuring a monkey on bass and an alligator on keyboard. Ōshima later suggested that he came up with the design by combining Felix the Cat's head with Mickey Mouse's body.

With Sonic's basic design settled, AM8 had to come up with a game to showcase their hip new hedgehog. One of the few directives Sega gave the design team was to emphasize speed: it had to harness the power of the souped-up Genesis and present players with exhilarating gameplay that left *Super Mario Bros.* in the dust. Biologists might scoff at the idea of a lightning-fast hedgehog, but AM8 imbued their sleek creature with spiked hair and a whirlwind spin attack. To underscore his speed, the team renamed Mr. Needlemouse "Sonic," but Madonna, the band, and the fangs were later scrapped after some executives complained the character came off as too aggressive and mean. AM8 colored Sonic cobalt blue to match Sega's logo and outfitted him with large red shoes that evoked allusions to boots worn by Michael Jackson and Santa Claus. With Sonic's cool and hip personality—later described as a combination of Kurt Cobain's laid-back ease, Michael Jordan's grace under pressure, and Bill Clinton's "Get it Done" attitude—Sega hoped to cater to the older members of Generation X while still painting Nintendo as a company geared toward children.

The Sonic project was code-named "Defeat Mario." Initially, Sonic's slowest, default speed was deliberately set to match Mario's running speed. But as flickering, slow frame rates, and other technical problems became apparent, AM8—now called Sonic Team—was forced to repeatedly tweak the overall speed of the game. Players guided Sonic as he sprinted through loops, jumped over pits using springs, and destroyed his enemies with his signature spin attack. Sonic's mission was to defeat the evil Dr. Robotnik, who had captured the land's animal inhabitants. If Sonic gathered a hundred gold rings, he gained an extra life. They also acted as protection: Sonic survived when hit by an enemy if he had one or more rings, but when hit with zero rings, Sonic lost a life and the game restarted at a previous checkpoint.

Sales of the Sega Genesis console quadrupled when, under the leadership of Sega of America president and CEO Tom Kalinske, the company began bundling the console with *Sonic the Hedgehog* instead of the 1988 beat-'em-up game *Altered Beast*. Though popular in Japan, *Sonic* had the greatest appeal in North America, where the Genesis outsold the Super Nintendo two to one during the 1991 holiday season, marking the first time Nintendo lost its top standing in the console market since the debut of the NES in 1985. Today, with more than fifteen million copies sold, *Sonic the Hedgehog* remains the bestselling Sega Genesis game of all time. Its popularity led to a franchise of twenty-one core games and several spin-offs that collectively sold 150 million units worldwide. The series also spawned two American animated television shows and the Japanese anime *Sonic X*.

If Sonic's appearance at the 1993 Macy's Thanksgiving Day Parade heralded his arrival as the mascot of gaming, it also signaled an ominous future for Sega: as the float neared Columbus Circle, it struck a light pole and deflated. Despite dominating the 16-bit gaming market for a short time, Sega would eventually lose the console war to Nintendo. After the failure of its Dreamcast console in 2001, Sega restructured itself predominantly as a third-party game developer and has since found success with its line of mobile games for the iOS and Android operating systems. As for its famous mascot, Sega entered a partnership with its former nemesis, Nintendo, in 2013 to develop Sonic games for the 3DS and Wii U consoles.

Sonic the Hedgehog was designed as a visual representation of Sega's spirit; he was a swaggering underdog unafraid to challenge the natural order. Sega has reinvented itself countless times throughout its storied existence, and like its flagship character, has always charged full speed ahead into any obstacle in its path.

TODAY, WITH MORE THAN
FIFTEEN MILLION COPIES SOLD,
SONIC THE HEDGEHOG REMAINS THE
BESTSELLING SEGA GENESIS GAME
OF ALL TIME.

MORTAL KOMBAT

(1992)

Finish him! *Mortal Kombat*'s over-the-top gruesomeness made players laugh, critics cringe, and moral guardians cry again for regulation of the video game industry.

Street Fighter II popularized a new breed of edgy, martial arts–fueled fighting games. Instead of facing off against computer-controlled sprites, it allowed players to battle head-to-head against an equally skilled human opponent. Coupled with a system that allowed winners of a contest to keep playing without spending another quarter, Street Fighter II's high-octane combat created long lines at arcades and generated fierce tournament play. Among Capcom's competitors, the rush was on to release the next big fighting game, one that doubled down on violence, on blood, on gruesome finishing moves. The answer was Midway Games' Mortal Kombat, which pushed the boundaries of what players could do with their in-game characters and what video games could depict onscreen. Mortal Kombat held a mirror up to American standards of decency—and some did not like what they saw.

In 1991, Midway was ready for a makeover. Founded in 1958 as a manufacturer of coin-operated amusements, it was purchased by the pinball giant Bally in 1969. After dabbling in various electromechanical games including puck bowling and Western shootout simulators, Midway shifted its focus to electronic gaming in the 1970s, eventually becoming the lead American distributor for Japanese arcade games. In 1978, Midway introduced American gamers to Taito's wildly successful Space Invaders (page 107), and two years later followed with the decade-defining game Pac-Man (page 131). Aided by a merger with Williams in 1988, Midway became the leading producer of arcade games in the United States by 1990. That dominance was short lived. Soon, Street Fighter II rocketed to the top of the earnings charts and a flurry of similar games, including SNK's Fatal Fury, continued to chip away at Midway's dominance.

Midway tasked two of its star developers, John Tobias and Ed Boon, to quickly create a fighting game. Tobias had helped design some of Williams's bestselling titles, such as Smash T.V. and Total Carnage, while Boon had started his career in Williams's pinball division before moving over to game design, helping to develop series such as High Impact Football. Initially, Midway was hoping to create a video game version of the 1992 film Universal Soldier starring Jean-Claude Van Damme. The game would simply feature Van Damme as he fought villains depicted from the movie. "We wanted to call it Van Damme," Ed Boon told Game Informer in 2016. "We just wanted to see huge letters, 'Van Damme' when you walked by. You couldn't pass that up." When the deal fell through with the film's distributor, TriStar Pictures, Tobias and Boon looked for other inspiration. One idea was to call their game "Dragon Attack," based on the song of the same name by Queen. Other possibilities, including "Death Blow" and "Final Fist," were too clichéd even by arcade standards. The team eventually decided the title should include "combat," which during a brainstorming session changed to "kombat" because, according to Boon, it seemed "unique or something like that." At the suggestion of a coworker, the team settled on the name Mortal Kombat.

The duo also did not want to make just another Street Fighter II clone that rewarded players for how fast they could mash buttons. Tobias and Boon decided to simplify Street Fighter II's controls slightly and to add a component they knew players were thirsting for: blood and gore. Street Fighter II was violent in its own right, but it was bound by the same honor code that imbued the ancient martial arts it so effectively portrayed: players could not kick opponents when they were on the ground; there was no blood; and when a character lost a fight, he or she lived to fight another day. To make their "bad-boy version" of *Street Fighter* stand out, Tobias and Boon needed to throw out the rule book and appeal to mankind's far more primitive instincts.

Inspired by Chinese mythology, kung fu, and action movies such as *Zu Warriors from the Magic Mountain* (1983), *Big Trouble in Little China* (1986), and *Bloodsport* (1988), Boon and Tobias centered *Mortal Kombat* around a martial arts tournament set on a fictional island in the Earthrealm. Players could choose from a cast of seven characters, including Shaolin martial artist Liu Kang, U.S. Special Forces officer Sonya Blade, undead ninja specter Scorpion, and a Jean-Claude Van Damme parody named Johnny Cage. Each character featured his or her own special combat moves, backstory, and motivation for entering the "Mortal Kombat" tournament. Players could compete against each other or battle computer opponents with the hope of defeating the evil sorcerer Shang Tsung and winning the tournament.

Released into early 1990s arcades overloaded with fighting games, *Mortal Kombat* instantly set itself apart by appearing familiar yet new all at once. Players accustomed to *Street Fighter II*'s joystick and six-button control configuration found *Mortal Kombat*'s joystick and four-button configuration (a fifth button added the ability to block attacks), easy to adapt to. At the same time, the game's use of digitized images of real-life actors differentiated it from the more traditional cartoonlike graphics of most other fighting games.

MORAL PANICS IN AMERICAN MEDIA

The moral panic over violent video games such as *Mortal Kombat* and the creation of an industry code to categorize and regulate content replicated a familiar pattern in American history.

In the nineteenth century, for instance, critics sounded the alarm over the potentially damaging influence of novels. Yes, novels, were once thought to be corrupting. In the twentieth century, movies and comic books came under censure, and in both cases producers, threatened with government regulation, adopted industry codes to control what was produced and to give audiences a clearer idea of media content. As society adjusted to these new forms of media, gradually the fears over them subsided. *Mortal Kombat* was part of the natural process of media evolution.

Mortal Kombat's combination of more realistic graphics and over-the-top violence raised its profile with gamers and critics alike. The game's notorious "fatalities" gave quick and skillful play-

589000 PUSH START

KANO WINS

TIME BONUS 84,000

FLAWLESS VICTORY

100,000

FATALIT 100,000

ers enough time to make specific joystick moves and button presses to "finish him" (or "finish her") in gruesome fashion, including Kano tearing out an opposing character's still-beating heart or Raiden firing lightning bolts that made an opposing character's head explode. Although many players didn't take the exaggerated violence very seriously, in December 1993, the U.S. Congress held hearings on video game violence in which politicians and media critics charged that *Mortal Kombat* and other violent games corrupted the nation's youth.

Despite a lack of evidence suggesting that

video game violence caused real-world violence, the hearings and increasing government and media scrutiny led the video game industry to create the Entertainment Software Rating Board (ESRB) in 1994. The self-regulating body established a rating system ranging from "content intended for young children" to "adults only" to help consumers determine a game's suitability. Ultimately, the creation of the ESRB allowed developers to create more mature content for a specifically older audience, helping video games shed their image as a medium for children.

And yet, beyond its controversial content and

role in triggering debate about the role of violent video games in society, *Mortal Kombat*'s compelling gameplay and iconic characters have proven enormously popular and enduring. Midway sold twenty-four thousand units of the arcade game, leading to successful home console versions and numerous game sequels and reboots, including *Mortal Kombat II* (1993), *Ultimate Moral Kombat 3* (1995), *Mortal Kombat vs. DC Universe* (2008), *Mortal Kombat* (2011), and *Mortal Kombat XL* (2016). The game's initial success also led to a music album, action figures, a collectible card game, comic books, animated television shows, and even a theatrical stage show titled *Mortal Kombat: Live Tour*. A 1995 film grossed $122 million worldwide at the box office and was the first commercially successful Hollywood film adapted from a video game. Collectively, the franchise has sold more than thirty-five million copies and its games span arcade, console, personal computer, and mobile formats over nearly two-and-a-half decades.

With blistering gameplay, memorable characters, and a healthy dose of gore, *Mortal Kombat* shepherded gamers into a bolder, bloodier age.

"YOUR *FREE* COPY OF DOOM SHAREWARE"

DOOM™

id

DOOM Shareware Owner

After you have installed this shareware program, please read the README file. This will tell you all about DOOM and will help you with any questions you might have about running and using the program.

To acess the README file change to the DOOM directory: CD C:/ DOOMSW, <enter>. Once in the DOOMSW directory type README <enter>.

DOOM

(1993)

Doom's success lay not only with its addicting gameplay and technical innovations, such as its introduction of a game engine, but also in its innovative digital distribution. Note the prominent "shareware" advertisement on the top front of the game packaging. This groundbreaking game earned a spot in the inaugural class of the World Video Game Hall of Fame.

n the early 1990s, the video game industry was still dominated by that Italian-American plumber named Mario. The gaming giant Nintendo was not just restricting the number of third-party titles that could be released for its NES and SNES consoles, but it was also enforcing a strict moral code for its games. The SNES port of the wildly popular (and gratuitously violent) arcade game *Mortal Kombat*, for instance, replaced blood with sweat and substituted the game's notorious fatalities with decidedly less violent "finishing moves." Many game designers felt suffocated by Nintendo's sanitized ecosystem and began returning to the wild west of video game development, the personal computer, to create exciting new games that challenged graphical and moral boundaries. Then, in 1993, a space marine blasted his way through hordes of invading demons, blazing a new path for games in the process. id Software's *Doom* was a seminal release in video game history, influencing the form, feel, and perception of so many first-person shooters that followed.

Doom's story begins with id Software, and id Software's story begins with a company called Softdisk. Softdisk created disk magazines, which were electronic publications distributed on 5¼" floppy disks that provided readers with an interactive experience using graphics, games, music, and puzzles. In the late 1980s, computer programmer John Romero was working at Softdisk, creating games that would be included alongside magazine articles. One such game was *Dangerous Dave* (1988), which Romero created to accompany an article about the GraBASIC programming language. *Dangerous Dave* was a simple game heavily inspired by *Super Mario Bros.* in which players collected gold cups and defeated monsters.

While working on *Dangerous Dave* and other titles, Romero's friend and fellow programmer, John Carmack, developed a novel way to produce rapid side-scrolling graphics called adaptive tile refresh, allowing developers to compensate for the relatively poor graphical capabilities of early '90s PCs. Thrilled with the possibilities, Romero, Carmack, and their coworker Tom Hall spent evenings creating a knock-off version of *Super Mario Bros. 3* for the PC, substituting Dangerous Dave for Mario; they later dubbed it "Dangerous Dave in Copyright Infringement." Hoping to convince Nintendo to bring their games to PC, the trio put together a working demo of *Super Mario Bros. 3*, but the Japanese gaming giant promptly turned them down. However, their technological breakthrough caught the attention of an entrepreneur named Scott Miller, who encouraged them to publish original titles with his company, Apogee Software. Working in secret using Softdisk's computers, Romero, Carmack, and Hall produced the side-scrolling platform game *Commander Keen* in 1990 for Microsoft's MS-DOS operating system, the precursor to Windows. The game was an immediate success, but invariably caught the attention of Softdisk, who claimed they owned *Commander Keen*'s intellectual property. In a legal settlement, Romero, Carmack, and Hall agreed to leave Softdisk and license it a number of video games.

In February 1991, the three friends formed id Software, short for the phrase "in demand." The company's Commander Keen titles were distributed via shareware—demo software that is free to play and distribute but must eventually be purchased to unlock full functionality. They also detached the game's core source code, known as the "engine," and licensed it to other companies. This practice would later become an important feature of id's business model. After the success of the Commander Keen series, id poured its resources into *Wolfenstein 3D*. Released in May 1992 for MS-DOS, the game had players assuming the role of an Allied spy during World War II who must battle Nazis and escape from a castle. *Wolfenstein 3D* was a massive success for id, selling more than two hundred thousand copies by the end of 1993.

While most of the id team was focused on *Wolfenstein 3D*, John Carmack was hard at work on a more ambitious project. *Wolfenstein 3D* had featured impressive graphics, but they were very limited: the shadow textures were crude, doors and walls were mostly uniform colors, and there were no sloping surfaces. Enemies in *Wolfenstein 3D* were never below or above the player, and nearly every level looked alike. Carmack wanted id's next game to feature bright and dark textures, curved passageways, elevators, and other elements that would truly make the game three-dimensional. After the release of a *Wolfenstein* prequel called *Spear of Destiny*, production on Carmack's project began in earnest. One idea was to license a game based on the hit science-fiction thriller *Aliens*, but id abandoned negotiations with the movie studio, 20th Century Fox, when it became clear its creative vision would be severely restricted.

Instead, Carmack decided to make their next-generation game a mashup of *Aliens*, the cult-classic B movie *Evil Dead II*, and a failed *Dungeons & Dragons* campaign in which demons overran Carmack's team. The game, which id dubbed *Doom*, would also feature an intricate story. Unlike *Wolfenstein 3D*, whose Nazi-battling gameplay was essentially plotless, *Doom* was developed with a compelling backstory: A base operated by the Union Aerospace

Corporation on the Martian moon Phobos is overrun by demons from Hell after its top-secret teleportation experiments go awry. A detachment of space marines is sent to investigate, but all are slaughtered except for one. It's up to the player to fight through the hoard of demons on Phobos and, eventually, Hell itself, to prevent a massive invasion of Earth.

In developing *Doom*, id's programmers made a number of crucial decisions that affected the future of gaming. First, they employed a first-person perspective they had developed for earlier titles such as *Wolfenstein 3D*, powered by a highly efficient graphics engine, the id Tech 1. By using smart programming techniques and simplified design choices to maximize speed, *Doom's* creators achieved texture-mapping and lighting that had never before been accomplished for PCs. Even more significantly, by separating the game engine from many of *Doom's* artistic assets, the creators gave players the ability to heavily modify the game. *Doom* also pioneered online multiplayer gaming over DWANGO—Dial-up Wide-Area Network Game Operation—service, which launched in 1994, though the most popular (and most fun) way of playing was to have a LAN (local area network) party in which players tethered their computers and blasted away at one another. The game's multiplayer "deathmatch" play contributed to the game's ongoing success and spurred on the popularity of multiplayer titles.

Doom's creators also tapped into newly emerging trends in digital distribution by making the first three episodes of the game available for free and then asking users to pay for further levels. By bypassing the traditional retail outlets and hooking players with a substantial body of free content, id became an early leader in a business model that today dominates much of the video-gaming world, especially in mobile, where "lite" versions of games provide players with incentives to purchase more content.

And yet even as *Doom*'s technical features and distribution model broke new ground, in many ways the game harkened back to older forms of play. Kids have been playing imaginary first-person shooters in the backyard for decades—cops and robbers, cowboys and Indians, and war games of all kinds. Nevertheless, *Doom*'s bloody battles with demonic monsters alarmed critics and politicians already on high alert about media violence. Although research still does not support claims that playing video games increases the propensity for real-life violence, *Doom* became emblematic of the debate over the role of games and violence in society, especially in the wake of the 1998 Columbine shootings, after which investigators discovered that the two gunmen, like tens of millions of other people, had played the game.

Doom was more than just a technically proficient game with a smart business plan. Its thematic, visual, and ludic elements hooked into players' minds and culture as a whole. The game's bloody battles with demonic monsters were set to the score of a heavy metal soundtrack that fueled players with adrenaline and critics with outrage. It brought players to Hell and back—and in the process forever changed how we experience games.

IN 1993, A SPACE MARINE
BLASTED HIS WAY THROUGH
HORDES OF INVADING DEMONS,
BLAZING A NEW PATH FOR GAMES
IN THE PROCESS.

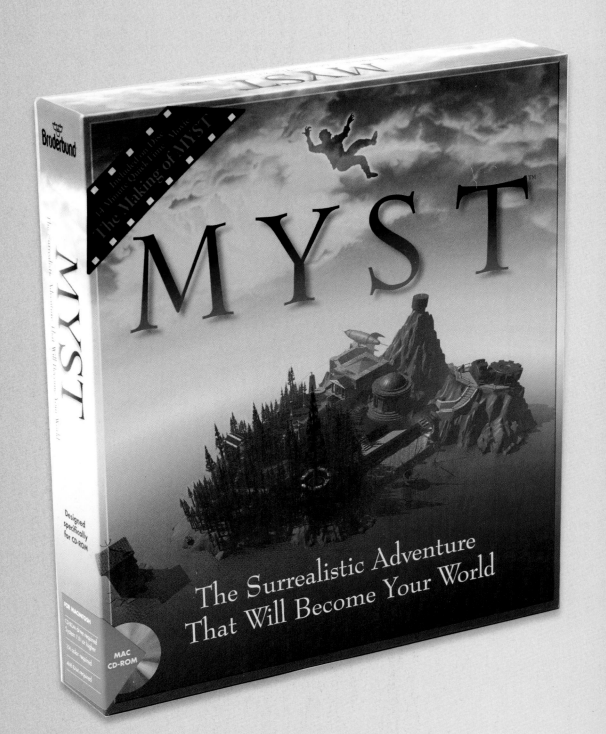

MYST

(1993)

Myst showed the power of the personal computer to immerse players in a haunting world of mystery. This copy of the best-selling game was donated to The Strong by Doug Carlston, the founder of the game's publisher, Brøderbund.

By the early 1990s, home video game consoles were once again flying high. Companies such as Electronic Arts, which helped transform the personal computer into a powerful gaming platform, were abandoning their former medium for home consoles. Still, 1993 saw the release of two iconic computer games: id Software's *Doom* (page 229), a science-fiction horror-themed shoot-'em-up that popularized the first-person shooter genre, and a puzzle game called *Myst* that featured no guns, no enemies, and no action. The latter just so happened to become the bestselling PC game for nearly a decade.

In 1988, Robyn Miller was taking a year off from the University of Washington, hoping to establish state residency to lower his tuition payments. He was toying with a novel, but could never seem to get started. One day he received a call from his brother Rand, who was working as a computer programmer at a small-town Texas bank. Rand asked his brother if he wanted to work on an interactive storybook for children. It was an odd request; Robyn was not a computer expert and had only ever played a handful of games. Yet he was eager to set aside his foundering novel, so Robyn gamely agreed and began drawing pictures on the HyperCard application for his Macintosh.

Their eventual creation, under the company name Cyan, was *The Manhole*, an adventure game for children in which players open manholes to reveal enormous beanstalks leading to fantastical realms. Released on floppy disks, the game had no ending; the goal was to simply explore a virtual world. *The Manhole* won a Software Publishing Association Excellence Award in 1989 and inspired Robyn and Rand Miller to continue developing games. Their follow-up

children's titles, *Cosmic Osmo and the Worlds Beyond the Mackerel* and *Spelunx,* similarly featured black-and-white graphics, point-and-click navigation, and a vast world to explore. The games saw modest success, and the brothers decided to create a more challenging version for adults, one featuring characters and a complex storyline.

Robyn and Rand pitched their idea, "The Gray Summons," to Activision, but it was rejected and the company gently suggested the brothers stick to children's games. Facing financial difficulties, the brothers finally secured a deal with Brøderbund to create a nonlinear, story-driven game, and development began in 1991. They dubbed their project *Myst*, a name inspired by *The Mysterious Island* by Jules Verne, which followed the adventures of five Americans on an uncharted island in the South Pacific. Like in the Millers' previous games, the player would have no weapons or lives, and could not die because there were no enemies to fight. Inspiration came from Verne's novels and the text-based adventure game *Zork* (page 97). For months, the Miller brothers obsessed over the gameplay, halting production repeatedly as they agonized over the look and difficulty of the game's many puzzles.

Building *Myst* was a technologically daunting task. To overcome graphical limitations, Robyn and Rand Miller took advantage of the latest software and hardware tools, notably CD-ROMs, which were first introduced in the mid-1980s and offered greatly enhanced storage capacity compared to floppy disks. But early CDs were limited by very slow access speeds, which factored into the Millers' decision to program discrete islands that could be called up one at a time. To achieve their beautiful imaging, the Cyan team used StrataVision 3D to render maps that were too complex to draw by hand. HyperCard allowed designers to make adjustments to the game relatively easily in the course of development, while a new technology called QuickTime allowed for embedded video—a key element of *Myst*'s many puzzles. The Miller brothers insisted that *Myst* appeal to non-gamers, a decision reflected by the game's lush environments and the way puzzles became integral to the gameplay, rather than separate. (A 2006 study among a sample of baby boomer Americans revealed that *Myst* was their favorite and most commonly played game.) Auditory and visual clues were consonant with the game's geography and story, rather than arbitrarily placed to slow down the player's progress.

In the game, players assumed the role of the Stranger, a silent, nameless adventurer who comes across a book with a detailed description of an island called Myst. After placing his hand on the final page, the Stranger is suddenly teleported to the island itself. The island is deserted, and the player has no choice but to begin exploring. Soon, he discovers that the island was developed by a mysterious man named Atrus and his wife, Catherine. Atrus is long dead, but his two sons, Sirrus (portrayed by Robyn Miller) and Achenar (portrayed by Rand Miller), are imprisoned inside two books. Each brother blames the other for the death of their father, and both plead with the player to rescue him. Gameplay involves exploring the island of Myst and its "ages"— dimensions that are accessible via various linking books scattered throughout the island—in search of red and blue pages, which could be used to free Sirrus or Achenar, respectively. By the end of the game, the player must decide to free one of the two brothers, or neither.

Featuring more than 2,500 haunting, evocative screens, *Myst* boasted a level of depth and immersion never before seen in computer games. It was an immediate commercial success, and along with the interactive movie puzzle adventure game *The 7th Guest*, is widely credited with jumpstarting the wave of CD-ROM–based games. Despite lacking weapons, items, or any characters aside from two disgruntled book-imprisoned scions, *Myst* resonated with a new generation of gamers, many of whom had never played a computer game before. *Myst* sold an astounding six million copies and would remain the bestselling computer game of all time until its sales were surpassed by *The Sims* in 2002.

"*Myst* seems to reflect the condition of the video game itself, poised at the brink of something new even before it has finished mastering something old," Edward Rothstein wrote in the *New York Times* in 1994. Unlike *Doom*, which pioneered the first-person shooter, *Myst* did not really help create a new genre; indeed, many *Myst* clones attempted to replicate its gameplay without success. In the years that followed its release, few other games could match *Myst*'s ability to open imaginative worlds, though Cyan itself produced sequels such as *Riven* and *Myst III: Exile* (along with many books, a soundtrack, and other tie-in products).

Myst proved that players do not need guns, enemies, characters, or even a jump button to become engrossed by a video game. Sometimes all it takes is an imagination and the will to explore an unknown world.

NINTENDO VIRTUAL BOY

(1995)

Throughout its history, Nintendo has shown a willingness to experiment with new play forms. The Nintendo Virtual Boy was one such attempt, with an immersive interface that harkened back to nineteenth-century stereoscopes. Unfortunately, it was a commercial failure.

The Game Developers Conference is the largest annual gathering of professional video game developers, often serving as the springboard for the latest cutting-edge technology. Since 2015, perhaps no technology has been more hyped and showcased than virtual reality (VR). Each year, attendees stand in line to demo the newest tech from companies like Oculus Rift, Sony Morpheus, and Steam VR, each offering state-of-the-art immersive experiences. For years, VR has represented the final frontier in game development, able to truly transport players to lush, three-dimensional worlds. But while today's VR tech might seem wildly advanced, VR has existed in one form or another for many years. In 1995, the gaming giant Nintendo released its Virtual Boy console, which was capable of producing "true 3-D graphics" and represented a major leap forward in gaming technology. And yet the Virtual Boy was a colossal failure, one that raises questions about whether today's VR tech can succeed among a population not yet finished exploring their own world.

Nineteenth-century inventors tried to create virtual reality devices that fully occupied the range of vision. Some, such as the mutoscope, were coin-operated machines that people used in public arcades to watch animated sequences of still images. But even more widespread was the stereoscope, a handheld contraption that gave viewers three-dimensional images when they looked through it. Manufacturers produced millions of slides of natural wonders from around the world, pictures of battlefields of the Civil War, views of factories, and often more scandalous images of Victorian beauties in various stages of undress. Meanwhile, at the performance theater,

the lights dim and the stage blazes with light to focus the attention of theatergoers on the production and minimize outside distractions. This physical setup lets audiences more easily slip into the suspension of disbelief that makes the experience compelling. And while 3-D is now ubiquitous in movie theaters, the technology has existed since the 1950s, when a succession of B movie monsters seemed to jump into people's laps when they wore special glasses.

The story of Nintendo's venture into VR begins in 1985 in Cambridge, Massachusetts, a year before the game company's NES console entered the American market. That year, an engineer named Allen Becker came up with an idea for a portable high-definition display that people could use on airplanes. Laptops did exist, in a manner of speaking, but their screens were bulky and offered terrible battery life. Becker conceived of a device that instead of displaying an image on a screen, projected it onto a user's retina. (The technology was inspired by the famed futurist Ray Kurzweil's invention of the flatbed scanner.) Becker's device used a series of LEDs that oscillated at extremely fast speeds using a mirror. The only problem was that only red LEDs were cheap enough to mass produce, so his display was only able to project red-on-black images. The eventual prototype resembled a pair of goggles and was called the Private Eye, produced by Becker's new company Reflection Technology, and was capable of simulating a twelve-inch display as seen from eighteen inches away. Numerous companies licensed the display—Hughes Aircraft, for instance, wanted to make a heads-up display for pilots—but nothing substantial reached the market.

By the early 1990s, virtual reality was all

the rage—or at least the idea of it was. NASA founded a VR research lab in 1990, and the 1992 film *The Lawnmower Man* told the story of a greenskeeper who becomes entangled in a virtual-reality experiment and develops telekinetic powers. Reflection Technology pitched the Private Eye to consumer electronic companies such as Hasbro, Mattel, and Sega, but failed to reach a deal due to concerns about motion sickness. Moreover, many companies were turned off by the device's single-color display. As Tom Kalinske, the former president and CEO of Sega of America, reflected, "Our problem with it was it was just one color. We were already promoting Game Gear in all colors."

Yet one man was intrigued by Becker's invention: Gunpei Yokoi. The head of Nintendo's research and development division, Yokoi was the brains behind Nintendo's Game & Watch handhelds as well as the Game Boy. Worried that games were increasingly geared toward hardcore gamers by sacrificing gameplay for extravagant graphics, Yokoi saw the Private Eye as a revolutionary product that could appeal to mainstream consumers. He even thought the red-on-black color scheme underscored the immersive experience. With the blessing of Nintendo Chairman Hiroshi Yamauchi, Yokoi arranged to purchase a worldwide exclusive license to the Private Eye for use in video games.

Initially, Nintendo hoped its next-generation console could be contained in a pair of goggles, but engineers were wary of placing a high frequency microchip so close to a player's head, as few studies on electromagnetic radiation had been conducted by that time. Ultimately, Nintendo decided to abandon the goggle setup in favor of a heavier device that rested on a table-top bipod. Pitching the device as an evolution of its Game Boy, Nintendo dubbed it the Virtual Boy—a fateful decision that also meant its sales would be measured against its wildly successful handheld cousin.

To operate the Virtual Boy, users peered downward into a binocular-like interface as a series of LEDs rapidly scanned across the eye's field of view using tiny vibrating mirrors, which created a distinctive hum. While not actually portraying virtual reality, the Virtual Boy could create an impression of depth by projecting slightly different angles of the same image onto each eye—essentially the same technology, known as stereoscopy, used with 3-D movies. In *Wario Land* for the Virtual Boy, for instance, players could move Wario left and right, but special blocks allowed Wario to leap onto platforms in the background, and boss fights often featured attacks that seemed to stop inches from the player's eyes.

The Virtual Boy was a commercial failure for many reasons. For one, Nintendo struggled to receive confirmation from doctors that its device was safe. The Virtual Boy box bore a prominent red disclaimer—IMPORTANT! BEFORE USING YOUR SYSTEM, CAREFULLY READ THE INSTRUCTION AND PRECAUTIONS BOOKLET—and the manual warned that children under the age of seven should not operate it. In part because of a built-in timer that reminded users to rest their eyes every fifteen minutes, the Virtual Boy developed a reputation that it could damage eyesight. In addition, Nintendo's budget was increasingly devoted to its next-generation console, the Nintendo 64 (released in 1996), and the company's best designers were wrapped up in projects like *Super Mario 64* and *Star Wars: Shadows of the Empire*. Ultimately forced to

revamp 2-D games into 3-D, many of the Virtual Boy's launch titles were hastily designed, uninspired, and failed to harness the system's advanced capabilities. Only twenty-two games were produced for the Virtual Boy, and just fourteen made their way to the United States. All told, the Virtual Boy sold approximately seven hundred seventy thousand units worldwide before it was discontinued barely a year after it was introduced—a pittance for a company accustomed to shipping hundreds of millions of NES, SNES, and Game Boy units.

But perhaps the Virtual Boy's biggest obstacle was one that challenges today's VR tech.

Game franchises like Madden NFL or Mario Kart succeed because they invite players to come together, to compete, to share an experience. Even an observer can cheer his friend on from the couch as she wages battle against a boss from The Legend of Zelda: Breath of the Wild. At their heart, video games are just another form of play—and play is most often a social experience. Virtual reality tech may enable us to lose ourselves in amazingly detailed worlds, but when the goggles come off we look at the people around us and are reminded that, indeed, there is no place like home.

THE VIRTUAL BOY SOLD APPROXIMATELY
SEVEN HUNDRED SEVENTY THOUSAND
UNITS WORLDWIDE BEFORE IT WAS
DISCONTINUED BARELY A YEAR AFTER
IT WAS INTRODUCED.

POKÉMON

(1996)

Inspired by the developer's childhood love of bug-collecting, *Pokémon Red* and *Green* became breakout Japanese hits for a series that extended beyond video games to include trading cards, animation specials, and movies. The widespread recognition of *Pokémon* explains why it is in the World Video Game Hall of Fame.

As a child, Satoshi Tajiri was known by his friends as "Dr. Bug." Growing up in Machida, a suburb of Tokyo, Japan, he explored lush rivers, forests, and rice paddies in search of insects. He was fascinated with how they crawled and climbed, how they hid under rocks and wiggled into impossibly small cracks. He learned new ways to catch them, such as placing honey on tree trunks. But as Japan industrialized throughout the 1970s, the lush forests of Tajiri's childhood turned into malls, offices, and parking lots. As he ventured farther and farther to find new and exciting insects, he gained an appreciation for the fragility of life and the need to conserve. Just as famed Nintendo designer Shigeru Miyamoto's boyhood explorations led to the development of the Legend of Zelda franchise, "Dr. Bug's" obsession with tiny insects would one day spark the worldwide sensation known as Pokémon, which has become the second-highest-grossing media franchise of all time behind Super Mario Bros.

As a teenager, Tajiri's obsession with insects morphed into an obsession with coin-operated arcade games, especially *Space Invaders*. His passion for blasting pixelated aliens became so great that he nearly failed to graduate high school. When he later purchased a Nintendo Famicom game system, he repeatedly took it apart to learn how it worked. Known as wildly creative but eccentric by his friends, Tajiri was not a fit for traditional college, and so he attended Tokyo Technical College to study electronics. There he founded a fanzine called *Game Freak*, its crumpled, handwritten pages hastily stapled together and distributed to his fellow video game enthusiasts. Despite its crude appearance, *Game Freak* developed a steady following and gained the attention of a young artist named Ken Sugimori.

Tajiri and Sugimori became fast friends. Together they continued to grow *Game Freak*, reviewing games and providing critical commentary on the nascent video game industry. They soon reached a conclusion: video games were hot and getting hotter, but most were poorly designed. Instead of reviewing games, the friends reasoned, they should make their own. Tajiri began studying a dialect of the BASIC computer language used for NES games, known as Family BASIC, while Sugimori sketched out character and level designs. By 1989, they'd established a company, also called Game Freak, and released their first NES game, a puzzle-style arcade game called *Mendel Palace*, the same year with Namco.

But everything changed in 1990, when Tajiri witnessed two Nintendo Game Boys tethered together with a link cable, which allowed players to play multiplayer games such as *F-1 Race*. "That cable really got me interested," he later said in an interview. "I thought of actual living organisms moving back and forth across the cable." All at once, memories from his childhood flooded back to him—of collecting insects, cataloging them, and hunting down new and exciting species. Tajiri envisioned a game wherein players could exchange mythical monsters, much like an entomologist might show off her insect collection. Players could even direct them into battle.

Tajiri excitedly pitched his idea for "Pocket Monsters," or *Pokémon*, to Nintendo. The company was not sold on the idea, but admired Tajiri's passion and encouraged him to develop it. Nintendo's chief designer, Shigeru Miyamoto, also advocated for the project and mentored Tajiri throughout the six-year design process.

Slowly the design for *Pokémon* took form: with a third-person, overhead perspective, players would navigate Kanto, based on the Japanese region of the same name, searching out the 151 rare creatures known as Pokémon, each designed and drawn by Sugimori. Players could find these creatures in cities, caves, beaches, and other terrain. They would not come willingly, of course; when encountering a wild Pokémon, the player would have to battle it with her existing stable of Pokémon to weaken and catch it with a Poké Ball. As the player collected increasingly powerful Pokémon, she could send them into battle at special gyms to acquire badges and gain ranking in elite Pokémon leagues. With a link cable, players could trade Pokémon with other players and even battle them. Gamers leveled their Pokémon through battles with other trainers, including Gym Leaders and elite members of the official Pokémon League. The game concluded with a final battle between the player and his or her rival, the current Pokémon League Champion.

Pokémon nearly bankrupted Game Freak, who could often barely afford to pay its employees. Tajiri eventually decided to release two versions of *Pokémon* for the Game Boy—*Pokémon Red* and *Pokémon Green*—which would allow the developers to design a richer world with more Pokémon while compelling players to purchase both games in order to "catch them all." (In the U.S., *Green* was released as *Blue*.) Despite initial concerns that "cute monsters" would not appeal to non-Japanese audiences, *Pokémon* quickly took the world by storm after its release in 1996. *Red*, *Green*, and *Blue* sold more than twenty-three million copies worldwide, and in 2009 they

appeared in the *Guinness Book of World Records* as the bestselling role-playing game of all time.

The Pokémon series now consists of roughly thirty core games containing more than seven hundred individual Pokémon, along with various spin-offs, such as the battle simulation *Pokémon Stadium* (1999), the virtual pet game *Hey You, Pikachu!* (1998), and the rogue-like *Pokémon Mystery Dungeon* (2005). With approximately 280 million units sold, *Pokémon* remains one of the bestselling video game franchises of all time. The series' immense popularity led to the creation of an entire transmedia franchise, now regulated by the Pokémon Company International, which includes the wildly popular *Pokémon Trading Card Game*, first published in 1996 by Media Factory. Since then, nearly fifteen billion Pokémon playing cards have been published worldwide.

A large portion of *Pokémon*'s appeal derives from its focus on collecting. While the games can be completed without finding every monster, many fans find the hunt just as essential as the game's plot. In the process, individual Pokémon have become pop-culture icons. The lightning-based Pikachu, arguably the most famous Pokémon of all, has appeared as a large balloon in the Macy's Thanksgiving Day Parade. In 2016, twenty years after the release of *Pokémon Red* and *Blue*, Niantic and Nintendo released *Pokémon Go*, an augmented reality game for mobile platforms that has been downloaded 500 million times (page 305). From mobile games to magazine covers to TV shows, Satoshi Tajiri's childhood obsession with insects has morphed into a multibillion-dollar juggernaut.

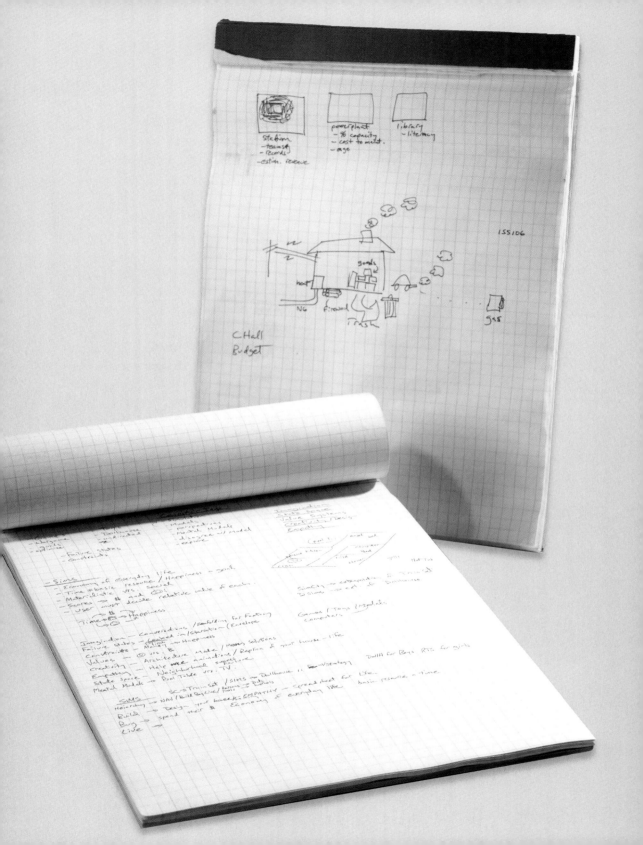

THE SIMS

(2000)

Will Wright's real-life simulator *The Sims* updated the age-old doll-house for the modern computer. It particularly appealed to girls and women, which helped it break sales records and earn a place in the World Video Game Hall of Fame. Wright donated the notebooks he used to create this game to The Strong.

On October 19, 1991, a massive firestorm swept through the hillsides of Oakland, California, inflicting $1.5 billion in damage and reducing nearly three thousand homes to ash. One of the very first homes to burn belonged to a video game designer named Will Wright. After grabbing a few precious photographs, Wright managed to safely flee the fire with his wife, but when he returned to his home a week later, all that remained was a chimney and the smoldering remnants of a Weber grill.

"The interesting part was to find out that I wasn't really that attached to much," he later said in an interview. "I started assessing my material needs: a toothbrush, underwear, a car, a house . . . I was surprised how I didn't miss stuff. The fact we got out and none of our family was hurt seemed so much more important." As Wright picked through the pieces of his home, he reflected on the seemingly small decisions people make on a daily basis that snowball into a life: what clothes to wear, what shoes to buy, what job to choose, whom to date and then marry, where to live. Wright came to think, what if we could see our lives from a top-down perspective and filter out the decisions that matter from the ones that don't? As it happened, this simple idea would become the nucleus for *The Sims*, the first game in the bestselling PC game series of all time.

Years before he conceived of *The Sims*, Wright was a restless student at Louisiana State University. After dabbling in architecture, mechanical engineering, computers, and finally robotics throughout college, Will Wright began trying his hand at game design in the early 1980s. In 1984, he put the finishing touches on *Raid on Bungeling Bay*, an action game for the Commodore 64 in which players piloted attack helicopters over enemy territory. *Raid* was a surprise hit, selling over twenty thousand copies in the United States and more than a million copies for the Nintendo Famicom in Japan. With a steady stream of income, Wright could work on his next, more ambitious project.

While creating *Raid on Bungeling Bay*, Wright had found that he was far more drawn to designing enemy forts than destroying them with helicopters. He began turning the design software he used to create *Raid on Bungeling Bay*'s maps into a game itself, one that allowed players to create roads and buildings, levy taxes, and tackle real-life problems like crime and poverty. He dubbed the game "Micropolis" and showed it to numerous publishers, but none were interested. They wanted to see another action title, and did not believe a game could be made out of the seemingly mundane job of city planning. From games like *Space Invaders* to *Missile Command*, destroying things was all the rage—not building.

Wright tabled his city simulator idea for a time, but his fortunes changed after attending "the world's most important pizza party" in 1987. There, at the house of a mutual friend, Wright met entrepreneur Jeff Braun, who was hoping to jump into the video game industry with a new company. After striking up a conversation over pizza and beer, Wright offered to show him "Micropolis." "I died," Braun later said. "This was what I was looking for." Braun urged Wright to move ahead with the game, and the two formed a company, Maxis—a name suggested by Braun's father, who believed a proper game company should have two syllables and include an *x*—in Walnut Creek, California. Its first title would be Wright's "Micropolis," published in 1989 and renamed *SimCity*. Wright's creation was, in many ways, more a toy than a game, affording players the chance to build and design their own city with no specific goals and with no way to win or lose. It was a surprise hit, selling a million copies by 1992. Over time, *SimCity* especially resonated with adults who previously associated video games with teenagers, as well as teachers who used the game to teach their students resource management and urban design.

The success of *SimCity* led Maxis to experiment with a long line of "Sim" games. Nineteen ninety-one saw the release of *SimAnt*, in which players took control of an ant colony nestled in a suburban backyard and defended the queen against other invading ants, spiders, and clumsy humans with large feet. Two years later came *SimFarm*, in which players built up farm land, managed livestock, planted crops, and guided the farm through natural disasters such as tornadoes, pests, droughts, and dust storms. In 1994, Maxis licensed a Japanese game called *The Tower*, renamed *SimTower* for the American market, where players built and managed their own skyscraper in hopes of turning it into a five-star facility complete with offices, condos, restaurants, and a hotel.

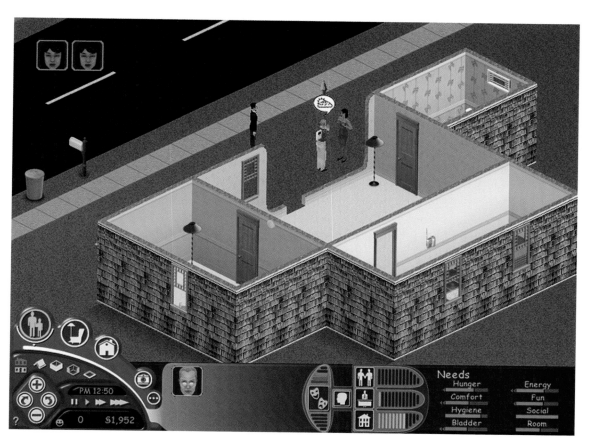

DOLLHOUSE DREAMS

The Sims invited players to do in the digital world what many young girls had done for centuries playing with dollhouses in the physical world. As early as the 1500s, wealthy European women had replica miniature "baby houses" made of their own homes. By the nineteenth century, dollhouses had become common playthings for affluent young girls. When dollhouses arrived in middle-class homes in the early twentieth century, these miniature dwellings were viewed by parents as a tool to prepare their daughters for modern homemaking and motherhood. But as *The Sims* illustrated, there's often more to a dollhouse then mimicry. With the freedom to create their own scenarios and furnish their own fantasies, girls and boys alike regularly created play far removed from the expectations of the adult world.

As Maxis became increasingly profitable, and after Wright nearly lost everything in the 1991 Oakland firestorm, he became focused on building a simulation for people. Much like his ants had to protect their colony and farmers had to manage their homestead, Wright envisioned a game where humans had to pay bills, keep a job, and tend to a family. He called his concept "Dollhouse" and pitched it to Maxis executives, including Braun. The reception was cold: few believed young men and boys would be attracted to a game with a "feminine" name, and Wright's idea was derided as "The Toilet Game" because players would be expected to guide their characters to the bathroom among other mundane tasks.

Maxis nixed the idea, but Wright was not ready to give up. He pulled aside a programmer and the two began working on the game in secret, which he now called *The Sims*. Then, in 1997, Maxis was acquired by Electronic Arts.

With a new board of directors, Wright once again pitched his idea. This time it was well received, and three years later *The Sims* hit store shelves nationwide. The game put players in control of a family of semi-autonomous characters—or "sims"—with little direction and no obvious goals to accomplish. It wasn't the first game to simulate the tasks of suburban existence; Rich Gold and David Crane's 1985 game *Little Computer People* did the same. But where *Little Computer People* allowed players to interact with computer-generated "peeps" in a cross-section of a three-story, two-dimensional house, *The Sims* empowered players to create, customize, and experiment with their sims in a vivid three-dimensional world.

Allowing players to create their own play style made *The Sims* extremely appealing. Those curious about playing "watchmaker" and creating social experiments could construct their sims, adjust how they looked, and even program their personality with five personality attributes—active, neat, nice, outgoing, and playful—before watching how they responded to various conditions. Players often put characters based on themselves and their families into the game. Many players took care of their sims like virtual pets, closely managing their needs for food, sleep, entertainment, fellowship with friends and family, and occasional trips to the restroom. Some players embraced the building and conspicuous consumption aspects of the game, spending their time renovating their homes with countless new pools, ornate columns, exotic plants, and colorful wallpaper.

With more than two hundred million copies sold in sixty countries and in more than twenty languages, *The Sims* and its many sequels and expansion packs have achieved worldwide popularity for its fun, innovative, and flexible gameplay. As video game critic Chris Baker wrote, "*The Sims*, to a greater extent than anything else released, broadened the definition of what a game could be."

SONY

PLAYSTATION 2

(2000)

The PlayStation 2 became the bestselling console of all time because it offered developers unprecedented tools for bringing their visions to life. Stormfront Studios used this test and debugging unit to help develop its games for the system.

ony's PlayStation 2 (PS2) reigns as the bestselling video game console of all time, surpassing the Atari 2600 (which sold thirty million units over a fifteen-year production life), the Nintendo NES (60 million units), and even the Game Boy series (a staggering 119 million units from 1989 to 2003). With over 150 million consoles sold over a thirteen-year lifespan and thousands of available games, the PS2 is the most popular game system ever built and remains a staple of living rooms and college dorms years after its discontinuation.

Ironically, the PlayStation series may never have existed without the help of Sony's chief competitor, Nintendo. In the mid-1980s, Sony signed a deal with Nintendo to produce audio chips for the company's upcoming Super Nintendo Entertainment System (SNES) console. The successful partnership spurred Nintendo to ask Sony to produce an optical disk add-on for the SNES called the Super NES CD-ROM, a peripheral designed to expand the console's storage capabilities, much like the Famicom Disk System had for the original NES, known as the Famicom in Japan (page 185). As a matter of fact, the project was known internally as the Nintendo "Play Station." Sony, which had pioneered the development of the CD-ROM alongside Philips Electronics, was uninterested in creating its own game system until Nintendo canceled the project, fully committing to the aging but reliable cartridge format. Sony briefly considered bringing its disk technology to Sega, but the game company did not believe Sony had the expertise to follow through.

Finally, Sony decided to continue with its own CD-ROM–based console. When Nintendo caught wind that its former partner was developing a console based on what was originally intended to be a SNES peripheral, it filed a lawsuit against Sony in federal court claiming breach of contract. The lawsuit failed, however, and the judge allowed Sony to continue its development. Before Sony launched its PlayStation in Japan in December 1994, game industry journalists and critics seriously questioned whether the company could compete with game-console titans Nintendo and Sega. Having never produced a dedicated video game console of any kind, Sony learned from their own missteps with the Betamax video cassette recorder and the stumbles of Atari's Jaguar (1993) and 3DO's Interactive Multiplayer (1993) game systems, which failed from a mixture of design flaws, high pricing (the Interactive Multiplayer retailed for $599 at launch), stiff competition, and a lack of third-party software developer support. Sony offered a superior CD-ROM console for $299 at launch ($100 below the Sega Saturn) with a wide selection of third-party software developers to produce games.

Although the PlayStation boasted a graceful gray case, groundbreaking technology, and an innovative ergonomic controller, it would never have succeeded without high-quality launch titles such as the 3-D fighting game *Battle Arena Toshinden* (1995), a conversion of the wildly popular coin-op game *Ridge Racer* (1994), and the downhill racing game *ESPN Extreme Games* (1995). While Nintendo and Sega took an isolationist approach to third-party developers, Sony's ability to generate quality in-house (by allying itself with game developer Namco and purchasing developer Psygnosis) and third-party software at competitive prices helped transform the company into a video game industry powerhouse. Ultimately selling more than 100 million units with more than 1,500 games in its stable, the Sony PlayStation was the king of 1990s consoles, paving the way for its hotly anticipated successor.

Sony began development on the PS2 shortly after the release of the original PlayStation. From the start, the company was committed to maintaining backward compatibility with the PS1 and its enormous portfolio of games. Unlike the SNES, which Nintendo designed with all-new cartridges and controllers, the PS2 could run any PlayStation game. Even the PS2 controller, known as the DualShock 2, was fully backward compatible and nearly identical to the previous generation save for a few cosmetic changes. Perhaps the most important decision was one that had nothing to do with video games at all: the inclusion of a DVD player. Compared to VHS tapes, DVDs offered vastly superior resolution and sound quality and were quickly being adopted by consumers. Retailing for $299, the PS2 cost as much as many stand-alone DVD players. By positioning the PS2 not just as a video game console, but a home theater system, Sony appealed to a much larger demographic.

Despite the immense hype surrounding the PS2, it launched in March 2000 to brisk but slower-than-expected sales. According to reports, third-party game developers were having trouble writing code for the PS2's finicky hardware, while component shortages meant the console wasn't on enough store shelves. Meanwhile, players unaccustomed to the PS2's next-generation 3-D graphics vocally grumbled about the console's "jagged" graphics. Nevertheless, the PS2's problems were short-lived. By the end of the year it had sold 6.4 million units worldwide, and nearly 25 million by the end of 2001, aided by blockbuster games like *Grand Theft Auto III*, *Gran Turismo 3: A-Spec*, and *Metal Gear Solid 2: Sons of Liberty*.

Sony was also aided by the demise of the Sega Dreamcast. Released in 1998 in Japan (and a year later in North America), the Dreamcast was the first of the consoles capable of 128-bit graphics. Although the Dreamcast sold well initially, a lack of titles hamstrung sales (especially a lack of participation by gamemakers Electronic Arts and Squaresoft), and the immense hype surrounding the PS2 ultimately helped sink the Dreamcast. When Sega discontinued the console in March 2001, Sony had the only 128-bit console on the market until Nintendo and Microsoft launched the GameCube and Xbox, respectively, at the end of the year. By that point, the PS2 had achieved dominance with a burgeoning stable of games.

The PS2 would never look back, maintaining strong sales long after the release of more advanced consoles including the Xbox 360 (released in 2005) and the PlayStation 3 (released in 2006). Software development for Sony's plucky console remained so robust that even in 2008, more games were released for the PS2 than the PS3. The venerable PS2 would sell and sell and sell, outlasting the George W. Bush administration and enduring through the first term of the Obama administration. When it was finally discontinued in 2013, the PS2 had sold approximately 153 million units over a thirteen-year production life, and big-name publishers like Konami and Electronic Arts were still producing games for it. From the numerous Grand Theft Auto games to *Kingdom Hearts* to *Final Fantasy X*, the PS2 was home to many of the greatest video games of all time.

GRAND THEFT AUTO III

(2001)

The Grand Theft Auto series has acquired notoriety for its violent content, but the true appeal of *Grand Theft Auto III* lay in an open world format that offered players unprecedented freedom. Its innovations earned it a spot in the 2016 class of the World Video Game Hall of Fame.

Who says crime doesn't pay? When it comes to notoriety, no game can touch the Grand Theft Auto franchise. In 2001, when Rockstar Games released the third installment of its bloody, vulgar, splendidly offensive series, the video game industry found itself barreling toward its next moral crisis. Having survived public outrage over *Death Race* (page 83), *Mortal Kombat* (page 223), and *Doom* (page 229), the industry now faced charges of glorifying crime, cheerleading police brutality, and extoling prostitution. *Grand Theft Auto III* (*GTA III*) wasn't the first 3-D "sandbox" game to allow players to freely interact—or destroy—an open virtual world, but it was the first game of its kind to achieve massive mainstream popularity and widespread critical acclaim. *GTA III* has sold some 17 million copies and represented the first breakout hit in a series that has sold more than 250 million units. Appealing to a new generation of players who relished the freedom to push the boundaries of what their in-game characters could do (or steal) in an open world, *GTA III* imbued Rockstar Games' seminal franchise with notoriety that lasts to this day.

In the mid-1980s, the epicenter of the video game industry was far, far away from the Central Lowlands of Scotland—yet that is where a young programmer named David Jones decided to make his start. As a full-time student at the Dundee Institute of Technology, Jones started his own company, DMA Design (short for Direct Mind Access), and spent his free hours in his parents' basement coding on his personal computer, the Commodore Amiga. His eventual creation was a side-scrolling shooter game called *Menace* in which players pilot an alien spaceship as it blasts enemies on the planet Draconia. Published by Psygnosis and released in 1988, *Menace* was a modest hit, selling some fifteen thousand copies and earning Jones about £20,000—which he promptly spent on a new car. DMA Design quickly produced two more games: The first, *Blood Money*, was another shooter game that saw even greater success, and the third game, *Lemmings*—a puzzle platform game in which players guided anthropomorphized lemmings through an obstacle course—equaled on its first day on sale the total units sold of *Menace* and *Blood Money* combined. All told, *Lemmings* would eventually sell more than fifteen million copies, making David Jones one of the wealthiest game designers of his time.

Yet Jones soon found that the video game landscape was changing. When DMA Design was invited by Nintendo to join Midway, LucasArts, and Rare in its content "Dream Team" for its upcoming Nintendo 64 console, Jones began working on a game called *Body Harvest*, in which players roamed the earth jumping into vehicles and killing aliens to save the last vestiges of humanity. The violent game was nixed by Nintendo's lead designer Shigeru Miyamoto, who wanted simpler, family-friendly games with decidedly less blood. But Jones knew he had come up with gold—maybe not with aliens, but with his idea for an open-world environment in which players could do anything they wanted. The idea soon morphed to a cops-and-robbers game set in a large city. Except this time, the players wouldn't be the good guys.

The idea was too risqué for Jones's old publisher, Psygnosis, so Jones reached out to BMG Interactive, the electronic gaming wing of BMG Music, which was looking to make a splash with a controversial game much like its rap artists were in the United States. Jones pitched his game as

"Race-n-Chase," in which players assumed the role of a low-level thug clawing his way up the organized crime ladder by stealing cars, carrying out hits, and many more acts of mayhem. But the key feature was freedom: Players could follow the general story arc, but they could also beat up and mug random pedestrians and instigate a massive police manhunt in between jobs. BMG was smitten and immediately licensed the game, changing the title to *Grand Theft Auto*.

Released in 1997 for MS-DOS and Microsoft Windows, the game's 2-D, top-down graphics were fairly crude even by standards of the time. Yet the game was a success, thanks in no small part to a massive wave of controversy. *Grand Theft Auto* was banned outright in Brazil, and it was condemned by moral guardians in Germany,

France, and the U.K. Nevertheless, the game was a bestseller in Britain, and DMA Design (now known as Rockstar Games after a series of sales) quickly put out a sequel in 1999. *Grand Theft Auto 2* was very similar to the original, with slightly improved graphics and a higher-octane storyline. The game was a commercial hit as well, but many critics believed it failed to break new ground. Rockstar knew the third installment in the series would need to push boundaries— graphical and moral—if the series were to remain relevant at the dawn of the twenty-first century.

For *GTA III*, Rockstar was without its star designer, David Jones, who had left the company shortly after the release of *Grand Theft Auto 2*. The *GTA III* team decided to license an established

AMERICAN GANGSTER

Controversy swirled around the Grand Theft Auto franchise, but the game's raw content made it a subject of much cultural commentary outside of video games, and observers noted that the game could be understood as the latest expression in a long line of cultural productions that explored the lives of outlaws, gangsters, and mafiosi.

The gangster genre coalesced in the 1930s as filmmakers responded to the inequities and failures of the capitalist system revealed by the Great Depression. From the scrappy bootlegger Tom Powers (James Cagney) in *The Public Enemy* (1931) to the chemistry-teacher-turned-neo-gangster-kingpin Walter White (Brian Cranston) in the *Breaking Bad* (2008–2013) television series, these stories explored the social origins of crime and the nation's myths about individual success. Like warped versions of the characters populating nineteenth-century author Horatio Alger's rags-to-riches novels, the gangster typically rose from hardship to amass power and wealth through crime and violence before ultimately falling at the hands of the police or rivals.

In a sense, Grand Theft Auto is the heir to outlaws like Jesse James and Billy the Kid, and to beloved movies such as *Scarface* and *The Godfather*.

game engine instead of developing their own. Using Criterion Games' RenderWare engine, the company developed a truly three-dimensional open-world Liberty City, based on New York City. Designed for Sony's PlayStation 2, which used high-capacity DVDs allowing for expansive terrain, *GTA III* featured a truly massive sandbox-style map using a revolutionary third-person camera. Players could now see in all three dimensions, scoping out distant cars to hijack or alleyways to escape police. *GTA III* also had a rich storyline centering around Claude, a silent thug who found himself increasingly intertwined with Liberty City's warring gangs, from the Leone Mafia family to a Colombian cartel to the Japanese yakuza.

But in many ways, *GTA III*'s plot played second fiddle to its vast, open world. Thanks to *GTA III*'s powerful new game engine, the weather changed, the time of day changed, and the violence was badder and bloodier than ever before. Players could use melee attacks, guns, and explosives to fight everyone from rival gang members to police to the elderly. They could boost a car and spend the day drag racing for cash, or—controversially—visit prostitutes to boost their health level after a particularly nasty run-in with the police. (Players could also mug them to reclaim their cash.) Fueled by a firestorm of controversy—*GameSpy* "awarded" *GTA III* Most Offensive Game of the Year (as well as Game of the Year), labeling it "absolutely reprehensible"—*GTA III* became the bestselling game of 2001 despite being released in October.

The game's crude content outraged critics, many of whom dubbed it a "thug simulator," believing the gameplay rewarded bad behavior and corrupted youth. Others defended the game as gritty social commentary and satire that lampooned many aspects of American culture through its faux radio commercials, talk radio show parodies, over-the-top violence, and sexual explicitness. *SimCity* and *The Sims* creator Will Wright has described the game as one of his favorites, explaining that,

You can actually be very nice in [*GTA III*] and drive an ambulance around saving people, or you can be very mean. The game doesn't really force you down one path or the other unless you're playing the missions. For me, it's not really about the missions, it's about the open-endedness . . . going out and living life in this little simulated city. It's like a big playground.

GTA III would go on to win numerous honors as the best game of the year and multiple awards from the Academy of Interactive Arts and Sciences, including Outstanding Achievement in Game Design and Outstanding Achievement in Game Play Engineering. It also inspired a wave of "anti-hero" games, including *Mercenaries: Playground of Destruction* (2005), *The Godfather: The Game* (2006), and the Assassin's Creed franchise (2007–present) that explored moral ambiguity in open world environments. *GTA III*'s success signaled not only a new emphasis on free-form exploration, but it also helped demonstrate that video games were a significant form of play for adults. Most important, *GTA III* heralded a new generation of games that broke free of traditional story, graphical, and moral boundaries, one felony at a time.

HALO: COMBAT EVOLVED

(2001)

Halo propelled the Xbox platform to popularity with its intoxicating first-person shooter fun. It joined the World Video Game Hall of Fame in 2017.

The halls of the Macworld Expo in New York were buzzing. It was July 1999, and Steve Jobs, back at the helm of Apple after a dozen-year hiatus, was set to make a big announcement. After sitting through a report of rosy sales figures and a preview of Apple's upcoming operating system, Mac OS 9, game journalists in the audience crept to the edge of their seats. "We are starting to see some great games come back to the Mac," Jobs said coyly, pausing for effect. "But this is one of the coolest I've ever seen. This game is going to ship early next year from Bungie, and this is the first time anybody has ever seen it."

The game was called *Halo: Combat Evolved*, and it was set to be released exclusively for the Mac the following year. A select group of journalists had seen a demonstration of *Halo* a few months earlier at the Electronic Entertainment Expo in Los Angeles, but thanks to a nondisclosure agreement they could not tell the world what they were bursting to say: "heavenly," *IGN* gushed after Macworld, one that brought "new meaning to the [word] 'fantastic.'" Yet Microsoft, Apple's chief competitor, committed a coup in June 2000 by purchasing Bungie and announcing that *Halo* would not initially be available for the Macintosh; instead it would be the lead title for Microsoft's upcoming Xbox console. Known as the Xbox's "killer app," *Halo: Combat Evolved* became one of the most popular first-person shooter games of all time, selling more than six million copies and launching a franchise behemoth that has sold more than sixty-five million games and generated $4.6 billion in profits.

In the early 1990s, University of Chicago student Alex Seropian produced a *Pong* clone called *Gnop!* ("Pong" spelled backward). Convinced he could make a go of this video game thing, Seropian established a company, Bungie Software, and quickly produced a tank shooter called *Operation: Desert Storm*, which managed to sell a modest 2,500 copies despite Seropian producing the game disks and boxes himself. In 1992, he teamed up with his fellow undergrad Jason Jones to publish *Minotaur: The Labyrinths of Crete*, a dungeon-crawling role-playing game with the tagline "Kill your enemies. Kill your friends' enemies. Kill your friends." The game also sold modestly, but it developed a loyal following due to its novel multiplayer functionality using internet modems. Inspired by id Software's *Wolfenstein 3D*, in 1993, Bungie released *Pathways into Darkness*, a first-person shooter for the Macintosh in which players solve puzzles and blast enemies to prevent an evil being from destroying the world. *Pathways* was a surprising hit and represented Bungie's first commercial success, becoming one of the most popular Mac games of 1994.

Following two more commercial hits, the first-person shooter *Marathon* (1994) and the real-time tactics game *Myth: The Fallen Lords* (1997), Bungie found itself near the pinnacle of the fledgling band of Macintosh game developers. With money pouring in from the Myth franchise, Jones had time to focus on his pet projects, namely a game called *Blam!* which would blend *Myth*'s real-time strategy component with Jones's love for science fiction, especially novels by Larry Niven and Iain M. Banks. Jones and one of Bungie's top programmers, Marcus Lehto, put together a demo that showcased the company's latest high-fidelity graphics. The game was later dubbed *Halo*, morphing into a third-person shooter game in which humans crash-land onto a mysterious world and must battle marauding bands of aliens. Increasingly exotic weapons found their way into the game, in addition to an ability for players to pilot vehicles. Steve Jobs was so impressed with the game's progress that he chose to feature it at the 1999 Macworld expo to showcase the graphical capabilities of the Mac.

Jobs's exuberance was short-lived. In 2000, Microsoft acquired Bungie and transformed *Halo* into not just a first-person shooter, but an exclusive title for the new Xbox console. According to reports, Jobs was so furious that he phoned Microsoft's then-CEO, Steve Ballmer, to rage about the injustice; Ballmer told his counterpart to calm down and offered to port other games to the Mac. Nevertheless, Ballmer's shenanigans proved crucial for the future of the Xbox. In an era when PC games dominated the first-person shooter (FPS) genre, *Halo* proved a

console could be just as effective, if not more so. The game's intricate storyline and memorable characters led players to become deeply involved in the game's universe, and its world-building was almost unprecedented in the genre. *Halo* also boasted one of the strongest multi-player experiences of its time, even though it was released prior to the launch of Xbox Live and therefore required LAN parties to make up a full team.

In *Halo: Combat Evolved*, players assumed the role of Master Chief John-117, an enhanced super-soldier of the twenty-sixth century. Accompanied by a synthetic intelligence character called Cortana, Master Chief battled members of the evil Covenant while searching for information on the artificial ring-shaped world known as Halo. The unique weaponry in *Halo* is also considered a hallmark of the series. Unlike other FPS games, players were only able to equip two weapons at a time, a limitation that forced

COWBOYS AND ALIENS

Games often reflect the cultures that produce them. *Halo: Combat Evolved* and the Halo universe cultivated in its sequels and novels echoes the legacy of exploration and conquest in the history of the American West. Set in the twenty-sixth century, many humans have left an overpopulated earth to settle new worlds in the final frontier of space. But when humans colonize planets once inhabited by a sacred, extinct alien race known as Forerunners, the Covenant attacks without warning. The aggression sparks an intergalactic war in which space marine gunslingers fight a war of extermination to save humanity in the wilderness of space.

Like all great works of fiction, the Halo universe blends compelling storytelling with parallels to our own world that are all too real.

constant assessment of scenarios. All weapons were extremely individualized and included believable limitations, such as plasma weapons that overheated and traditional bullet guns that required extra time to reload. All weapons fired at different speeds and could also be used to bludgeon enemies. *Halo* also introduced the concept of a rechargeable shield that absorbed damage from both enemy fire and physical impact.

For Microsoft, *Halo*'s most immediate impact was on Xbox console sales. The game was sold alongside nearly half of all consoles, leading critics to name it Microsoft's "killer app"—a term describing a program so valuable that its loss would deplete the overall desirability of the hardware. The terms "Halo Clone" and "Halo

Killer" soon followed, referring to games that attempted to duplicate *Halo*'s success. Hardcore fans of the franchise referred to themselves as the "Halo Nation," and the game's influence can also be seen in the creation of *Red vs. Blue*, a fan-made web series that popularized *machinima*, the technique of combining gameplay video with voiceovers to create short films or web series.

Halo sold more than one million copies within five months—faster than any other Xbox game. It won Game of the Year in the 2001 AIAS awards, and *Rolling Stone* awarded it with "Best Original Soundtrack." *Variety* magazine called it the *Star Wars* of video games, while *The Escapist* likened it to Virgil's epic *Aeneid*. The characters also left a lasting impression: a wax figure of Master Chief appeared in Madame Tussauds in Las Vegas, and the A.I. helper Cortana received so much praise that Microsoft bestowed the name on its now-ubiquitous virtual assistant, even using the character's original voice actress, Jen Taylor, for the U.S. version of the software. *Halo*'s popularity was such that the release of its sequel was treated as a cultural event, in much the same way as a highly anticipated film release.

With five main series games and a variety of sequels and spin-offs, not to mention novel, comic book, and web series adaptations, the Halo franchise has grossed more than $4 billion and sold over sixty-five million games, with members of the Halo Nation still clamoring for more.

DENSHA DE GO! CONTROLLER

(2002)

Video games give players the chance to have experiences unattainable in real life. For Japanese players of *Densha de Go!*, the thrill is in playing with a highly realistic train simulator.

According to the Bureau of Transportation Statistics, there are more than 250 million registered automobiles in the United States. The "American love affair with the automobile," as the old saying goes, began at the turn of the twentieth century, when "horseless carriages" powered by internal combustion engines first began appearing on American roads. Today, the average household owns about two cars, while each American drives more than thirteen thousand miles per year. As a result, passenger trains, which were the predominant mode of transportation in the nineteenth century, have largely been relegated to urban areas. Amtrak, the partially government-funded passenger train service that operates creaky intercity routes, is a favorite political football of lawmakers and is perennially starved for funds in a country that has wholly embraced the automobile. Yet in Japan, nearly seventeen thousand miles of track help transport 7.2 billion people every year efficiently and punctually. In fact, the country is home to forty-six of the world's fifty busiest stations. It comes as no surprise, therefore, that while driving games like *Need for Speed* are among the bestsellers in America, a train simulator named Densha de Go! is a beloved series in Japan.

At first glance, driving a virtual passenger train may not seem like compelling gameplay. While racing games let you control supercars as you swerve and drift and drag or flight simulators place you in the cockpit of an F-16 fighter jet to dogfight at supersonic speeds, trains measure their zero-to-sixty times in minutes, not seconds, and can only move in two directions. Yet there is a long history of playing with trains. In 1900, Joshua Lionel Cowen and Harry C. Grant formed the Lionel Corporation in New York City, special-izing in fans, simple lights, and other electrical novelties. For Christmas season, Lionel created its first train, the Electric Express. For countless families, snapping together steel O-gauge track, twisting together electrical wire, and oiling miniature locomotives was a staple holiday tradition.

While rail travel stagnated in America after World War II, a decimated Japan embraced the train as a means to move its people. In 1964, the Tōkaidō Shinkansen line opened, providing high-speed service between Tokyo and Shin-Osaka. From high-speed bullet trains to levitating maglevs that glide at more than three hundred miles per hour, the Japanese rail system has developed a reputation for speed and reliability. Since the mid-1990s, the Densha de Go! franchise has enabled gamers to take control of Japan's sleek fleet of locomotives. Featuring real-life trains on actual routes, the game challenges players to drive a train to its destination while adhering to a strict timetable. Beginning with an arcade version in 1995, publisher Taito has released numerous home versions for platforms including PC and Sony PlayStation. Many Densha de Go! games also came with sophisticated controllers that accurately depicted real life, such as throttle levers, brake controls, foot pedals, and knobs to open and close passenger doors.

Densha de Go! was not merely a simulator, however. The games awarded points for maintaining speed limits, running on time, stopping within centimeters of a designated point, slowing down and speeding up gradually so as not to anger passengers, and countless other variables that made it a demanding arcade game. Many versions also included changing weather patterns, such as rain and snow, which affected how quickly players could stop their train. At the end of each route, players were awarded points depending on how effectively they piloted their train from station to station. While arcades have largely gone the way of the locomotive in the United States, Japanese arcades remain alive and well. In 2016, celebrating the twentieth anniversary of its train-simulator franchise, Taito announced a brand-new arcade cabinet that realistically reproduced an actual train cockpit. Inside it, players could gaze upon four displays representing a train engineer's windows, while the virtual control panel accurately depicted the real-life controls used to guide a train.

In many ways, the specialized Densha de Go! controllers represented a link between old and new play: the PlayStation 2 controller for the game, with its large speed-control lever, resembled 1950s-era Lionel transformers. *Densha de Go!* is also representative of how play can be highly localized. While *Super Mario Bros.*, *Space Invaders*, and *Pokémon*, among countless other games, have been easily exported to the West, the DNA of *Densha de Go!* is so uniquely Japanese that it would be unlikely to succeed anywhere else. Indeed, Taito has never attempted to sell its simulator outside of Japan. Other well-known video games often have similar local, but not universal, appeal. For example, while Electronic Arts' Madden NFL is a juggernaut franchise in the United States, its sales are meager in Europe, where the company's FIFA soccer series is far more popular. Likewise, World War II–era first-person shooters are a perennially popular genre for American developers like Activision, but audiences are more apprehensive about these games in Germany and Japan.

In short, *Densha de Go!* is a testament to how play can simultaneously transcend and be shaped by geographic and cultural boundaries.

WORLD OF WARCRAFT

(2004)

World of Warcraft secured a spot in the inaugural class of the World Video Game Hall of Fame because its massive audience of millions of players built robust online relationships. This server blade represents part of the real-life hardware that makes these virtual communities possible.

In September 2001, Bill Roper, a vice president at the game company Blizzard Entertainment, arrived in London at the annual European Computer Trade Show (ECTS). Open to industry professionals and journalists, ECTS was commonly used by game companies to launch hotly anticipated titles. A celebrated and highly secretive company, Blizzard had two years earlier announced the third installment of Warcraft, its blockbuster real-time strategy (RTS) franchise, and speculation was rampant that Blizzard was about to announce a sequel to its other popular real-time-strategy game, *StarCraft*, which was the bestselling game of 1998 and was considered by many to be one of the greatest games of all time. Instead, Blizzard shocked the gaming world, announcing its intention to produce *World of Warcraft*, a massively multiplayer online role-playing game (MMORPG) set in the Warcraft universe. It would become the most-subscribed-to MMORPG of all time—a title it continues to hold today, well over a decade after its launch.

In 1991, three recent UCLA grads, Michael Morhaime, Allen Adham, and Frank Pearce, each contributed $10,000 to form the game design firm Silicon & Synapse. To acclimate themselves to video game development and art design, their early games were ports of existing titles, such as *Battle Chess* and *The Lord of the Rings*. In 1993, Silicon & Synapse released two original titles, *Rock n' Roll Racing* and *The Lost Vikings*, both of which were received to lukewarm reviews and modest sales. For their next games, Morhaime, Adham, and Pearce took inspiration from the 1992 game *Dune II: The Building of a Dynasty*, released by Westwood Studios, which became the blueprint for many RTS games. In *Dune II*, play-

ers commanded one of three races—the Atreides, the Harkonnen, or the Ordos—against the other two in a bid for interplanetary domination. Players were required to mine spice, the planet's most valuable resource, to pay for armies and expand their territory. While not the first real-time strategy game, this dynamic would form the basis for all RTS games that followed.

Eager to rebrand their company as a producer of RTS games, Morhaime, Adham, and Pearce changed their name to Chaos Studios before settling on Blizzard on 1994. That year, Blizzard released *Warcraft: Orcs & Humans* for PC and Macintosh, meant to be a direct competitor to Westwood Studio's line of RTS games. Set on the planet Azeroth, players took control of either the humans or the invading orcs. In the single-player campaign, missions required players to build towns, harvest resources, and win increasingly elaborate skirmishes with the enemy. Using the same top-down perspective as *Dune II*, the game also allowed players to battle friends over a modem or LAN. It was this multiplayer dynamic that finally showcased the full potential of RTS games. With the success of *Warcraft: Orcs & Humans*, its blockbuster sequel, *Warcraft II: Tides of Darkness*, and its equally popular cousin, *StarCraft*, Blizzard had reached the pinnacle of game development in only a few short years.

And yet, in 2001, Blizzard decided to move in an entirely new direction by announcing *World of Warcraft*, an MMORPG. In 1997, developer Richard Garriott coined the term "massively multiplayer online role-playing game" for his game *Ultima Online*. Similar games had often been previously identified as graphical multi-user dungeons (MUDs), which referred to multiplayer virtual worlds with real-time combat that combined

NEVERWINTER NIGHTS

What was the first MMORPG? Some point to *MUD* (1980), a text-based adventure game hosted on Essex University's servers and later introduced to the ARPAnet. Others say *Ultima Online* (1997), which, while not the first online multiplayer game, was arguably the first "massive" one, with more than two hundred fifty thousand subscribers at its peak.

Yet six years before *Ultima Online* appeared on the internet, game developer Don Daglow (creator of *Utopia*, page 147) released *Neverwinter Nights*, one of the most important games in the history of the industry. The first true online multiplayer game to feature a graphical interface, *Neverwinter Nights* was developed by Daglow's outfit, Stormfront Studios, along with America Online (AOL), Strategic Simulations, and TSR, the publisher of *Dungeons & Dragons*. Daglow's team had to overcome numerous technical hurdles to produce the game. Dial-up modems, for instance, operated at a fraction of the speed of today's broadband connections. Game instructions and content crossed phone lines in packets of information, and severe limits on the size of these packets made it difficult for programmers to coordinate the simultaneous actions of all the players. When *Neverwinter Nights* launched in 1991, each server hosted fifty players, which meant the computer had to calculate and convey the impact of each player's actions and conversation to forty-nine other players. Doing this seamlessly required skilled programming on the part of programmers Cathryn Mataga and Craig Dykstra.

Hosted on AOL servers, *Neverwinter Nights* pioneered gameplay that is ubiquitous today. Players began by creating a character based on *Dungeons & Dragons* races, including elves, dwarves, and gnomes; and classes, such as fighters, clerics, and thieves. In the land of Neverwinter, players could team up and explore dangerous dungeons, defeat monsters, and loot treasure. But what made *Neverwinter Nights* great was the social aspect. Fans created in-game factions, known as guilds, and organized player-versus-player tournaments to establish a hierarchical "ladder" of the most powerful players. (Reportedly, AOL's then-CEO Steve Case often logged in as the immensely powerful avatar "Lord Nasher.")

AOL ran *Neverwinter Nights* until 1997. When the online service provider shut down the game after six years to focus on other business, the subscriber base exceeded one hundred thousand users. *Neverwinter Nights* established a new style of gameplay and popularized features of MMORPGs that remain fixtures of the multiplayer online experience. In 2010, Daglow donated game-development materials to The Strong that reveal how he developed *Neverwinter Nights*, providing historians and others with crucial sources for understanding the origins of MMORPGs.

elements of role-playing, hack-and-slash, and interactive fiction games.

In an MMORPG, players create a virtual avatar to represent themselves, generally choosing a "job" or "class" based on *Dungeons & Dragons*–like roles such as fighters, mages, rangers, and thieves. While playing, gamers chat with one another, engage in player vs. player combat, and complete quests to further the game's storyline. As a persistent world, the game continuously evolves even when the player logs off. Sony's *EverQuest* (1999) is credited with mainstreaming the genre, but *World of Warcraft* dominates the field as the largest and bestselling MMORPG ever created.

World of Warcraft players take on the roles of either members of the Alliance or the Horde in the fantasy world of Azeroth. Following the traditional flow of MMORPGs, players complete quests, battle enemies, and unlock storylines across the virtual realm. But its massive popularity stems from the comparative ease with which players complete their tasks, making the game suitable for both casual and hardcore gamers alike. Many MMORPGs, for example, exact high penalties when an avatar dies, whereas *World of Warcraft* allows gamers to swiftly return to their missions. Recovery time between battles is also shorter than average, and the game provides a higher than normal number of experience-giving quests, allowing players to level up quicker. This is especially useful for gamers who want to swiftly catch up with friends who have been playing longer.

MMORPGs like *World of Warcraft* offer a particularly immersive experience not often found in other multiplayer genres. Gamers become deeply invested in and connected to the worlds in which they play, and many form lasting friendships through "guilds"—groups of gamers who band together to defeat high-level monsters and assist one another in earning special gear and accessories. Blizzard hosts *World of Warcraft* servers throughout the world, allowing gamers to forge relationships with players in many countries and from all walks of life. Such a virtual world provides experiences that translate into real-life connections, with digital avatars becoming direct extensions of the players' bodies. This is especially poignant for gamers with physical or cognitive disabilities, who may feel more comfortable establishing friendships from behind the safety of a computer screen.

World of Warcraft is the highest-grossing video game ever created. By 2015—a full eleven years after its release—the game boasted over ten million subscribers, only slightly reduced from its peak of twelve million in October 2010. By 2016, more than one hundred million accounts had been created since the game's release. In an era when free-to-play gaming is swiftly gaining ground, *World of Warcraft*'s ability to entice players to pay a $15 monthly fee speaks volumes to its lasting popularity.

SONY'S *EVERQUEST* (1999) IS CREDITED WITH MAINSTREAMING THE GENRE, BUT *WORLD OF WARCRAFT* DOMINATES THE FIELD AS THE LARGEST AND BESTSELLING MMORPG EVER CREATED.

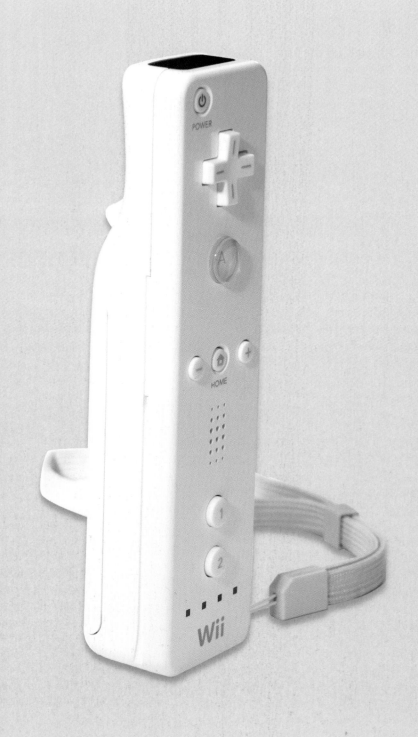

WII REMOTE

(2006)

Nintendo broadened the definition of who was a gamer with its crowd-pleasing Wii console. The Wii-mote let people operate the game with arm gestures that mimicked natural movements. Soon virtual bowling leagues and tennis tournaments sprung up around the country.

onsider the humble, traditional controller. While its shape and complexity have changed over the decades, the essential functions have remained the same. From the NES's four-button layout to the PlayStation 3's eight-button, two-joystick arrangement, controllers have largely retained the same basic idea. While aiming a sniper in the latest *Call of Duty* for Xbox One may require a more complex series of inputs compared to navigating *Sonic* for the Sega Genesis, both rely on opposable thumbs and a dexterous use of fingers; the rest of the body remains a passive observer. In 2006, however, Nintendo forever changed how we interact with our games with its Wii console. In fact, its controller was *not* a controller—Nintendo dubbed it a "remote"—and it featured only two primary buttons. And yet the Wii remote was the most revolutionary device of its day, for its most important interactive component lay not in a button or directional pad, but in the human body itself.

After dominating the console wars during the 1990s, Nintendo found itself steadily losing market share during the early 2000s. For years, the gaming giant was used to blockbuster sales: it had sold nearly 62 million NES consoles worldwide, 49 million SNES consoles, and a staggering 118 million Game Boy units. Yet its Nintendo 64 console, despite having a stable of blockbuster games such as *Super Mario 64* and *GoldenEye 007*, sold a modest 33 million units, lagging far behind the Sony PlayStation's 102 million. A contributing factor was Nintendo's choice to retain its venerable but graphically limited cartridge format, long after discs had become the industry standard. Moreover, its thin list of third-party games meant players were flocking to the PlayStation's massive library of award-winning

franchises such as Metal Gear Solid and Final Fantasy. Nintendo released its GameCube console in 2001, featuring optical mini-discs and PlayStation-style controllers, but sales of the charming purple cube (21 million) were swamped by Sony's PlayStation 2, which would become the bestselling console of all time with 155 million units sold.

With Sony now the undisputed king of video games and game heavyweight Microsoft entering the market with its Xbox console, Nintendo knew it could not rival the raw graphical horsepower of its wealthy competitors. But Nintendo's chief game designer, Shigeru Miyamoto, saw an opening. "Power isn't everything for a console," he later said in an interview. "Too many powerful consoles can't coexist. It's like having only ferocious dinosaurs. They might fight and hasten their own extinction." For decades, Nintendo had prided itself on gameplay, not power. Its NES and SNES consoles had won their respective console wars not because they outmuscled the competition, but because they had thoughtful, beautifully designed games.

Nintendo's president at the time, Iwata Satoru, challenged his engineers to create a console that was no thicker than three DVD cases and could easily nestle into a crowded living room entertainment center. But more important, it had to appeal to people who never considered themselves gamers. "A mom has to like it," Satoru argued, and he believed this revolution would begin and end with the controller—indeed, the codename for its next-generation console was "Revolution." Instead of using D-pads, joysticks, buttons, and triggers to control the action, the player's primary input device would be the controller itself. Nintendo eventually called its new console the "Wii," a name meant to evoke the communal aspect of games. (The two "i" characters were meant to resemble two players standing side-by-side.)

Using accelerometers, Nintendo engineers developed a "remote" that could register when a player moved her hand up, down, left, and right, as well as acceleration in any direction. As the spiritual successor to Nintendo's famed NES Zapper gun, the remote would allow a player to manipulate virtual objects by simply pointing at them onscreen. But the true genius of the Wii remote lay in its ability to take the shape of whatever object it was intended to replicate onscreen. For *Mario Kart* and other racing games, the remote could be turned sideways and used like a steering wheel. For flight simulators, it could be a joystick. In *Fishing Master*, the remote doubled as a fly-fishing pole.

Bundled with Nintendo Wii home video game consoles sold outside of Japan, *Wii Sports* best demonstrated how Nintendo redefined how video games could be played. Relying on a motion-sensitive Wii remote, *Wii Sports* distilled five sports—tennis, baseball, bowling, golf, and boxing—into essential gestures that could be acted out by the player with the Wii remote. *Wii Sports* baseball, then, was a game of hitting and pitching, swinging and throwing, while tennis was played with forehand flicks and well-timed overhand slams. The intuitive nature of *Wii Sports* meant that players who had never touched a video game could quickly and easily grasp the gestures necessary to play.

Wii Sports exemplified what game critic and theorist Jesper Juul calls the "casual revolution" or "the moment in which the simplicity of early video games is being rediscovered, while new flexible designs are letting video games fit into

the lives of players." Much like *Pong* and other early video games, *Wii Sports* operated in a casual space where a set of tennis or a baseball game could be played in minutes. Instead of having to memorize a series of buttons to swing a virtual baseball bat or roll a digital bowling ball, *Wii Sports* matched the actions of the player—a swing of the arm in this case—with what happened on screen.

Nintendo intentionally sought to broaden the base of "gamers." Even the company's marketing campaign drove this message home by circumventing the stereotypical young male gamer for a much wider audience. Nintendo's first Wii commercials showed two Japanese businessmen playing games on the Wii with other men and women, young and old, and people of varying races and ethnicities. The message was clear: the Wii could be played not only with your friends, but also with your mother and father—and even your grandparents. Indeed, as the console surged in popularity, senior centers routinely offered *Wii Sports* bowling leagues for members who found the pastime too physically demanding to hurl an actual ball down a lane. In 2011, health insurer Aetna even sponsored a *Wii Sports Resort* (the successor to *Wii Sports*) Senior Bowling Championship.

By broadening its base of players with simple, intuitive games, Nintendo sold more than one hundred million Wii consoles, outselling the Microsoft Xbox 360 and Sony PlayStation 3 and pushing the rival companies to introduce their own motion-sensing control devices in 2010. After years on the sidelines, Nintendo had once again regained its perch atop the video game world by enticing a new generation of gamers from every possible walk of life.

CALL OF DUTY:
MODERN WARFARE 2

(2009)

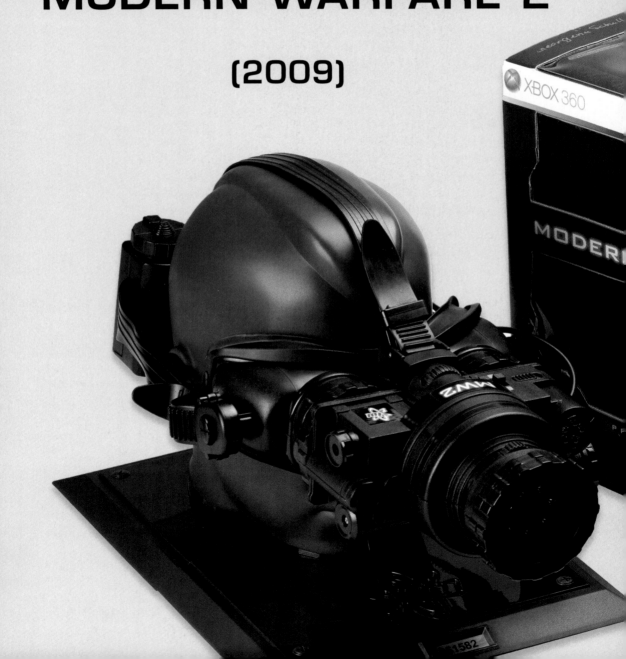

At a time when fear of terrorism dominated the headlines, *Call of Duty: Modern Warfare 2* sent players to wage virtual battle in Central Asia with gameplay that struck some as a bit too realistic. Designer Charles Wiederhold donated this edition of the game autographed by the development team.

For as long as humans have waged war, we have tried to reimagine a more civilized version of it through play. Chess, for instance, is believed to be descended from the sixth-century Indian strategy game chaturanga, in which players direct elephants, chariots, cavalry, and infantry toward their enemy along a checkered board. During the mid-nineteenth century, the Prussian army used a form of wargaming called kriegspiel to train its officers. For civilians wishing to play the role of a military general, two German brothers, Johann Gottfriend Hilpert and Johann Georg Hilpert, created the first mass-produced tin soldiers during the late eighteenth century as a tribute to Frederick the Great. The English writer H.G. Wells even helped codify the rules of playing war with toy soldiers in his book *Little Wars* (1913).

The interest in playing with World War II themes began shortly after the war started. Flipping through 1940s issues of *Playthings* magazine, the leading publication of the toy industry, reveals that toymakers moved quickly to produce toy soldiers, planes, tanks, boats, and other playthings that would enable kids to fight the good fight in which so many of their parents were involved. Electromechanical coin-operated games, dress-up costumes, and even simple handheld ball games exploited the war for ludic effect. Certainly, the little green army man was the most iconic toy to emerge during this period. With the advent of cheap plastics as a malleable production material, toymakers turned out these tiny soldiers by the millions and sold them to children for pennies each. Kids arranged these soldiers into elaborate battle scenes, engaging in play that was more imaginative than rule-based.

For most players, individual soldiers were just that—green plastic men with no personalities, no backstories, no family. For years, the heroes of World War II were the generals who planned daring battles like the invasion of Normandy and the Guadalcanal Campaign, not the soldiers who actually won them. This began to change in the 1990s with a slew of bestselling books by historian Stephen Ambrose, including *Band of Brothers* (1992) and *Citizen Soldiers* (1997), which celebrated the heroism and ingenuity of the ordinary G.I. These stories and others were made into blockbuster films, such as *Saving Private Ryan* (1998), and award-winning TV series such as HBO's *Band of Brothers* (2001).

Video games were not far behind. In 1999, DreamWorks Interactive and Electronic Arts released *Medal of Honor* for the Sony PlayStation. The game was conceived by Steven Spielberg, who had directed *Saving Private Ryan* and produced *Band of Brothers* and wanted to create a video game that captured the individual soldier's experience during World War II. In *Medal of Honor*, players assumed the role of fictional Lieutenant Jimmy Patterson from the Air Transport Command during the tail end of the war. Critics heralded the game for its impressive graphics and realistic storytelling.

In October 2003, Activision released *Call of Duty*, a first-person shooter similar to *Medal of Honor* but featuring multiple storylines from the American, British, and Soviet perspectives. Just months earlier, the United States had invaded Iraq, and war coverage dominated TV news each night. In a country eager to experience the life of a soldier (albeit from the safe confines of their living room), *Call of Duty* was an immediate hit despite depicting a theater of war that bore little resemblance to America's conflicts in the Middle East. While previous shooters typically emphasized "lone wolf" gameplay in which players took on the full force of the enemy alone, *Call of Duty* pioneered the use of computer-controlled allies who provided covering fire and other support, helping to create a more immersive style of play that more accurately reflected the heat of battle. Released for PC, Xbox 360, and PlayStation 3, *Call of Duty* was a bestseller and spawned its similarly World War II–themed sequel, *Call of Duty 2*, in 2005.

Several factors explain why World War II was (and remains) a popular setting for games. First, the tactics and weaponry of the Second World War were well suited for adaptation to gameplay. The conflict prized diverse technological development and the shifting of forces, something that has been easily adapted to established game mechanics. World War I, for example, notable for the grinding attrition of its trench warfare, has proved less appealing for game developers interested in movement and maneuverability. Additionally, World War II was largely seen as a "good war," with clear heroes and aggressors. The concept of a war fought by "the greatest generation" has proved perennially appealing to new generations of players who often see in World War II–era fighters the embodiment of admirable virtues of toughness and righteousness.

Soon the market was saturated with World War II shooters, including numerous *Medal of Honor* sequels, *Battlefield 1942*, *Brothers in Arms*, and many others. With American wars in Afghanistan and Iraq still dominating newspaper headlines, Activision chose to breathe new life into the *Call of Duty* franchise with a decidedly closer-to-home release. In *Call of Duty 4: Modern Warfare*, released in 2007 for the PlayStation 3, Xbox 360, and PC, Activision dragged its popular series sixty years into the present, replacing M1 Garand rifles and M1A1 Thompson submachine guns with AK-47s and Barrett M82A1 sniper rifles. Instead of 1944, *Modern Warfare* took place in 2011, when conflict in the Middle East set off a chain of events that ignited a civil war in Russia. The game was the bestselling title of the year, selling seven million copies by 2008.

RATED M
FOR MATURE

Although video games are often associated with children, according to the Entertainment Software Association, the average age of video game players is thirty-five, and nearly three-quarters of the video game–playing population is eighteen or older. As gamers have come of age, so have the games they choose to play. While lovable Mario and Pac-Man remain perennial video game powerhouses, popular games such as *Call of Duty: Modern Warfare 2*, *The Last of Us*, *The Walking Dead*, and *Grand Theft Auto V* appeal to adult players looking for more mature, ethically complex stories and worlds to interact with.

The series reached its crescendo with *Call of Duty: Modern Warfare 2*, released in 2009. Taking place five years after events in *Modern Warfare*, the game features many of the same characters as its predecessor. After ultranationalists seized control of Russia, terrorists seek revenge on the West by staging attacks throughout Europe. Playing through various storylines involving the elite British counter-terrorist unit Task Force 141 and the United States Army Rangers, players must infiltrate deep into enemy territory and stop the ultranationalists from inciting global war. *Modern Warfare 2* controversially included a mission in which players, controlling an undercover CIA operative attempting to gain the trust of a Russian terrorist group, participate in a mass shooting at a Moscow airport. While gamers were not forced to actually shoot pedestrians, and were given the option of skipping the mission, the game warned the content might be found "disturbing or offensive."

Despite the controversy, *Modern Warfare 2* was a massive bestseller, selling nearly five million copies within twenty-four hours. Grossing more than $310 million on its first day on sale in the U.S. and U.K., the game was the biggest game launch of its time, and eventually brought in more than $1 billion in revenue. The recipient of numerous Game of the Year awards, *Modern Warfare 2* is credited with reinventing the first-person shooter genre by injecting a degree of realism and international intrigue rarely seen in games.

MODERN WARFARE 2 IS CREDITED WITH REINVENTING THE FIRST-PERSON SHOOTER GENRE BY INJECTING A DEGREE OF REALISM AND INTERNATIONAL INTRIGUE RARELY SEEN IN GAMES.

MINECRAFT

(2011)

Kids have played with construction toys for hundreds of years, but *Minecraft* gave them the tools to build an unimaginable array of fantastical buildings, brick by 8-bit brick.

One of the earliest forms of play is also one of the most complex: construction. As the famed American pediatrician Dr. Benjamin Spock once said, "A child loves his play not because it's easy, but because it's hard." The building block has long been a favorite toy. In the nineteenth century, toy manufacturers such as F. Ad. Richter of Germany and S.L. Hill of New York City began producing building toys in mass quantities for children. Soon vast quantities of construction materials filled children's nurseries—the physical playgrounds of middle-class and more affluent children. In the twentieth century, Erector Sets, LEGO blocks, Tinkertoys, and other new forms of building toys delighted kids.

This curious impulse to build follows us to adulthood, and even to the digital realm. The building game *Minecraft* has become a global phenomenon with endless gameplay possibilities enabling players to make their own creations using sets of pixilated blocks that they mine and use to build fabulous structures. *Minecraft* has also become a worldwide community in which gamers of all ages don't just play but also chat, share videos, ask questions, kibitz, and learn from one another. The game has sold more than 120 million copies across all platforms and continues to provide new and exciting ways for children and adults to build.

"Losing is fun!" is the unofficial motto of *Dwarf Fortress*, an indie video game in various stages of de-velopment since 2002 in which players controlled a merry band of dwarves who attempt to create an opulent underground fortress—and, invariably, find new and spectacular ways to die. For many, the game came across as gobbledygook; the graphics were made up of letters, numbers, and other keyboard characters. An invading spider, for instance, was represented by the letter *S*, while mineable minerals were designated with the British pound symbol. From a distance, *Dwarf Fortress* looked like the green cascading source code from the Matrix films. Nevertheless, the game developed a cult following, and one of its biggest fans was a Swedish computer programmer named Markus Persson. A lover of

LEGOs as a child, Persson was enthralled by the game's "fortress mode," which allowed players to construct battlements and assign tasks to individual dwarves. For Persson, detailed graphics meant leaving less to the human imagination. The simpler the graphics, the better he could imagine them.

Persson was also in love with the indie gaming scene as much as he was with *Dwarf Fortress* itself. Without money-grubbing corporate raiders hampering creative vision, he reasoned, a truly independent developer could do whatever he or she wanted. For Persson, who had worked at two of Sweden's most successful software publishers, Jalbum and Midasplayer, that meant a truly open game with no rules besides having fun. He began to dream up his own idea for a game, one that combined the simplistic graphics of *Dwarf Fortress* with the construct-whatever-you-want dynamics of his two other favorite games, *RollerCoaster Tycoon* and *Dungeon Keeper*. The former was an amusement park simulator that let players build and manage roller coasters, while the latter tasked players with building caves and populating them with monsters and traps to ward off treasure hunters.

Persson's initial sketches were for an open-ended game controlled via a top-down perspective, much like *Dwarf Fortress* and most other strategy games. However, after happening upon an indie game called *Infiniminer* one evening, he suddenly changed his mind. *Infiniminer* took place in a LEGO-like 3-D world in which players carved tunnels into the ground to extract minerals. But instead of being guided by an overhead perspective, players navigated the world like in a first-person shooter, but with axes instead of guns. Unfortunately, just weeks after its release,

hackers breached *Infiniminer*'s source code and posted it on the internet, allowing anyone to make changes and release their own version. Zachary Barth, *Infiniminer*'s creator, lost control of the game and ultimately gave his blessing to fans to make their own changes.

Persson had his opening. He hastily reengineered his build-anything game into a first-person perspective and made his already blocky graphics even more LEGO-like. In a few frenzied weeks, the game that would become *Minecraft* took form. The world was composed almost entirely of cubes representing everything from dirt to ore to lava. Players could then "mine" cubes by breaking them and placing them in new locations using a 3-D grid. *Minecraft*'s world was essentially infinite, with new terrain generated the more players explored. From underground labyrinths to vast cathedrals to imposing castles to sky fortresses to replicas of the White House and Taj Mahal, the possibilities were endless.

While there were traditional video game elements in *Minecraft*, such as hostile monsters in survival mode who attack players as they build, the objectives were self-generated and the tasks self-assigned. Psychologists note that intrinsic motivation is almost always a more powerful spur to effort than extrinsic motivation, and *Minecraft* offered self-motivation in spades, as players concentrated on what they could create rather than on what score they achieved. In single-player mode, players could choose to build their own personal world of one, while multiplayer mode allowed them to join private or public servers to interact with (or battle) others in a single world.

Persson released *Minecraft* to the public in May 2009 via the TIGSource forums, a popular hangout for indie game developers. Known on the forums as "Notch," Persson invited his fellow gamers to test *Minecraft* and offer criticisms. He constantly blogged about his updates to the game, publicizing bug fixes and soliciting feedback from amateur and professional developers alike. But *Minecraft* was not destined to be just an oasis for indie gamers who detested rules; Persson also intended to make money from it. A lot of money. For the first stable public release of the game, known as the alpha phase, he charged players a one-time fee of $13—a price that would double once the game was complete. He did not base this pay model on any sort of established formula, but merely a hunch that he should begin charging for the game early. "I knew that I would never feel that it was good enough to put a price tag on. So I charged from the start," he later told *Wired*.

Minecraft fostered a community in which individuals played and socialized with friends on dedicated servers or with strangers from all around the world. The game has become a powerful introduction not only to computers but to the creation process, especially for children. It was this diverse and devoted community that impelled Microsoft to purchase Mojang, Persson's company, for $2.5 billion, a testament to *Minecraft*'s ability to serve as a gateway into the digital world—which it is for more than 120 million people. As of 2017, *Minecraft* is the second bestselling video game of all time behind *Tetris*.

In the end, *Minecraft*'s power is not measured in sales but in compelling gameplay that is both new in its digital form and old in its basic structure. Rather than a high-octane graphical engine, *Minecraft* is powered by the same imaginative wonder that has fueled play for millennia. In 1910, the pioneering fantasy writer Edith Nesbit described a lonely boy playing with blocks in a strange house in much the same way a similar boy could interact with *Minecraft* today:

> By armfuls, two and three at a time, he carried down the boxes of bricks and the boxes of blocks, the draughts, the chessmen, and the box of dominoes.
> . . . He cleared a big writing-table of such useless and unimportant objects as blotting-pad, silver inkstand, and red-backed books, and there was a clear space for his city.
> He began to build.
> . . . He worked hard and he worked cleverly, and as the cities grew in beauty and interestingness he loved them more and more. He was happy now. There was no time to be unhappy in.

SKYLANDERS

(2011)

Toys come to life in the hit video game series Skylanders. For kids, the effect felt magical. In reality, it was the result of the artful use of technology. This prototype of the game's portal was cobbled together from a paper bowl and basic electronics.

n recent decades, the idea of childhood play has shifted to the virtual world as video games introduce children to magical creatures and wondrous new worlds. Yet until a division of Activision called Toys for Bob debuted *Skylanders: Spyro's Adventure*, no form of play had bridged the divide between the physical and the virtual. It began with a simple question: Can toys come to life?

In the early 1980s, before he thought about a career in game design, Paul Reiche III wanted to be a geologist. A student at the University of California, Berkeley, he loved studying rocks, glaciers, waterfalls, and other wonders of the natural world. These plans were dashed when he discovered that poison oak, to which he was extremely allergic, was especially prevalent in ravines, where field geologists make their living studying fault lines. "I puffed up like a giant bright red marshmallow," he told *Polygon* in 2014. "I had to do something else, so I started making games." Just as he loved studying the geological building blocks of Earth, Reiche was fascinated with the makeup of fictional worlds. In particular, he obsessed over *Dungeons & Dragons* (page 61) and daydreamed about its world and the creatures who lived there. It was through the legendary role-playing game that he met Fred Ford, connecting over a mutual love for fantastical monsters.

After graduation, Ford worked as a programmer for various game companies while Reiche worked at TSR, then the publisher of *Dungeons & Dragons*, and later Electronic Arts, where he worked on *Mail Order Monsters*, a monster-making action strategy game, and *Archon: The Light and the Dark*, a chess-based strategy game featuring pieces that fight each other to determine which player wins a square. But the two

friends never forgot their love of creating virtual worlds, and they decided to join forces to create their own company in 1989.

They called their company Toys for Bob, although they didn't make toys and there was no one named Bob affiliated with the company; Reiche's wife, Laurie, chose the name to help the studio stand out in a crowded video game market. Their first title was a dogfighting game set in outer space called *Star Control,* released in 1990 for MS-DOS and the Commodore Amiga. For the next ten years, Toys for Bob dabbled in 3-D fighting games, action strategy games, and platformers before taking on contracts to produce licensed games such as Eidos Interactive's *102 Dalmatians* and *Extreme Skate Adventure* by Disney and Activision, respectively. In 2005, Activision purchased Toys for Bob outright and set them up with a steady stream of contract work, including two games based on DreamWorks Animation's *Madagascar* films. Toys for Bob was good at quickly pumping out licensed games, but revenues plummeted as the market became saturated with what many considered a very formulaic genre. Activision not-too-subtly hinted to Reiche and Ford that they needed to come up with an original idea, and fast.

As the Toys for Bob team brainstormed ideas, Reiche and Ford kept returning to their old love of fantastical monsters. "Then somewhere along the line, somebody came up with the idea of 'making toys come to life,'" Robert Leyland, a technical engineer at Toys for Bob later said in an interview. "And we thought: That's good, that's fantastic, in hindsight the best idea we've ever had." In short, players would be able to purchase a monster figurine, hook it up to a game console, and interact with it in a video game. I-Wei Huang, a designer who dabbled in physical toy construction in his spare time, began drafting ideas for monsters and modeling them with computer software. But it was up to Leyland to figure out how to link the toys to a gaming system. To make the toys sleek and elegant, they would have to connect wirelessly while not using cumbersome batteries. But how?

Like Huang, Leyland had a side hobby that proved useful: he loved taking electronics apart and putting them back together. Over the years he had discovered ways to hack the Nintendo Wii's motion-control remote, and he quickly cobbled together a "portal" that could connect to the Wii. Then, using embedded radio-frequency identification (RFID) chips—the same technology used in electronic tolls and identification implants for pets, among countless other uses—the monster figurines could be placed on the portal and appear virtually in a video game. Leyland's first working prototype was rather crude: a paper plate scribbled with the word PORTAL hastily attached to an RFID sensor. But it worked—the program could determine which figurine was standing on the portal at any moment.

Reiche and Ford's bosses were thrilled with the idea and encouraged them to marry the technology to any brand in Activision's large stable of intellectual property. Reiche and Ford chose Spyro, a purple dragon who was featured in an eponymous line of video games in the late 1990s for the Sony PlayStation. By the time they plucked Spyro out of mothballs, he had been all but forgotten. But he had just enough name recognition to catch the market's attention while allowing Toys for Bob to create an all-new world for him. The eventual game was called *Skylanders: Spyro's Adventure*, in which players assumed the role of a powerful portal master able to control thirty-two mythical creatures called Skyland-

ers, who have been expelled from their world, Skylands, by an evil portal master named Kaos. Frozen in our own world as toys, the player must use her portal to send them back to Skylands to fight Kaos and save the land from destruction.

Released for the Wii, PlayStation 3, 3DS, and Wii U in October 2011, *Skylanders* invaded the toy and video game markets. It was the third most profitable game by the following summer, and by December 2012 had grossed more than $500 million in U.S. retail sales. *Skylanders* vastly outperformed Activision's expectations, with the series' six core titles topping $3 billion in sales and over 250 million toys sold by 2017. By requiring players to purchase the *Skylanders* game in addition to individual Skylander figures, the franchise has proved to be a gold mine for Activision and has inspired numerous toys-to-life series including *Disney Infinity*, *LEGO Dimensions*, and Nintendo's *Amiibo*. There are now scores of playable Skylander characters aligned to a single element: air, dark, earth, fire, life, light, magic, tech, undead, or water—each with its strengths and weaknesses. The game used a rock-paper-scissors dynamic, with, for example, Smolderdash (fire) strong against Whirlwind (air) who was strong against Slobber Tooth (earth) who was strong against Chopper (tech), and so on.

Skylanders was the right game at the right time, arriving in an era witnessing a convergence of the real and the virtual, from A.I. assistants like Alexa and Cortana to augmented-reality devices to driverless cars to homes that can be controlled from a smartphone app. The Skylander figures could be tossed around the carpet like traditional toys and then booted into a virtual world where their personalities truly came to life. By merging the digital with the tactile, *Skylanders* has shepherded play into a new era.

NANCY DREW:

TOMB OF THE LOST QUEEN

(2012)

What's the power of a game? The Make-A-Wish Foundation helped Rachel Vaughn, a seventeen-year-old girl with terminal cancer, meet the Her Interactive team, which produced the bestselling line of Nancy Drew computer games. After Rachel passed away, her family wrote this note to the development team to express their thanks.

Rachel Elysse Vaughn loved mysteries. In particular, she loved the Nancy Drew Mystery Stories series, first published in 1930 and by the 2000s comprising more than 150 books that had collectively sold tens of millions of copies. Rachel also loved computer games, none more than Her Interactive's catalog of Nancy Drew mystery games. The Nancy Drew books and games helped Rachel endure a year-long battle with kidney cancer, which tragically cut her life short at just seventeen years old. In her last year, the Make-A-Wish Foundation arranged to have Rachel meet the Her Interactive team, who dedicated their upcoming title, *Nancy Drew: Tomb of the Lost Queen*, to her.

Nancy Drew has captured the imagination of girls since her fictional debut in 1930. Originally created by Edward Stratemeyer—whose Stratemeyer Syndicate also produced the Hardy Boys, the Bobbsey Twins, Tom Swift, and other mainstays of popular juvenile literature—Nancy Drew epitomized the "new woman" of the era. The Nineteenth Amendment gave the sexes equality in voting in 1920. Soon after, female participation in workplaces and universities soared, and the automobile offered many women newfound mobility and freedom. Nancy Drew fired the imagination of her readers as she raced across the countryside in her blue roadster, hunting clues, collaring bad guys, and solving mysteries.

In the 1930s and '40s, she was depicted as an assertive, outspoken sixteen-year-old wunderkind who balanced her crime-solving with arts, athletics, and volunteer work. The 1950s saw Nancy's tomboy affect somewhat tamed as bowdlerized versions of the books made her more deferential to adults, particularly men. In the 1980s, she became more interested in boys and dating. Despite her many changes over the twentieth century, Nancy Drew remained a heroic example to young girls who admired her courage, adventurousness, and quick-thinking.

The late 1990s finally saw the release of a video game adaptation. While boys and girls alike have enjoyed the most popular video games of all time, game designers have often oriented their business toward one demographic: boys. Even Nintendo, a company that famously appealed to the entire family, featured very few female protagonists in its games, with some notable exceptions, such as Samus Aran from *Metroid* (although the player must complete the game in under five hours for this secret to be revealed).

Sixty-nine years after Nancy Drew's literary debut, Her Interactive began creating games infused with her trademark smarts and spunk. The company had released its first game in 1995, a dating sim targeted at girls called *McKenzie & Co.*, followed a year later by *The Vampire Diaries*, based on Lisa Smith's series of teen romantic thrillers, but it found its true subject when it turned to the teenage sleuth. In 1998, it released *Nancy Drew: Secrets Can Kill*, the first of more than twenty titles about the girl detective. Collectively, they have sold more than nine million copies. Her Interactive's singular focus on games for girls separates it from almost every other game company over the last two decades. Guided for many years by Megan Gaiser, Her Interactive has persevered in the face of conventional wisdom that gaming was for boys—an early company slogan proclaimed that Her Interactive made "games for girls who aren't afraid of a mouse."

Tomb of the Lost Queen was the twenty-sixth installment in Her Interactive's Nancy Drew series. Like the other games, it was a point-and-click adventure game in which players assume the first-person perspective of Nancy Drew. As in the blockbuster game *Myst* (page 235), players navigated with the mouse to solve puzzles and discover clues. Set in Cairo, *Tomb of the Lost Queen* follows Nancy Drew as she joins a group of archaeologists unearthing a tomb purported to hold the final resting place of Egypt's fabled Lost Queen. Nancy must discover the cause of a recent spate of suspicious accidents while uncovering the mysteries of the tomb, which was rumored to be cursed and booby-trapped. This game and many others in the Nancy Drew series was the product of extensive focus testing. For their games, Her Interactive convened an advisory panel of young girls to test the puzzles and other gameplay features. With a strong set of data, Her Interactive could determine what sort of game elements its audience desired, leading fans like Rachel Vaughn to come back again and again for more.

In 2013, Her Interactive donated to The Strong a large collection of games, design drafts, memoranda, press materials, focus group studies, player correspondence, and other materials documenting the company's history, the development of its Nancy Drew games, and the attitudes of girls toward gaming over the past two decades. Her Interactive enjoyed an especially close relationship with its fans, and the company's donation encompasses fan mail, walkthroughs, business studies, surveys, and countless other materials that show how integral young women were to developing what would become a blockbuster franchise. One such document is a card from Rachel's mother and father, who thanked Her Interactive for granting Rachel's final wish. When Rachel could not visit the company's headquarters due to her deteriorating condition, some of the team members traveled to the hospital to meet Rachel and fulfilled her wish to be featured as a character in an upcoming *Nancy Drew* computer game. Their note is a testament to the power of games to move us in deep and meaningful ways.

"Though Rachel passed away shortly after her wish was granted," her parents wrote, "we are confident she was aware and held on just long enough to experience it. . . . We will remember the way you honored our family and treasure the experience."

POKÉMON GO

(2016)

Augmented reality became a pop-culture phenomenon with the explosive success of *Pokémon Go*. Adults and kids alike took their phones into previously unexplored places in the real world to hunt for virtual creatures like Pikachu, Squirtle, and the elusive Dragonite.

At first, it seemed like any other July weekend in 2016: In New York City, a scorching heat wave had passed and the weather was sunny and cool. In San Francisco, Madison Bumgarner twirled a magnificent one-hit, fourteen-strikeout gem as the Giants defeated the Arizona Diamondbacks four to nothing during a pleasant late Sunday afternoon. But something was off. This was the modern era, of course, and seeing people buried in their smartphones was nothing new—yet this weekend, Americans nationwide seemed especially glued to their screens. Although Bumgarner had sustained a no-hitter until the eighth inning, the normally frenzied fans seemed distracted, gazing into their phones as they twisted and contorted in their seats. In New York, hordes of pedestrians stormed into quiet, rarely trodden corners of Central Park. In Daytona Beach, Florida, a marauding band of smartphone-wielding hunters appeared at the Supreme Beans Coffee Shop. "Because you're a gym," they testily informed the owner, who asked why her normally sleepy café was suddenly awash in patrons. Indeed, this was no normal weekend—*Pokémon Go* had arrived, and mobile gaming would never be the same.

Today's smartphones offer a cornucopia of choices inconceivable to users who back in the late 1990s were satisfied playing *Snake*, a clone of the arcade game *Blockade* (1976), on their Nokia phone. Before mobile phones, portable video game systems like the Game Boy, PSP, and 3DS proved the best option for gameplay, Nintendo's Game Boy line dominated portable gaming after its debut in 1989 because it excelled in providing great content at an affordable price, with long-lasting battery performance.

This all changed in July 2008, when Apple opened the floodgates for mobile app development with its App Store. While the company's popular smartphone, the iPhone, had been available for a year, third-party developers were not allowed to create their own mobile programs. The App Store officially unshackled the iPhone, and the library of apps exploded from barely five hundred in 2008 to more than two million today. Google soon followed suit with the launch of its Android operating system, which was designed from the ground up to include third-party apps and now counts nearly three million apps. And, every year, games prove to be the single biggest moneymaker for app developers. In 2016, for instance, more than 80 percent of revenue in the App Store was from games, with the average owner spending $27. One of the earliest blockbuster games was *Angry Birds*, a series of games that have been downloaded more than two billion times since 2010.

Pokémon Go's story begins with a company called Niantic Labs, which was originally formed as a startup wholly owned by Google. Experimenting with location-based technology, Niantic believed the ultimate virtual world could be our actual world. Using GPS, players could turn their own lives and neighborhoods into a video game. The result was a game called *Ingress*, an augmented-reality game in which players sought "portals" based on real-life landmarks such as public art installations, libraries, and museums. Players joined one of two opposing factions, the Enlightened and the Resistance, in hopes of capturing enemy portals and establishing control fields over certain geographic areas. As the game became more popular, players populated some fifteen million real-life sites with portals. While the dynamics of *Ingress* could be complex, the premise was simple: players had to physically move to locations to play it, where they might meet anyone (including, in some cases, future spouses).

In 2014, Nintendo's affiliate, the Pokémon Company, teamed up with Google to create an April Fools' Day joke in which mobile phone users caught Pokémon using Google Maps. It was a short-lived gag, but it piqued the interest of John Hanke, chief executive of Niantic Labs. What if, Hanke thought, people could catch Pokémon in real life using the same augmented-reality technology that powered *Ingress*? He pitched the idea to Tsunekazu Ishihara of the Pokémon Company, who was a fan of *Ingress* and immediately saw the potential for ordinary people to "catch" Pokémon using their mobile phones. Using Google Maps data and crowd-sourced portal locations from *Ingress*, Niantic began designing its new venture, *Pokémon Go*.

Players started by creating a game account and customizing an avatar with their iPhone or Android-equipped smartphone. A map overlay based on Google Maps pinpointed the player's location, with landmarks and businesses replaced with Pokéstops and Pokémon gyms. The former provided players with items, such as berries, potions, and Poké Balls (used to catch Pokémon), while the latter served as battle arenas for the game's three rival factions, Team Valor, Team Mystic, and Team Instinct—one of which a player could join upon reaching level five.

But the true genius of *Pokémon Go* lay in its augmented reality. As players moved throughout their real-world surroundings, the *Pokémon Go* app used their individual smartphone's GPS and internal clock to determine when and where they confronted wild Pokémon. For players wandering around parks, for instance, they were more likely to confront grass- and bug-type Pokémon, such as Bulbasaurs and Metapods, respectively. As for those trudging by lakes and ponds, Squirtles and Poliwags were much more likely to be con-

PIGS IN CLOVER

Hanheld games have had a long history. During the late nineteenth century, a handheld ball game called *Pigs in Clover*—in which players rolled small balls, or "pigs," through a maze to a "pen" at the center—became the must-have toy. In 1889, New York Senator William M. Evarts purchased the game from a street vendor and brought it to work the next day. Before long, the game had supposedly impeded the work of the United State Senate, stalling President Benjamin Harrison's agenda as lawmakers became obsessed with the game's ball-rolling challenge. A few days later the *New York World* lampooned their lack of productivity with a political cartoon depicting lawmakers as pigs and the White House as a pig pen. The caption read: "Will Mr. Harrison be able to get all these hungry pigs in the official pen?"

fronted. In augmented-reality mode, the *Pokémon Go* app used the smartphone's camera and gyroscope to superimpose a wild Pokémon on the screen as if it were in the real world. And by tapping on a Poké Ball and flicking it upward, a player could attempt to catch it.

Pokémon Go was quite literally an overnight sensation, skyrocketing to the top of the App Store's "Top Grossing" and "Free" charts—a reflection of the game's "freemium" model, which allowed users to play for free while purchasing in-game power-ups. *Pokémon Go* was the most downloaded app on the App store by the end of its first week, and SurveyMonkey determined it had become the most active mobile game *ever*, with twenty-one million users. Within two days it had been downloaded on 5 percent of all Android devices in the U.S., and reached one hundred million downloads on Google Play after barely a month. In August 2016, *Guinness World Records* awarded *Pokémon Go* five world records for achieving various revenue and download milestones, including fastest mobile game to gross $100 million—a feat it accomplished in just twenty days.

Criticism inevitably followed in the wake of *Pokémon Go*'s success. Some stories claimed that the game led to increased car accidents due to distracted driving or that thieves were using the game to lure players into dark alleys to be mugged. Such fears are common every time large numbers of people engage in a new fad. And controversy was nothing new to the Pokémon franchise. During the height of the Pokémon playing-card phase, many U.K. school districts banned the cards, worried about the effect of "bullying, intimidation and 'aggressive trading' among children desperate to complete their collections of 150 cards," while some police organizations in the U.S. denigrated Pokémon as "America's most dangerous hobby."

More interesting were critiques about the game's unique, real-world location features. Especially noteworthy were concerns over the game's initial use of cemeteries and memorials—including the United States Holocaust Museum and the National September 11 Memorial & Museum—as sites to catch Pokémon. Game designers quickly moved to eliminate these sites from the game. Other commentators, while glad that players were out and about, lamented how kids were staring at their phones looking for fictional monsters rather than observing real nature.

Perhaps there is no going back to a time when we experienced the real world unmediated from our devices. *Pokémon Go*'s strange, cute virtual monsters have brought players together to revolutionize a new form of play, one in which the virtual and the real have become inseparable. In that way, maybe *Pokémon Go* is not merely a game, but a foretaste of an augmented-reality future.

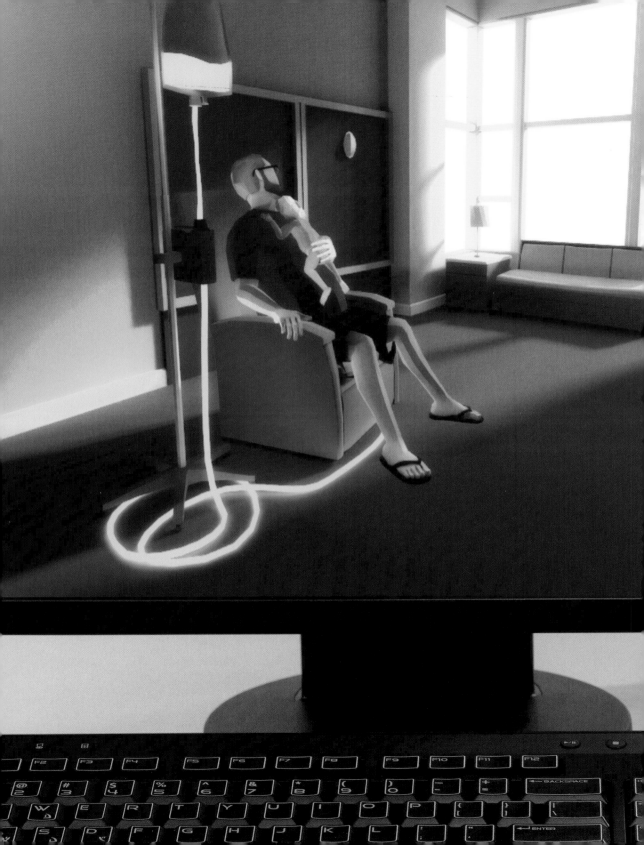

THAT DRAGON, CANCER

(2016)

Over their long history, video games have inspired us not only with their technological prowess, but with their deep stories. *That Dragon, Cancer* showed that games could speak to even the rawest of human emotions.

At the 2013 PAX Prime, the largest annual video game expo in the U.S., an unusually large crowd lingered in a far corner of the fourth floor, where indie developers were showing off their latest releases. The majority of gamers typically meander their way between the big-ticket booths, such as Activision or Electronic Arts, to play the latest release of Call of Duty or Madden NFL. But during that day in early September, a stream of players cautiously wandered to game developer Ryan Green's booth. As they left, many were in tears and grabbing for the Kleenex box strategically placed next to the game monitor. For the demo did not involve blasting aliens or shooting Nazis; it was an autobiographical game depicting the Green family's experiences raising their son, Joel, who was diagnosed with terminal cancer at his first birthday.

Ryan, a developer for Soma Games, began working on *That Dragon, Cancer* in November 2012, when Joel was nearly four years old. After doctors gave Joel just four months to live in 2010, the boy endured crushing rounds of chemotherapy, steroids, and tumors that impacted his ability to see and eat. These and countless other setbacks would have incapacitated adults, much less a toddler. And yet Ryan and his wife, Amy, both devout Christians, were overjoyed that their son had continued to live on despite a terrible prognosis. For Ryan, the idea to build a game based on his family's experiences came to him in church, when he reflected on a particularly bad night when Joel was having a terrible reaction to his cancer treatment. "There's a process you develop as a parent to keep your child from crying, and that night I couldn't calm Joel," Ryan told *Wired* in 2016. "It made me think, 'This is like

a game where the mechanics are subverted and don't work.'"

With the help of his friend and developer Josh Larson, Ryan began building a simple game in which players were in a hospital room with Ryan, helping him ease Joel's suffering. But no matter what they tried, from gently rocking Joel to feeding him, they could not calm him down. The scene ended with Ryan's voice becoming increasingly strained, despairing over his lack of power to help Joel. For Ryan, the game acted as a catharsis, helping him to express his overwhelming pain in an artistic medium he was comfortable working with. The game also resonated deeply with players, many of whom were parents and could relate to the struggles of putting a child to sleep and feelings of powerlessness in the face of health problems.

The demo of *That Dragon, Cancer* was widely celebrated within the indie game community for taking risks that no major publisher would dare take. As Jenn Frank wrote after playing the game at the 2013 Game Developer's Conference, "We will all meet this thing, or have already met it. Maybe that should be scary, but *That Dragon, Cancer* is about sustaining the hope and joy of life for just as long as we can." Joel's condition continued to worsen, so Ryan took time off from his full-time job to finish the game. As Amy, Ryan, and Larson devoted ever more of their time to expanding the game, they formed the studio Numinous Games in hope of creating a distribution network. *That Dragon, Cancer* morphed into an exploration game using both the first- and third-person perspective, reliving various vignettes that captured some of the most profound moments of the Greens' experience with their son.

Joel died in the early hours of March 14,

2014. After five years of enduring tumors that had grown and shrunk and grown again, he'd had enough. In the wake of his death, Amy, Ryan, and Larson decided to change the tenor of the game, one that more effectively honored Joel's life and recreated the good moments as well as the bad. "We decided to focus more on who Joel was and what it was like to be with him and to love him," Larson told *The New Yorker*'s Simon Parkin in 2015. "We moved from focusing on the plot of Joel to focusing on the character of Joel." *That Dragon, Cancer* beautifully synthesized animation with magical realism to depict the Greens' journey as they learned of their son's diagnosis, cherished the rare, happy moments, and, like so many other families facing heartbreaking adversity, ventured into the unknown.

There were no dragons to be slain in *That Dragon, Cancer*, for it was made clear early in the game that the cancer would win. The game had no objectives, and unlike *Super Mario Bros.*, there were no extra lives to be gained. There was only one life in Ryan and Amy Green's masterpiece, and it was tragically cut short. While many video games make players feel powerful by equipping them with spectacular weapons to fight evil monsters, *That Dragon, Cancer* challenged them to be powerless. As players attempted to comfort Joel as he convulsed in his hospital bed from the toxic cocktail of chemotherapy drugs, there was no potion they could use to comfort him, no com-bination of buttons they could push to make it all better. The game was experienced, not beaten. Malika Zouhali-Worrall, a filmmaker who made a documentary called *Thank You for Playing* about the Greens' experience, later noted that one particular scene, set in a playground, seemed to resonate with players. "Nothing happens; you just hear Joel's laughter," she told *The New Yorker*. "Time and again, I've watched people just stay there, quietly pushing Joel's avatar on the swing. That opportunity to linger can be profound."

"Can a computer make you cry?" Electronic Arts posed this question in an advertisement in 1983 when the company, now a multibillion-dollar brand and the second-largest video game producer in the world, was a fledgling upstart trying to raise the bar for electronic games. "Until now, the people who asked such questions tended not to be the same people who ran software companies," EA's ad said. "Instead, they were writers, filmmakers, painters, musicians. They were, in the traditional sense, artists." In the decades since, video game designers have made strides to redefine the definition of "art." In their eyes, a video game can be just as affecting as a tear-jerking song, a haunting poem, or a tragic novel. It's not the medium that matters, but the stories they tell. The Green family proved in perhaps the most heartbreaking way imaginable that video games could indeed be an art form—one that could most certainly make you cry.

Acknowledgments

Thank you to the many people who contributed to *A History of Video Games in 64 Objects*. The Strong's World Video Game Hall of Fame acknowledges and appreciates Nicholas Bromley for his contributions. He was a wonderful writing partner throughout this process. Matthew Daddona at Dey Street Books first approached us about doing this book and ably guided its production. Walter Colley, with the assistance of Maria Spinelli, made the artifacts shine with his skilled photography. At The Strong, many people contributed greatly to this book's production. Shannon Symonds, Andrew Borman, Martin Reinhardt, Hillary Ellis, Julia Novakovic, and Beth Lathrop all played crucial roles, not only in working on this book but also in acquiring, caring for, and conserving the objects featured in it. Other members of the collections team, especially Victoria Gray, Chris Bensch, Nicolas Ricketts, Michelle Parnett-Dwyer, and Tara Winner-Swete, have also contributed enormously. Suzanne Seldes worked tirelessly to master innumerable essential details, while Shane Rhinewald and Noelle McElrath-Hart played key roles steering publicity and marketing efforts. Kelly Lucyszyn was indispensable, guiding photography and design, as well as helping to edit the manuscript in its final stages. Mike Rae helped with cover design brainstorming. This book was made possible because of the leadership of The Strong's president and CEO, Steve Dubnik, as well as that of his predecessor, G. Rollie Adams, who spearheaded The Strong's establishment of the International Center for the History of Electronic Games and the World Video Game Hall of Fame. Everything we do at The Strong is a team effort and we want to thank all of our colleagues who help make the museum the ultimate play destination. Lastly, thank you to all the people and companies who have donated artifacts and supported The Strong's efforts to collect, preserve, and interpret the history of video games. This book is a testament to your support.

With gratitude,
Jon-Paul Dyson and Jeremy Saucier

Notes

HUMPTY DUMPTY (1947)

2 "slimy crews of tinhorns": Conor Friedersdorf, "The Mayor Who Took a Sledgehammer to NYC's Pinball Machines," *The Atlantic*, posted January 18, 2013, https://www.thatlantic .com/politics/archive/2013/01/the-mayor-who-took-a -sledgehammer-to-nycs-pinball-machines/267309/

TENNIS FOR TWO (1958)

6 "convey the message that our scientific endeavors have relevance for society": Brookhaven National Laboratory, "The First Video Game?" https://www.bnl.gov/about/history /firstvideo.php

7 "The real innovation in this game": Brookhaven National Laboratory, "The First Video Game?"

7 "it didn't seem likely that anyone would want to spend much time": Kristen J. Nyitray, "William Alfred Higinbotham: Scientist, Activist, and Computer Game Pioneer," *IEEE Annals of the History of Computing*, vol. 33, no. 00 (April–June 2011), 96–101, https://pdfs.semanticscholar.org/01eb /cfc6ec7186a21b2504483ee5861d2cf3ce8f.pdf

JOHN BURGESON'S BASEBALL GAME (1960)

11 "I am sorry you have felt it necessary to remove novelty type programs from the library": Jon-Paul Dyson, "The Oldest-Known Computer Baseball Simulation," *Play Stuff Blog*, posted June 20, 2014, http://www.museumofplay.org /blog/chegheads/2014/06/the-oldest-known-computer -baseball-simulation/

RALPH BAER'S BROWN BOX (1967)

23 "A piece of Jewish chutzpah": Arthur Molella, "How a WWII Refugee Became the Father of Video Games," *Slate*, posted December 7, 2015, http://www.slate.com/articles /technology/future_tense/2015/12/ralph_baer_father _of_video_games_was_a_german_jew_who_escaped _the_nazis.html

NINTENDO LOVE TESTER (1969)

27 "The Love Tester came from me wondering": Osamu Inoue. *Nintendo Magic: Winning the Videogame Wars*. New York: Vertical, 2010.

THE OREGON TRAIL (1971)

34 "Instead of shaking dice to determine how far you went": Kevin Wong, "The Forgotten History of *The Oregon Trail*, As Told by Its Creators," *Motherboard*, posted February 15, 2017, https://motherboard.vice.com/en_us/article/qkx8vw/the -forgotten-history-of-the-oregon-trail-as-told-by-its-creators

"SPACEWAR: FANATIC LIFE AND SYMBOLIC DEATH AMONG THE COMPUTER BUMS" IN *ROLLING STONE* (1972)

38 "the most advanced, imaginative, expensive pinball machine the world has seen": Levy, Stephen. *Hackers: Heroes of the Computer Revolution,* 25th anniversary edition (Sebastopol, CA: O'Reilly Media, Inc., 1984), 46.

38 "I discovered that drugs were less interesting than computers": Chris Baker, "Stewart Brand Recalls First *Spacewar* Video Game Tournament," *Rolling Stone*, posted May 25, 2016, http://www.rollingstone.com/culture /news/stewart-brand-recalls-first-spacewar-video-game -tournament-20160525

PONG (1972)

50 "But I thought it was too big a step for him": David Pescovitz, "Atari's 40th Anniversary," *Boing Boing*, posted June 27, 2012, https://boingboing.net/2012/06/27/ataris-40th -anniversary.html

101 BASIC COMPUTER GAMES (1973)

57 "It is practically impossible to teach good programming to students that have had a prior exposure to BASIC": Edsger W. Dijkstra, *Selected Writings on Computing: A Personal Perspective* (Springer-Verlag, 1982), 129–131.

BREAKOUT (1976)

72 "If I put Jobs on the night shift, I'd get two Steves for the price of one": Sam Colt, "A Young Steve Jobs Smelled So Bad He Had To Be Put On The Night Shift At Atari," *Business Insider*, posted August 22, 2014, http://www.businessinsider.com/steve-jobs-on-the-night-shift-at-atari-2014-8

72 "We worked day and night": Brian Ashcroft, "The Time Steve Jobs Got 'the Kissing Disease' (He Wasn't Making Out!)" *Kotaku*, posted October 26, 2011, https://kotaku.com/5853409/the-time-steve-jobs-got-the-kissing-disease-he-wasnt-making-out

73 "Since Jobs didn't really understand [*Breakout*]": Conor Murphy, "The History of *Breakout*," *Big Fish* (blog), posted May 30, 2012, http://www.bigfishgames.com/blog/the-history-of-breakout/

FAIRCHILD CHANNEL F (1976)

78 "I want you to go to Connecticut": Benj Edwards, "The Untold Story of the Invention of the Game Cartridge," *Fast Company*, posted January 22, 2015, https://www.fastcompany.com/3040889/the-untold-story-of-the-invention-of-the-game-cartridge

DEATH RACE (1976)

84 "In this game a player takes the first step to creating violence": Blumenthal, R., "*Death Race* Game Gains Favor, but Not with the Safety Council," *New York Times*, 1976, http://www.proquest.com.ezproxy.lib.utexas.edu/, retrieved September 22, 2010.

ATARI VIDEO COMPUTER SYSTEM (1977)

88 "In order to go into the consumer marketplace, we just needed much deeper pockets": David Becker, "The Return of King Pong," *CNET*, posted July 26, 2005, https://www.cnet.com/news/the-return-of-king-pong/

89 "In the beginning, all games were casual": John Gaudiosi, "Interview: Bushnell's NeoEdge Becomes Big Player with Yahoo! Games," *GameDaily* (July 10, 2008), http://archive.li/hWiYJ

SIMON (1978)

105 "More than a few youngsters are sure to be wearing long faces Christmas morning": "*Simon*, No. 1 Hit of Game Season, Is Sold Out," *Chicago Tribune*, December 20, 1978.

SPACE INVADERS (1978)

109 "*Space Invaders*. Before I saw it, I was never particularly interested in video games": Carolyn Sayre, "10 Questions for Shigeru Miyamoto," *Time*, posted July 19, 2007, https://web.archive.org/web/20070826025748/http://www.time.com/time/magazine/article/0%2C9171%2C1645158%2C00.html

ADVENTURELAND (1978)

112 "I had done it": "*Pirate's Adventure*," *Byte Magazine*, December 1980, 192, https://archive.org/stream/byte-magazine-1980-12/1980_12_BYTE_05-12_Adventure#page/n193/mode/2up

112 "Once she hid them in the oven": "*Pirate's Adventure*," *Byte Magazine*, December 1980, 192, https://archive.org/stream/byte-magazine-1980-12/1980_12_BYTE_05-12_Adventure#page/n193/mode/2up

SPEAK & SPELL (1978)

114 "As the business grew I learned as I went": Benj Edwards, "VC&G Interview: 30 Years Later, Richard Wiggins Talks *Speak & Spell* Development," *Vintage Computing and Gaming*, posted December 16. 2008, http://www.vintagecomputing.com/index.php/archives/528

ASTEROIDS (1979)

122 "little flying ship as in *Computer Space*": "The Making of *Asteroids*," *Retro Gamer*, September 2009, http://ataricade.videoarcade.it/Making_of_Asteroids.pdf

123 "I thought, okay, if he's dying three times and still putting in another quarter, he must think it's his fault": "The Making of *Asteroids*," *Retro Gamer*, September 2009, http://ataricade.videoarcade.it/Making_of_Asteroids.pdf

124 "*Asteroids* is a classic man-against-machine game": "The Making of *Asteroids*," *Retro Gamer*, September 2009, http://ataricade.videoarcade.it/Making_of_Asteroids.pdf

PAC-MAN (1980)

132 "In nightmares and in real life": Peter Gray, Ph.D., "Chasing Games and Sports: Why Do We Like to Be Chased?" *Psychology Today*, posted November 5, 2008, https://www.psychologytoday.com/blog/freedom-learn/200811/chasing-games-and-sports-why-do-we-be-chased

132 "In the late 1970s, there were a lot of games in arcades which featured killing aliens": Matt Peckham, "This Is What *Pac-Man*'s Creator Thinks 35 Years Later," *Time*, posted May 22, 2015, http://time.com/3892662/Pac-Mans-35-years/

MISSILE COMMAND (1980)

138 "Make me a game that looks like this": Alex Rubens, "The Creation of *Missile Command* and the Haunting of Its Creator, Dave Theurer," *Polygon*, posted August 15, 2013, https://www.polygon.com/features/2013/8/15/4528228/missile-command-dave-theurer

138 "Realizing that the bombs would kill all of the people in the targeted city": Rubens, "The Creation of *Missile Command*."

139 "That was the whole point of the game": Rubens, "The Creation of *Missile Command*."

UTOPIA (1981)

149 "Our dreams pick us": Chris Baker, "Don Daglow's 8 Keys to a Long Career in the Game Industry," *Gamasutra*, posted March 21, 2016, https://www.gamasutra.com/view/news/268509/Don_Daglows_8_keys_to_a_long_career_in_the_game_industry.php

RIVER RAID (1982)

153 "By knowing the river": "*River Raid*—Atari 2600—Activision" instruction manual on *Atari Age* website, https://atariage.com/manual_page.php?SystemID=2600&SoftwareLabelID=409&maxPages=6&currentPage=4

E.T. THE EXTRA-TERRESTRIAL (1982)

158 "Guards kept reporters and spectators away from the area": "Atari Parts Are Dumped," *New York Times*, September 28, 1983, http://www.nytimes.com/1983/09/28/business/atari-parts-are-dumped.html

159 "Yeah, it's got some problems": Keith Phipps, "Interview: Howard Scott Warshaw," *AV Club*, posted February 2, 2005, https://www.avclub.com/howard-scott-warshaw-1798208406

ONE-ON-ONE: DR. J VS. LARRY BIRD (1983)

162 "I considered the 2600 a toy": Patrick Sauer, "How Dr. J and Larry Bird Helped Build a Video Game Empire," *Vice Sports*, posted May 25, 2017, https://sports.vice.com/en_us/article/wje9kq/how-dr-j-and-larry-bird-helped-build-a-video-game-empire

PINBALL CONSTRUCTION SET (1983)

170 "sheer torture": Sharon Darling, "Birth of a Computer Game," *Compute!*, September 1985, 48, http://www.atarimagazines.com/compute/issue57/computer_game.html

170 "Trip was really pushing, and I was kind of stubborn": Chris Kohler, "Trailblazing DIY Pinball Game Snags Pioneer Award for Bill Budge," *Wired*, posted January 21, 2011, https://www.wired.com/2011/01/bill-budge-pioneer/

KING'S QUEST (1984)

174 "didn't even know how to plug a computer in": Liane Nooney, "A Pedestal, a Table, a Love Letter: Archaeologies of Gender in Videogame History," *Game Studies*, vol. 13, issue 2 (December 2013), http://gamestudies.org/1302/articles/nooney

175 "The machine has the smell of death about it": Philip Elmer-Dewitt, "A Flop Becomes a Hit," *Time*, December 24, 1984, http://content.time.com/time/magazine/article/0,9171,951424,00.html

175 "One can be a better mother from a kitchen table": Nooney, "A Pedestal, a Table, a Love Letter."

175 "Please continue to create forever": Nooney, "A Pedestal, a Table, a Love Letter."

TETRIS (1984)

178 "Everybody who touched this game couldn't stop playing it": Jimmy Maher, "A Tale of the Mirror World, Part 3: A Game of Falling Shapes," *The Digital Antiquarian* (blog), posted June 30, 2017, http://www.filfre.net/2017/06/a-tale-of-the-mirror-world-part-3-a-game-of-falling-shapes/

181 "*Tetris* made Game Boy and Game Boy made *Tetris*": Phil Hoad, "*Tetris*: How We Made the Addictive Computer Game," *The Guardian*, posted June 2, 2014, https://www.theguardian.com/culture/2014/jun/02/how-we-made-tetris

NINTENDO ENTERTAINMENT SYSTEM (1985)

186 "This could be a miscalculation on Nintendo's part": Steve Bloom (ed.), "Nintendo's Final Solution," Hotline, *Electronic Games*, March 1985, 9.

186 "Atari collapsed because they gave too much freedom to third-party developers": Liz Finnegan, "*E.T. the Extra-Terrestrial* Was the Most Important Video Game Ever Made," *The Escapist*, posted June 30, 2015, http://www.escapistmagazine.com/articles/view/video-games/columns/pixels-and-bits/14240-Disastrous-ET-Game-Buried-in-Arizona-Desert-Landfill-Was-Actuall

THE LEGEND OF ZELDA (1986)

194 "She was a famous and beautiful woman from all accounts": Todd Mowatt, "In the Game: Nintendo's Shigeru Miyamoto," Interview with Amazon.com. https://www.amazon.com/exec/obidos/tg/feature/-/117177/

JOHN MADDEN FOOTBALL (1990)

208 "I picked John because I wanted a design partner that could help us make the game authentic": Jeffrey Fleming, "We See Farther—A History of Electronic Arts," *Gamasutra*, posted February 16, 2007, https://www.gamasutra.com/view/feature/130129/we_see_farther_a_history_of_.php?

208 "If it was going to be me and going to be pro football": Patrick Hruby, "The Franchise: The inside Story of How Madden NFL Became a Video Game Dynasty," *ESPN Outside the Lines*, http://www.espn.com/espn/eticket/story?page=100805/madden

209 "Before *Madden*, jocks did not play video games": Hruby, "The Franchise."

210 "I used to say": Hruby, "The Franchise."

STREET FIGHTER II (1991)

215 "I think the crazy personalities of the staff showed in the gameplay": Leone, "*Street Fighter II*: An Oral History," Chapter 2.

SONIC THE HEDGEHOG (1991)

218 "Few have heard of it, even fewer have played it": Chris Kohler, "Playing the SG-1000, Sega's First Game Machine," *Wired*, posted October 2, 2009. https://www.wired.com/2009/10/sega-sg-1000/

MORTAL KOMBAT (1992)

224 "We wanted to call it *Van Damme*": Suriel Vazquez, "The Early Names for *Mortal Kombat* Were as Cheesy as You'd Expect," *Game Informer*, posted December 1, 2016, http://www.gameinformer.com/b/news/archive/2016/12/01/the-early-names-for-mortal-kombat-were-as-cheesy-youd-expect.aspx

MYST (1993)

237 "*Myst* seems to reflect the condition of the video game itself": Edward Rothstein, "A New Art Form May Arise From the *Myst*," *New York Times*, December 4, 1994, http://www.nytimes.com/1994/12/04/arts/a-new-art-form-may-arise-from-the-myst.html?pagewanted=all

NINTENDO VIRTUAL BOY (1995)

241 "Our problem with it was it was just one color": Benj Edwards, "Unraveling The Enigma Of Nintendo's Virtual Boy 20 Years Later," *Fast Company*, posted August 21, 2015, https://www.fastcompany.com/3050016/unraveling-the-enigma-of-nintendos-virtual-boy-20-years-later

POKÉMON (1996)

246 "That cable really got me interested": "The Ultimate Game Freak," *Time*, November 22, 1999, http://content.time.com/time/magazine/article/0,9171,2040095,00.html

THE SIMS (2000)

250 "The interesting part was to find out that I wasn't really that attached to much": Tracey Taylor, "Will Wright: Inspired to Make *The Sims* after Losing a Home," *Berkeleyside*, posted October 17, 2011, http://www.berkeleyside.com/2011/10/17/will-wright-inspired-to-make-the-sims-after-losing-a-home/

250 "I died": Matthew Yi, "Profile: Will Wright," SF Gate, posted November 3, 2003, http://www.sfgate.com/business/article/PROFILE-Will-Wright-Unsimulated-success-2579300.php

253 "*The Sims*, to a greater extent than anything else released": Chris Kohler, "The 15 Most Influential Games of the Decade," *Wired*, posted December 24, 2009, https://www.wired.com/2009/12/the-15-most-influential-games-of-the-decade/

GRAND THEFT AUTO III (2001)

263 "You can actually be very nice in [*GTA III*]": Bill Loguidice and Matt Barton, *Vintage Games: An Insider Look at the History of "Grand Theft Auto," "Super Mario," and the Most Influential Games of All Time.* Burlington, MA: Focal Press, (2009), 112.

HALO: COMBAT EVOLVED (2001)

266 "new meaning to the [word] 'fantastic.'": "Heavenly *Halo* Announced from Bungie," *IGN*, posted July 21, 1999, http://www.ign.com/articles/1999/07/22/heavenly-halo-announced-from-bungie

WII REMOTE (2006)

282 "Power isn't everything for a console": Arthur Cios, "How Nintendo CEO Satoru Iwata Changed Video Games Forever," *Konbini*, posted 2015, http://www.konbini.com/us/entertainment/nintendo-ceo-satoru-iwata-changed-video-games-forever/

283 "the moment in which the simplicity of early video games":

Jesper Juul, *A Casual Revolution*. Cambridge, MA: The MIT Press (2012), 2.

MINECRAFT (2011)

293 "I knew that I would never feel that it was good enough": Daniel Goldberg and Linus Larsson, "The Amazingly Unlikely Story of How *Minecraft* Was Born," *Wired*, posted November 5, 2013, https://www.wired.com/2013/11/minecraft-book/

294 "pioneering fantasy writer": Edith Nesbit, *The Magic City,* New York: Macmillan (1910), 15–16.

SKYLANDERS (2011)

298 "I puffed up like a giant bright red marshmallow": Colin Campbell, "Toys for Bob and the story behind *Skylanders*," *Polygon*, posted April 16, 2014, https://www.polygon.com/2014/4/16/5614716/skylanders-story-toys-for-bob-skylanders-swap-force

298 "Then somewhere along the line, somebody came up with the idea of 'making toys come to life'": Blake Maloof, "Alt. GDC: Developing *Skylanders*' Innovative 'Portal of Power,'" *Make:*, posted March 13, 2012, https://makezine.com/2012/03/13/alt-gdc-developing-skylanders-innovative-portal-of-power/

POKÉMON GO (2016)

308 "bullying, intimidation and 'aggressive trading'": Lana Polansky, "The World's Most Dangerous Game: *Pokémon*'s Strange History with Moral Panics," *Vice*, posted September 5, 2016, https://www.vice.com/sv/article/yvepdx/pokemon-go-moral-panics-satanism-infosec

THAT DRAGON, CANCER (2016)

312 "There's a process you develop as a parent": Jason Tanz, "Playing for Time," *Wired*, January 2016, https://www.wired.com/2016/01/that-dragon-cancer/

312 "We will all meet this thing, or have already met it": Jenn Frank, "Cancer, the Video Game," *Kotaku*, posted May 9, 2013, https://kotaku.com/cancer-the-video-game-471333034

313 "We decided to focus more on who Joel was and what it was like to be with him and to love him": Simon Parkin, "A Father's Video Game About His Son's Terminal Cancer," *New Yorker*, posted July 22, 2015, https://www.newyorker.com/culture/culture-desk/a-video-game-about-terminal-cancer

313 "Time and again, I've watched people just stay there": Parkin, "A Father's Video Game."

Sources

HUMPTY DUMPTY (1947)

Cohen, Stanley. *Folk Devils and Moral Panics*. New York: Routledge, 2011.

Flower, Gary and Bill Kurtz. *Pinball: The Lure of the Silver Ball*. New York: Chartwell Books, 1988.

Friedersdorf, Conor. "The Mayor Who Took a Sledgehammer to NYC's Pinball Machines." *The Atlantic*, posted January 18, 2013, https://www.theatlantic.com/politics/archive/2013/01/the-mayor-who-took-a-sledgehammer-to-nycs-pinball-machines/267309/

June, Laura. "For Amusement Only: The Life and Death of the American Arcade." *The Verge*, posted January 16, 2013, https://www.theverge.com/2013/1/16/3740422/the-life-and-death-of-the-american-arcade-for-amusement-only

Markey, Patrick M. and Christopher J. Ferguson. *Moral Combat: Why the War on Violent Video Games is Wrong*. Dallas, TX: BenBella Books, 2017.

Nagy, Attila. "Not Safe for Play? The Evolution of Pinball Games." *Gizmodo*, posted June 16, 2015, http://gizmodo.com/not-safe-for-play-the-evolution-of-pinball-machines-1709936073

Saucier, Jeremy. "Pinball Lives at The Strong." *Play Stuff Blog*, posted May 23, 2014, http://www.museumofplay.org/blog/chegheads/2014/05/pinball-lives-at-the-strong/

Sharpe, Roger C. *Pinball!* New York: E.P. Dutton, 1977.

TENNIS FOR TWO (1958)

"First Video Game, The?" on Brookhaven National Laboratory's official website, https://www.bnl.gov/about/history/firstvideo.php

Guins, Raiford. "Follow the Bouncing Ball: 'Tennis for Two' . . . at The Strong!" *Play Stuff Blog*, posted January 13, 2017, http://www.museumofplay.org/blog/chegheads/2017/01/following-the-bouncing-ball-tennis-for-two-at-the-strong/

Guins, Raiford. *Game After: A Cultural Study of Video Game Afterlife*. Cambridge, MA: MIT Press, 2014.

Nyitray, Kristen J. "William Alfred Higinbotham: Scientist, Activist, and Computer Game Pioneer." *IEEE Annals of the History of Computing*, vol. 33, no. 2, April–June 2011, 96–101.

JOHN BURGESON'S BASEBALL GAME (1960)

Dyson, Jon-Paul. "The Oldest-Known Computer Baseball Simulation." *Play Stuff Blog*, posted June 20, 2014, http://www.museumofplay.org/blog/chegheads/2014/06/the-oldest-known-computer-baseball-simulation/

Kalb, Bess. "The Lost Founder of Baseball Video Games." *Grantland*, posted April 16, 2012, http://grantland.com/features/john-burgeson-ibm-computer-start-baseball-video-games/

DIGI-COMP COMPUTER (1963)

Cross, Gary. *Kids' Stuff: Toys and the Changing World of American Childhood*. Cambridge, MA: Harvard University Press, 1999.

"Digi-Comp 1 Toy Computer," on The National Museum of American History's official website, http://americanhistory.si.edu/collections/search/object/nmah_694610

Ensmenger, Nathan. *The Computer Boys Take Over: Computers, Programmers, and the Politics of Technical Expertise*. Cambridge, MA: MIT Press, 2010.

SUMERIAN GAME (1964)

Wing, Richard L. "Two Computer-Based Economics Games for Sixth Graders." In *Simulation Games in Learning*, edited by Sarane S. Boocock and E. O. Schild, 155–168. Berkeley, CA: Sage Publications, 1968.

Wing, Richard L., Mabel Addis, Walter Goodman, Jimmer Leonard, and William McKay. *The Production and Evaluation of Three Computer-Based Economics Games for the Sixth Grade*. Yorktown Heights, NY: U.S. Department of Health, Education, and Welfare, 1967.

RALPH BAER'S BROWN BOX (1967)

Baer, Ralph. *Videogames in the Beginning*. Springfield, NJ: Rolenta Press, 2005.

"Brown Box, 1967–68, The" on The National Museum of American History's official website, http://americanhistory.si.edu/collections/search/object/nmah_1301997

Dyson, Jon-Paul. "Remembering Ralph." *Play Stuff Blog*, posted December 12, 2014, http://www.museumofplay.org/blog/chegheads/2014/12/remembering-ralph

"Video Game History," on Ralph Baer's official website, retrieved January 12, 2018. http://www.ralphbaer.com/video_game_history.htm

NINTENDO LOVE TESTER (1969)

Ashcraft, Brian. "The Nintendo They've Tried to Forget: Gambling, Gangsters, and Love Hotels." *Kotaku*, posted March 22, 2011, https://kotaku.com/5784314/the-nintendo-theyve-tried-to-forget-gambling-gangsters-and-love-hotels

Gorges, Florent and Isao Yamazaki. *The History of Nintendo, 1889–1980: From Playing-Cards to Game & Watch*. Pix'n Love Publishing. 2008.

Inoue, Osamu. *Nintendo Magic: Winning the Videogame Wars*. New York: Vertical, 2010.

Plunkett, Luke. "The Nintendo Love Test Was More than a Vitality Sensor." *Kotaku*, posted July 1, 2010, https://kotaku.com/5576999/the-nintendo-love-tester-was-more-than-a-vitality-sensor

Sheff, David. *Game Over: How Nintendo Conquered the World*. New York: Random House, 1994.

COMPUTER SPACE (1971)

"*Computer Space*" on The Strong's official website, http://www.museumofplay.org/online-collections/22/67/109.17313

Donovan, Tristan. *Replay: The History of Video Games*. East Sussex, UK: Yellow Ant, 2010.

Edwards, Benj. "*Computer Space* and the Dawn of the Arcade Video Game." *Technologizer*, posted December 11, 2011, http://www.technologizer.com/2011/12/11/computer-space-and-the-dawn-of-the-arcade-video-game/

THE OREGON TRAIL (1971)

Dyson, Jon-Paul. "Four Decades on the Oregon Trail." *Play Stuff Blog*, posted February 8, 2010, http://www.museumofplay.org/blog/chegheads/2010/02/four-decades-on-the-oregon-trail/

Dyson, Jon-Paul. "MECC, the Company That Launched Educational Gaming." *Play Stuff Blog*, posted October 20, 2016, http://www.museumofplay.org/blog/chegheads/2016/10/mecc-the-company-that-launched-educational-gaming/

Misa, Thomas J. *Digital State: The Story of Minnesota's Computing Industry*. Minneapolis, MN: University of Minnesota Press, 2013.

Wong, Kevin. "The Forgotten History of *The Oregon Trail*, as Told by Its Creators." *Motherboard*, posted February 15, 2017, https://motherboard.vice.com/en_us/article/qkx8vw/the-forgotten-history-of-the-oregon-trail-as-told-by-its-creators

"SPACEWAR: FANATIC LIFE AND SYMBOLIC DEATH AMONG THE COMPUTER BUMS" IN *ROLLING STONE* (1972)

Baker, Chris. "Stewart Brand Recalls First *Spacewar* Video Game Tournament." *Rolling Stone*, posted May 25, 2016, http://www.rollingstone.com/culture/news/stewart-brand-recalls-first-spacewar-video-game-tournament-20160525

Brand, Stewart. "*Spacewar*: Fanatic Life and Symbolic Death Among the Computer Bums." *Rolling Stone*, No. 123, December 7, 1972, 50–58.

Levy, Stephen. *Hackers: Heroes of the Computer Revolution*. 25th anniversary edition. Sebastopol, CA: O'Reilly Media, Inc., 1984.

MAGNAVOX ODYSSEY (1972)

Baer, Ralph. *Videogames in the Beginning*. Springfield, NJ: Rolenta Press, 2005.

Dyson, Jon-Paul. "Ralph Baer Brings His Brown Box to NCHEG." *Play Stuff Blog*, posted June 29, 2009, http://www.museumofplay.org/blog/chegheads/2009/06/ralph-baer-brings-his-brown-box-to-ncheg/

Langshaw, Mark. "Magnavox Odyssey Retrospective: How Console Gaming Was Born." *DigitalSpy*, posted December 13, 2014, http://www.digitalspy.com/gaming/retro-gaming/feature/a616235/magnavox-odyssey-retrospective-how-console-gaming-was-born/

"Magnavox Odyssey," on *Pong-Story* website, http://www.pong-story.com/odyssey.htm

MAGNAVOX MINI THEATER (1972)

Huhtamo, Erkki. "What's Victoria Got to Do with It? Toward an Archeology of Domestic Video Gaming." In *Before the Crash: Early Video Game History*, edited by Mark J. P. Wolf, 30–52. Detroit: Wayne State University Press, 2012.

Leach, William R., *Land of Desire: Merchants, Desire, and the Rise of a New American Culture*. New York: Vintage, 1994.

"Magnavox Mini Theater and Odyssey Demonstration Film Cartridge," on The Strong's official website, http://www.museumofplay.org/online-collections/22/53/116.3633

"Magnavox Odyssey with Sound," YouTube (archival advertisement), https://www.youtube.com/watch?v=Dn5e8Fsabpc

Saucier, Jeremy. "Preserving the First Video Game Merchandising Display Unit." *Play Stuff Blog*, posted September 7, 2017, http://www.museumofplay.org/blog/chegheads/2017/09/preserving-the-first-video-game-merchandising-display-unit/?_ga=2.232886302.1499039691.1504811277–1958976795.1504811277

Saucier, Jeremy. "Selling Electronic Play in Video Game Television Commercials." *Play Stuff Blog*, posted February 6, 2016, http://www.museumofplay.org/blog/chegheads/2013/02/selling-electronic-play-in-video-game-television-commercials

PONG (1972)

Alcorn, Allan. "Oral History of Allan (Al) Alcorn." By Henry Lowood. Computer History Museum, April 26, 2008 and May 23, 2008, http://archive.computerhistory.org/resources/access/text/2012/09/102658257-05-01-acc.pdf

Isaacson, Walter. "The Birth of *Pong*." *Slate*, posted October 7, 2014, http://www.slate.com/articles/technology/technology/2014/10/the_invention_of_pong_how_nolan_bushnell_launched_the_video_game_industry.html

Lowood, Henry. "Videogames in Computer Space: The Complex History of Pong." *IEEE Annals of the History of Computing*, vol. 31, no. 3, July–September 2009, 5–19, https://pdfs.semanticscholar.org/07d2/52566f6dc928eaa4ce6848182f90a2f71f61.pdf

"Pong," on the World Video Game Hall of Fame's official website, http://www.worldvideogamehalloffame.org/games/pong

Vendel, Curt, and Marty Goldberg. *Atari Inc.: Business is Fun*. Carmel, NY: Syzygy Press, 2012.

"Welcome to PONG-Story," on *Pong-Story* website, http://www.pong-story.com/intro.htm

101 BASIC COMPUTER GAMES (1973)

Ahl, David H. "Birth of a Magazine." *The Best of Creative Computing, Volume 1*, 1976, http://www.atariarchives.org/bcc1/showpage.php?page=2

Digital Equipment Corporation. *101 BASIC Computer Games*. Maynard, MA, 1973, http://bitsavers.trailing-edge.com/pdf/dec/_Books/101_BASIC_Computer_Games_Mar75.pdf

Dyson, Jon-Paul. "Toys." In *Debugging Game History: A Critical Lexicon*, edited by Henry Lowood and Raiford Guins, 401–408. Cambridge, MA: The MIT Press, 2016.

"Fifty Years of BASIC, the Programming Language That Made Computers Personal." *Time*, posted April 29, 2014, http://time.com/69316/basic/

DUNGEONS & DRAGONS (1974)

Dyson, Jon-Paul. "The Influence of *Dungeons and Dragons* on Video Games." *Play Stuff Blog*, posted May 6, 2011, http://www.museumofplay.org/blog/chegheads/2011/05/the-influence-of-dungeons-and-dragons-on-video-games

Peterson, Jon. *Playing at the World: A History of Simulating Wars, Peoples, and Fantastic Adventures from Chess to Role-Playing Games*. San Diego, CA: Unreason Press, 2012.

Rausch, Allen. "Magic & Memories: The Complete History of *Dungeons & Dragons*." *Gamespy*, posted August 16, 2004, http://pc.gamespy.com/articles/538/538262p1.html

HOME PONG (1975)

"Atari *Pong*: The Home Systems," on *Pong-Story* website, http://www.pong-story.com/atpong2.htm

"Atari *Pong*," on Centre for Computing History's official website, http://www.computinghistory.org.uk/det/4007/Atari-PONG/

Dyson, Jon-Paul. "But Mom, I Wanted *Pong*!" *Play Stuff Blog*, posted January 18, 2013, http://www.museumofplay.org/blog/chegheads/2013/01/but-mom-i-wanted-pong/

"*Pong* for Your Home," on the Atari Museum website, http://www.atarimuseum.com/videogames/dedicated/homepong.html

Vendel, Curt and Marty Goldberg. *Atari Inc.: Business is Fun*. Carmel, NY: Syzygy Press, 2012.

BREAKOUT (1976)

Dyson, Jon-Paul. "Steve Jobs, Breakout Pioneer." *Play Stuff Blog*, posted October 7, 2011, http://www.museumofplay.org/blog/chegheads/2011/10/steve-jobs-breakout-pioneer

Hanson, Ben. "How Steve Wozniak's Breakout Defined Apple's Future." *Game Informer*, posted on October 9, 2015, http://www.gameinformer.com/b/features/archive/2013/06/27/how-steve-wozniak-s-breakout-defined-apple-s-future.aspx

Isaacson, Walter. *Steve Jobs*. New York: Simon & Schuster, 2011.

Murphy, Conor. "The History of Breakout." *Big Fish Games* (blog), posted on May 30, 2012, http://www.bigfishgames.com/blog/the-history-of-breakout/

Sudnow, David. *Pilgrim in the Microworld: Eye, Mind, and the Essence of Video Skill*. New York: Warner Books, 1983.

Vendel, Curt and Marty Goldberg. *Atari Inc.: Business is Fun*. Carmel, NY: Syzygy Press, 2012.

FAIRCHILD CHANNEL F (1976)

"Archival Collections Related to Video and Other Electronic Games," on The Strong's official website, http://www.museumofplay.org/collections/archival-video-game

Edwards, Benj. "The Untold Story of the Invention of the Game Cartridge." *Fast Company*, posted January 22, 2015, https://www.fastcompany.com/3040889/the-untold-story-of-the-invention-of-the-game-cartridge

Edwards, Benj. "VC&G Interview: Jerry Lawson, Black Video Game Pioneer." *Vintage Computing and Gaming*, posted February 24, 2009, http://www.vintagecomputing.com/index.php/archives/545/vcg-interview-jerry-lawson-black-video-game-pioneer

Saucier, Jeremy. "Collection Documents the Career of Video Game Pioneer Jerry Lawson." *Play Stuff Blog*, posted December 2, 2013, http://www.museumofplay.org/blog/chegheads/2013/12/collection-documents-the-career-of-video-game-pioneer-jerry-lawson

Whalen, Zach. "Channel F for Forgotten: The Fairchild Video Entertainment System." In *Before the Crash: Early Video Game History*, edited by Mark J. P. Wolf, 60–80. Detroit: Wayne State University Press, 2012.

DEATH RACE (1976)

"*Death Race*," on the International Arcade Museum website, https://www.arcade-museum.com/game_detail.php?game_id=7541

"*Death Race* Arcade Game," on The Strong's official website, http://www.museumofplay.org/online-collections/22/67/111.7002

Kocurek, Carly A. "The Agony and the Exidy: A History of Video Game Violence and the Legacy of *Death Race*." *Game Studies*, vol. 12, issue 1, September 2012, http://gamestudies.org/1201/articles/carly_kocurek

Kocurek, Carly A. *Coin-Operated Americans: Rebooting Boyhood at the Video Game Arcade*, Minneapolis, MN: University of Minnesota Press, 2015.

Mackey, Bob. "A Brief History of Video Game Violence, Part 1: *Death Race* to *Mortal Kombat*." *US Gamer*, posted on April 24, 2015, http://www.usgamer.net/articles/a-brief-history-of-video-game-violence-part-1-death-race-to-mortal-kombat

Plunkett, Luke. "*Death Race*, the World's First Scandalous Video Game." *Kotaku*, posted February 28, 2012. http://kotaku.com/5889166/death-race-the-first-scandalous-video-game

ATARI VIDEO COMPUTER SYSTEM (1977)

"Atari 2600," on The Strong's official website, http://www.museumofplay.org/online-collections/22/43/105.1898

Fulton. Steve. "The History of Atari: 1971–1977." *Gamasutra*, posted November 6, 2007, https://www.gamasutra.com/view/feature/130414/the_history_of_atari_19711977.php

Lapetino, Tim. *Art of Atari*. Mt. Laurel, NJ: Dynamite, 2016.

Montfort, Nick and Ian Bogost. *Racing the Beam: The Atari Video Computer System*. Cambridge, MA: MIT Press, 2009.

MATTEL FOOTBALL (1977)

Blumenthal, Howard J. *The Complete Guide to Electronic Games*. New York: New American Library, 1981.

"Gaming at Its Finest, Circa 1977." *Forbes*, posted on August 2, 2001, https://www.forbes.com/2001/08/02/0802tentech.html

Kaminski, Joseph. "Retro Tech: Mattel *Classic Football*." *CNET*, posted April 8. 2008, https://www.cnet.com/news/retro-tech-mattel-classic-football/

"Mattel's *Auto Race*," on the Handheld Museum website, http://www.handheldmuseum.com/Mattel/AutoRace.htm

"Mattel's *Football* (I)," on the Handheld Museum website, http://www.handheldmuseum.com/Mattel/FB.htm

Wheeler, Eric. "Are You Ready for Some (Electronic) Football?" *Play Stuff Blog*, posted January 7, 2011, http://www.museumofplay.org/blog/chegheads/2011/01/are-you-ready-for-some-electronic-football/

ZORK (1977)

Anderson, Tim and Stu Galley. "The History of *Zork*." *The New Zork Times*, http://samizdat.cc/shelf/documents/2004/05.27-historyOfZork/historyOfZork.pdf

Jerz, Dennis. "Somewhere Nearby is Colossal Cave: Examining Will Crowther's Original 'Adventure' in Code and in Kentucky." *Digital Humanities Quarterly*, vol. 1, no. 2

Lammle, Rob. "A Brief History of *Zork*." *Mental Floss*, posted on June 15, 2014, http://mentalfloss.com/article/29885/eaten-grue-brief-history-zork

Montfort, Nick. *Twisty Little Passages: An Approach to Interactive Fiction*. Cambridge, MA: MIT Press, 2003.

"*Zork* Map: The Great Underground Empire, Part 1," on The Strong's official website, http://www.museumofplay.org/online-collections/22/52/110.766

SIMON (1978)

Baer, Ralph. *Videogames in the Beginning*. Springfield, NJ: Rolenta Press, 2005.

Edwards, Owen. "The Not-So-Simple Simon Proved the Young Were Swifter than the Old." *Smithsonian Magazine*, September 2006, http://www.smithsonianmag.com/smithsonian-institution/not-so-simple-simon-proved-young-were-swifter-than-old-180953561/

"*Touch-Me*," on the International Arcade Museum website, https://www.arcade-museum.com/game_detail.php?game_id=12694

SPACE INVADERS (1978)

Bowen, Kevin. "The Gamespy Hall of Fame: *Space Invaders*." *Gamespy*, last modified April 8, 2008, https://web.archive.org/web/20080408152913/http://archive.gamespy.com/legacy/halloffame/spaceinvaders.shtm

"Looking at Taito's History as They Turn 60." *Arcade Heroes*, posted August 27, 2013, http://arcadeheroes.com/2013/08/27/taito-turns-60/

Paradis, Charles. "Insert Coin to Play: *Space Invaders* and the 100-Yen Myth." *Numasmatist*, March 2014.

"*Space Invaders*," *Giant Bomb*, posted February 15, 2013, https://www.giantbomb.com/space-invaders/3030–5099/

"*Space Invaders*," on The Strong's official website, http://www.museumofplay.org/online-collections/22/67/109.17111

"*Space Invaders*," on the World Video Game Hall of Fame's official website, http://www.worldvideogamehalloffame.org/games/space-invaders

ADVENTURELAND (1978)

"*Adventureland*," *Giant Bomb*, posted May 13, 2017, https://www.giantbomb.com/adventureland/3030-6189/

Campbell, Keith. *The Computer & Video Games Book of Adventure*. Tring, U.K.: Melbourne House, 1983.

"GameSetInterview: Adventure International's Scott Adams." *GameSetWatch*, posted on July 19, 2006, http://www.gamesetwatch.com/2006/07/gamesetinterview_adventure_int.php

"*Pirate's Adventure*," *Byte Magazine*, December 1980, https://archive.org/stream/byte-magazine-1980-12/1980_12_BYTE_05-12_Adventure#page/n193/mode/2up

Saucier, Jeremy. "Scott Adams Adventure International Collection Documents Early Commercial Computer Gaming." *Play Stuff Blog*, posted May 1, 2017. http://www.museumofplay.org/blog/chegheads/2017/05/scott-adams-adventure-international-collection-documents-early-commercial-computer-gaming/

SPEAK & SPELL (1978)

Blumenthal, Howard J. *The Complete Guide to Electronic Games*. New York: New American Library, 1981.

"Texas Instruments *Speak & Spell*," on the Datamath Calculator Museum website, http://www.datamath.org/Speech/SpeaknSpell.htm

Watters, Audrey. "*Speak & Spell*: A History." *Hack Education*, posted January 13, 2015, http://hackeducation.com/2015/01/13/speak-and-spell

ASTEROIDS (1979)

"*Asteroids*," on *AllGame* website, last modified March 8, 2009, https://web.archive.org/web/20090308030532/http://www.allgame.com/game.php?id=15438

"*Asteroids* (Atari)," on *Gaming History 101* website, posted March 19, 2012, https://gaminghistory101.com/2012/03/19/asteroids/

"The Making of *Asteroids*." *Retro Gamer*, September 2009, http://ataricade.videoarcade.it/Making_of_Asteroids.pdf

Wolf, Mark. *The Video Game Explosion: A History from "Pong" to PlayStation and Beyond*. Westport, CT: ABC-CLIO/Greenwood Press, 2008.

RALPH BAER'S LIGHT ANTI-TANK WEAPON (1979)

Baer, Ralph. *Videogames: In the Beginning.* Springfield, NJ: Rolenta Press, 2005.

"Bradley Trainer: Atari's Top Secret Military Project," on the *Arcade Blogger* website, https://arcadeblogger.com/2016/10/28 /bradley-trainer-ataris-top-secret-military-project/

Dyson, Jon-Paul. "From *Battlezone* to *World of Tanks.*" *Play Stuff Blog*, posted March 15, 2013, http://www.museumofplay.org /blog/chegheads/2013/03/from-battlezone-to-world-of-tanks

Saucier, Jeremy. "From Training, to Toy, to Treatment: The Many Lives of *Full Spectrum Warrior.*" *Play Stuff Blog*, posted October 5, 2012, http://www.museumofplay.org/blog/chegheads/2012/10/from-training-to-toy-to-treatment-the-many-lives-of -full-spectrum-warrior

PAC-MAN (1980)

Geoffrey R. Loftus and Elizabeth F. Loftus, *Mind at Play: The Psychology of Video Games.* New York: Basic Books, 1983.

Goldberg, Marty. "*Pac-Man*: The Phenomenon—Part 1." *Classic Gaming*, last modified March 16, 2007, https://web.archive.org /web/20071016203822/http://classicgaming.gamespy.com/View.php?view=Articles.Detail&id=249

"History of *Pac-Man*." *Mental Itch*, https://mentalitch.com/history-of-pac-man/

Iwatani, Toru. "How to Create a Good Game—From My Experience of Designing *Pac-Man*," *GDC Vault* (video; in Japanese), http://www.gdcvault.com/play/1014631/Classic-Game-Postmortem-PAC

"*Pac-Man*," on the World Video Game Hall of Fame's official website, http://www.worldvideogamehalloffame.org/games /pac-man

"*Pac-Man*—The Dot Eater," on the *Dot Eaters* website, http://thedoteaters.com/?bitstory=pac-man&all=1

Peckham, Matt. "This Is What *Pac-Man*'s Creator Thinks 35 Years Later." *Time*, posted May 22, 2015, http://time.com/3892662 /pac-mans-35-years/

Saucier, Jeremy. "The Lasting Appeal of Chase Games." *Play Stuff Blog*, posted September 11, 2014, http://www.museumofplay .org/blog/chegheads/2014/09/the-lasting-appeal-of-chase-games

Soble, Jonathan. "Mayasa Nakamura, Whose Company Created *Pac-Man*, Dies at 91." *New York Times*, posted January 30, 2017, https://www.nytimes.com/2017/01/30/business/pac-man-masaya-nakamura-dead.html?_r=0

MISSILE COMMAND (1980)

"Let's Talk About *Missile Command*," on the *Arcade Blogger* website, https://arcadeblogger.com/2016/02/19/lets-talk-about -missile-command/

"*Missile Command*," on The Strong's official website, http://www.museumofplay.org/online-collections/22/67/109.17116

Rubens, Alex. "The Creation of *Missile Command* and the Haunting of Its Creator, Dave Theurer." *Polygon*, posted August 15, 2013, https://www.polygon.com/features/2013/8/15/4528228/missile-command-dave-theurer

DONKEY KONG (1981)

deWinter, Jennifer. *Shigeru Miyamoto: "Super Mario Bros.," "Donkey Kong," "The Legend of Zelda."* New York: Bloomsbury, 2015.

Fahs, Travis. "The Secret History of *Donkey Kong.*" *Gamasutra*, posted on July 6, 2011, https://www.gamasutra.com/view /feature/134790/the_secret_history_of_donkey_kong.php?page=2

Kohler, Chris. *Power-Up: How Japanese Video Games Gave the World an Extra Life.* New York: Dover Publications, 2016.

Muldoon, Moira. "The Father of Mario and Zelda." *Salon*, posted on December 2, 1998, https://www.salon.com/1998/12/02 /feature_252/

UTOPIA (1981)

Baker, Chris. "Don Daglow's 8 Keys to a Long Career in the Game Industry." *Gamasutra*, posted March 21, 2016, https://www .gamasutra.com/view/news/268509/Don_Daglows_8_keys_to_a_long_career_in_the_game_industry.php

Barton, Matt and Bill Loguidice. "A History of Gaming Platforms: Mattel Intellivision." *Gamasutra*, posted May 8, 2008, https:// www.gamasutra.com/view/feature/132054/a_history_of_gaming_platforms_.php

Cassidy, William. "*Utopia.*" *Gamespy*, posted August 3, 2004, http://www.gamespy.com/articles/495/495918p1.html

Marks, Robert B. "The Most Important Pc Games of All Time: *Civilization.*" *PC Games*, posted August 11, 2016, https://www .pcgamesn.com/most-important-pc-games-civilization

RIVER RAID (1982)

Symonds, Shannon. "Preserving Carol Shaw's Trailblazing Video Game Career." *Play Stuff Blog*, posted July 19, 2017, http:// www.museumofplay.org/blog/chegheads/2017/07/preserving-carol-shaws-trailblazing-video-game-career

Edwards, Benj. "VC&G Interview: Carol Shaw, Atari's First Female Video Game Developer." *Vintage Computing and Gaming*, posted October 12, 2011, http://www.vintagecomputing.com/index.php/archives/800/vcg-interview-carol-shaw-female-video-game-pioneer-2

"*River Raid*—Atari 2600—Activision," game manual on *Atari Age* website, https://atariage.com/manual_page.php?SystemID=2600&SoftwareLabelID=409&maxPages=6&currentPage=4

E.T. THE EXTRA-TERRESTRIAL (1982)

"Atari 2600 *E.T. the Extra-Terrestrial*—Atari Dig," on The Strong's official website, http://www.museumofplay.org/online-collections/22/46/115.487

"Atari Parts Are Dumped." *New York Times*, September 28, 1983, http://www.nytimes.com/1983/09/28/business/atari-parts-are-dumped.html

"Buried Atari Cartridges." *Snopes*, last modified April 26, 2014, http://www.snopes.com/business/market/atari.asp

"Classic Gaming Expo 2000: Keynote Addresses: Atari 2600," on *Classic Gaming* website, last updated January 9, 2014, https://web.archive.org/web/20140109200808/http://classicgaming.gamespy.com/View.php?view=Articles.Detail&id=376

"Great Video Game Crash of 1983," on *BugSplat* website, https://www.bugsplat.com/great-video-game-crash-1983

Guins, Raiford. *Game After: A Cultural Study of Video Game Afterlife*. Cambridge, MA: MIT Press, 2014.

Phipps, Keith. "Interview: Howard Scott Warshaw." *AV Club*, posted February 2, 2005, https://www.avclub.com/howard-scott-warshaw-1798208406

ONE-ON-ONE: DR. J VS. LARRY BIRD (1983)

DeMaria, Rusel and Johnny L. Wilson. *High Score! The Illustrated History of Electronic Games*. Berkeley, CA: McGraw-Hill, 2002.

Maher, Jimmy. "Seeing Farther." *The Digital Antiquarian*, posted January 23, 2013, http://www.filfre.net/2013/01/seeing-farther/

Sauer, Patrick. "How Dr. J and Larry Bird Helped Build a Video Game Empire." *Vice Sports*, posted May 25, 2017, https://sports.vice.com/en_us/article/wje9kq/how-dr-j-and-larry-bird-helped-build-a-video-game-empire

"Trip Hawkins, MBA '78," on Stanford Graduate School of Business's official website, https://alumni-gsb.stanford.edu/get/page/magazine/article/?article_id=53339

PINBALL CONSTRUCTION SET (1983)

Barton, Matt and Bill Loguidice. "The History of the *Pinball Construction Set*: Launching Millions of Creative Possibilities." *Gamasatra*, posted February 9, 2009, https://www.gamasutra.com/view/feature/132316/the_history_of_the_pinball_.php

"Bill Budge Donates His Iconic Video Game Computer to the International Center for the History of Electronic Games," on The Strong's official website, http://www.museumofplay.org/content/bill-budge-donates-video-game-computer-icheg

Saucier, Jeremy. "Bill Budge, *Pinball Construction Set*, and the Popularization of User-Customized Video Games." *Play Stuff Blog*, posted September 18, 2012, http://www.museumofplay.org/blog/chegheads/2012/09/bill-budge-pinball-construction-set-and-the-popularization-of-user-customized

KING'S QUEST (1984)

Lammle, Rob. "From *King's Quest* to *Leisure Suit Larry*: A Brief History of Sierra On-Line." *Mental Floss*, posted April 24, 2012, http://mentalfloss.com/article/30538/kings-quest-leisure-suit-larry-brief-history-sierra-line

Loguidice, Bill and Matt Barton. *Vintage Games: An Insider Look at "Grand Theft Auto," "Super Mario," and the Most Influential Games of All Time*. Burlington, MA: Focal Press, 2009.

Nooney, Laine. "A Pedestal, a Table, a Love Letter: Archaeologies of Gender in Videogame History." Game Studies, vol. 13, issue 2, December 2013, http://gamestudies.org/1302/articles/nooney

TETRIS (1984)

Ackerman, Dan. *The Tetris Effect: The Game that Hypnotized the World*. New York: PublicAffairs, 2016

Check, Marc. "Russian-Born *Tetris* Illustrates Good Design." *Play Stuff Blog*, posted March 3, 2010, http://www.museumofplay.org/blog/chegheads/2010/03/russian-born-tetris-illustrates-good-design/

Dyson, Jon-Paul. "New Display Highlights the Worldwide Reach of *Tetris*." *Play Stuff Blog*, posted February 4, 2016, http://www.museumofplay.org/blog/chegheads/2016/02/new-display-highlights-the-worldwide-reach-of-tetris/

Juul, Jesper. *A Casual Revolution: Reinventing Video Games and Their Players*. Cambridge, MA: MIT Press, 2010

Maher, Jimmy. "A Tale of the Mirror World, Part 3: A Gaming of Falling Shapes." *The Digital Antiquarian*, posted June 30, 2017, http://www.filfre.net/2017/06/a-tale-of-the-mirror-world-part-3-a-game-of-falling-shapes/

"*Tetris*," on the World Video Game Hall of Fame's official website, http://www.worldvideogamehalloffame.org/games/tetris

Weisberger, Mindy. "The Bizarre History of *Tetris*." *Live Science*, posted October 13, 2016, https://www.livescience.com/56481
-strange-history-of-tetris.html

NINTENDO ENTERTAINMENT SYSTEM (1985)

Altice, Nathan. *I Am Error: The Nintendo Family Computer/Entertainment System Platform*. Cambridge, MA: The MIT Press, 2015.

Kohler, Chris. "October 18, 1985: Nintendo Entertainment System Launches." *Wired*, posted October 18, 2010, https://www
.wired.com/2010/10/1018nintendo-nes-launches/

Narcisse, Evan. "How Nintendo Made the NES (and Why They Gave It a Gun)." *Kotaku*, posted October 16, 2015, https://kotaku
.com/an-insiders-memories-of-making-the-nintendo-entertainme-1737014878

"Nintendo's Restrictive Licensing History." *Nerd Trek*, posted November 12, 2011, http://nerdtrek.com/nintendos-restrictive
-licensing-history/

Sheff, David. *Game Over: How Nintendo Conquered the World*. New York: Random House, 1994.

Stark, Chelsea. "How Nintendo Brought the NES to America—and Avoided Repeating Atari's Mistakes." *Mashable*, posted
October 19, 2015, http://mashable.com/2015/10/19/nintendo-nes-launch-atari/

Turner, Benjamin and Christian Nutt. "Nintendo Famicon: 20 Years of Fun!" *Gamespy*, last modified on August 5, 2004, https://
web.archive.org/web/20040805170336/http://archive.gamespy.com:80/articles/july03/famicom/index1.shtml

SUPER MARIO BROS. (1985)

Altice, Nathan. *I Am Error: The Nintendo Family Computer/Entertainment System Platform*. Cambridge, MA: The MIT Press, 2015.

deWinter, Jennifer. *Shigeru Miyamoto: "Super Mario Bros.," "Donkey Kong," "The Legend of Zelda."* New York: Bloomsbury, 2015.

McLaughlin, Rus. "IGN Presents: The History of *Super Mario Bros.*" *IGN*, posted September 13, 2010, http://www.ign.com
/articles/2010/09/14/ign-presents-the-history-of-super-mario-bros?page=2

Sheff, David. *Game Over: How Nintendo Conquered the World*. New York: Random House, 1994.

"*Super Mario Bros.*," on the World Video Game Hall of Fame's official website, http://www.worldvideogamehalloffame.org
/games/super-mario-bros

THE LEGEND OF ZELDA (1986)

Donovan, Tristan. *Replay: The History of Video Games*. East Sussex, UK: Yellow Ant, 2010.

Fahs, Travis and Lucas M. Thomas. "IGN Presents the History of *The Legend of Zelda*." *IGN*, posted July 5, 2012, http://www.ign
.com/articles/2012/07/06/ign-presents-the-history-of-the-legend-of-zelda?page=7

Loguidice, Bill and Matt Barton. *Vintage Games: An Insider Look at "Grand Theft Auto," "Super Mario," and the Most Influential
Games of All Time*. Burlington, MA: Focal Press, 2009.

"Nintendo *The Legend of Zelda*," on The Strong's official website, http://www.museumofplay.org/online-collections/22/46/110.8059

NES HANDS FREE CONTROLLER (1989)

Salvini, Kenny. "Todd Stabelfeldt: Titan of Tech." *New Mobility*, posted October 2, 2017, http://www.newmobility.com/2017/10
/todd-stabelfeldt-titan-tech/

Sheff, David. *Game Over: How Nintendo Conquered the World*. New York: Random House, 1994.

PRINCE OF PERSIA (1989)

Dyson, Jon-Paul. "Jordan Mechner Collection Documents Revolution in Game Graphics." *Play Stuff Blog*, posted October 29, 2014,
http://www.museumofplay.org/blog/chegheads/2014/10/jordan-mechner-collection-documents-revolution-in-game-graphics/

McLaughlin, Rus, Scott Collura, and Levi Buchanan. "IGN Presents: The History of *The Prince of Persia*." *IGN*, posted May 18, 2010.
http://www.ign.com/articles/2010/05/18/ign-presents-the-history-of-prince-of-persia?page=1

Mechner, Jordan. *The Making of "Prince of Persia" Journals 1985–1993* on his official website, http://www.jordanmechner.com
/downloads/makpopsample.pdf

Pham, Alex. "*Prince of Persia* Creator Jordan Mechner Is Still in the Game." *Los Angeles Times*, posted April 25, 2011, http://
articles.latimes.com/2011/apr/25/business/la-fi-himi-mechner-20110425

JOHN MADDEN FOOTBALL (1990)

DeMaria, Rusel and Johnny L. Wilson. *High Score! The Illustrated History of Electronic Games*. McGraw-Hill, 2002.

Fleming, Jeffrey. "We See Farther—A History of Electronic Arts." *Gamasutra*, posted February 16, 2007, https://www.gamasu-
tra.com/view/feature/130129/we_see_farther__a_history_of_.php

Harris, Blake J. "John Madden Hockey: How a Lousy Football Game Birthed a Bastard and Led to Greatest Hockey Game of All-
Time." *Read Only Memory*, http://readonlymemory.vg/john-madden-hockey

Hruby, Patrick. "The Franchise: The Inside Story of How Madden NFL Became a Video Game Dynasty." *ESPN Outside the Lines*, http://www.espn.com/espn/eticket/story?page=100805/madden

STREET FIGHTER II (1991)

Hendershot, Steve. *Undisputed Street Fighter: A 30th Anniversary Retrospective*. Dynamite, 2017.

Leone, Matt. "*Street Fighter II*: An Oral History." *Polygon*, posted on February 3, 2014, https://www.polygon.com/a/street-fighter-2-oral-history

McLaughlin, Rus. "IGN Presents the History of *Street Fighter*." *IGN*, posted February 16, 2009, http://www.ign.com/articles/2009/02/16/ign-presents-the-history-of-street-fighter

"*Street Fighter II*," on the World Video Game Hall of Fame's official website, http://www.worldvideogamehalloffame.org/games/street-fighter-ii

SONIC THE HEDGEHOG (1991)

Cohen, D. S. "History of *Sonic the Hedgehog* by Sega Genesis." *Lifewire*, last updated October 29, 2016, https://www.lifewire.com/history-of-sonic-the-hedgehog-729671

Harris, Blake. *Console Wars: Nintendo, Sega, and the Battle that Defined a Generation*. New York: Dey Street Books, 2014.

Hester, Blake. "*Sonic the Hedgehog*'s Long, Great, Rocky History." *Polygon*, posted February 8, 2016, https://www.polygon.com/2016/2/8/10756318/sonic-the-hedgehog-great-rocky-history

"Sega Genesis Sega Classic *Sonic the Hedgehog*—Product Package," on The Strong's official website, http://www.museumofplay.org/online-collections/22/46/109.6101

MORTAL KOMBAT (1992)

Dargenio, Angelo. "The History of Fighting Games, Part 3: Attack of the Clones." *Arcade Sushi*, posted January 31, 2014, http://arcadesushi.com/the-history-of-fighting-games-part-3-attack-of-the-clones/

Donovan, Tristan. *Replay: The History of Video Games*. East Sussex, UK: Yellow Ant, 2010.

Fahs, Travis. "The History of *Mortal Kombat*." IGN, posted May 5, 2011, http://www.ign.com/articles/2011/05/05/the-history-of-mortal-kombat

Vazquez, Suriel. "The Early Names for *Mortal Kombat* Were as Cheesy as You'd Expect." *Game Informer*, posted December 1, 2016, http://www.gameinformer.com/b/news/archive/2016/12/01/the-early-names-for-mortal-kombat-were-as-cheesy-youd-expect.aspx

Wilson, Aolfe. "The Glorious, Gory History of *Mortal Kombat*." *Vice*, posted October 29, 2014, https://www.vice.com/en_us/article/jmbnvd/why-all-the-fuss-over-mortal-kombat-322

DOOM (1993)

"*Doom*," on The Strong's official website, http://www.museumofplay.org/online-collections/22/52/110.5847

"id Software," *Giant Bomb*, posted June 27, 2013, https://www.giantbomb.com/id-software/3010–347/

Kushner, David. *Masters of "Doom": How Two Guys Created an Empire and Transformed Pop Culture*. New York: Random House, 2003.

Pinchbeck, Dan. *"Doom": Scarydarkfast*. Ann Arbor, MI: University of Michigan Press, 2012.

MYST (1993)

Carroll, Jon. "Guerrillas in the *Myst*." *Wired*, posted August 1, 1994, https://www.wired.com/1994/08/myst/

Wolf, Mark. *"Myst" and "Riven": The World of the D'ni*. Ann Arbor, MI: University of Michigan Press, 2011.

Yoshida, Emily. "Lost to the Ages." *Grantland*, posted September 24, 2013, http://grantland.com/features/looking-back-game-myst-20th-anniversary/

NINTENDO VIRTUAL BOY (1995)

Dyson, Jon-Paul. "Lessons from the Past for the Future of Virtual Reality." *Play Stuff Blog*, posted April 6, 2015, http://www.museumofplay.org/node/3940

Edwards, Benj. "Unraveling the Enigma of Nintendo's Virtual Boy, 20 Years Later." *Fast Company*, posted August 21, 2015, https://www.fastcompany.com/3050016/unraveling-the-enigma-of-nintendos-virtual-boy-20-years-later

"Nintendo Virtual Boy Electronic Sign," on The Strong's official website, http://www.museumofplay.org/online-collections/22/53/115.788

POKÉMON (1996)

Madnani, Mikhail. "A Brief History of *Pokémon*." *Live Mint*, last modified July 25, 2016, http://www.livemint.com/Sundayapp/Z7zHxltyWtFNzcoXPZAbjI/A-brief-history-of-Pokmon.html

Plunkett, Luke. "The Man Who Creates *Pokémon* for a Living." *Kotaku*, posted May 24, 2011, https://kotaku.com/5804919/the
-man-who-creates-pokemon-for-a-living/

Plunkett, Luke. "The Origins of *Pokémon*." *Kotaku*, posted May 30, 2011, https://kotaku.com/5806664/how-pokemon-was-born
-from-bug-collecting-and-aspergers-syndrome

THE SIMS (2000)

"2016 World Video Game Hall of Fame Inductees Announced," on The Strong's official website, http://www.museumofplay.org
/press/releases/2016/05/2688-2016-world-video-game-hall-fame-inductees-announced

Lammle, Rob. "A Brief History of *SimCity*." *Mental Floss*, posted January 30, 2013, http://mentalfloss.com/article/48610/ant
-city-and-beyond-history-all-things-sim

Taylor, Tracey. "Will Wright: Inspired to Make *The Sims* after Losing a Home." *Berkeleyside*, posted October 17, 2011, http://www
.berkeleyside.com/2011/10/17/will-wright-inspired-to-make-the-sims-after-iosing-a-home/

SONY PLAYSTATION 2 (2000)

Agnello, Anthony John. "RIP PlayStation 2: Sony Halts Production of the Most Successful Game Console in History." Digital
Trends, posted January 7, 2013, https://www.digitaltrends.com/gaming/rip-playstation-2-sony-halts-production-of-the
-worlds-most-successful-game-console/

Donovan, Tristan. *Replay: The History of Video Games*. East Sussex, UK: Yellow Ant, 2010.

Magnier, Mark. "Sony's PlayStation 2 Making Its U.S. Launch from a Shaky Platform." *Los Angeles Times*, October 3, 2000, http://
articles.latimes.com/2000/oct/23/business/fi-40746

"PlayStation 2 Console," on The Strong's official website, http://www.museumofplay.org/online-collections/22/43/111.2687

Saucier, Jeremy. "How Software Development Helped Make Sony's PlayStation the King of 1990s Consoles." *Play Stuff Blog*,
posted November 5, 2012. http://www.museumofplay.org/blog/chegheads/2012/11/how-software-development-helped
-make-sony%E2%80%99s-playstation-the-king-of-1990s

GRAND THEFT AUTO III (2001)

"David Jones: The Scot behind the Most Lucrative Game of All Time." *Money Week*, posted September 25, 2013, https://
moneyweek.com/profile-of-david-jones/

Garrelts, Nate. *The Meaning and Culture of Grand Theft Auto: Critical Essays*. Jefferson, NC: McFarland & Company, 2006.

"*Grand Theft Auto V*: Games Visionary behind Scotland's Biggest Cultural Export." *Daily Record*, last updated September 17,
2013, http://www.dailyrecord.co.uk/entertainment/video-games/video-games-news/grand-theft-auto-v-games-2275673

Kushner, David. *Jacked: The Outlaw Story of "Grand Theft Auto."* Hoboken , NJ: Wiley, 2012.

Loguidice, Bill and Barton, Matt. *Vintage Games: An Insider Look at the History of "Grand Theft Auto," "Super Mario," and the Most
Influential Games of All Time*. Burlington, MA: Focal Press, 2009.

McLaughlin, Rus and Lucas M. Thomas. "IGN Presents the History of *Grand Theft Auto*." *IGN*, posted May 6, 2013, http://www
.ign.com/articles/2013/05/06/ign-presents-the-history-of-grand-theft-auto-2?page=2

HALO: COMBAT EVOLVED (2001)

"*Halo: Combat Evolved*," on The Strong's official website, http://www.museumofplay.org/online-collections/22/52/110.10884

Hughes, Neil. "Apple's Steve Jobs 'Raged' at Steve Ballmer When Microsoft Bought *Halo*." *Apple Insider*, posted October 26, 2010,
http://appleinsider.com/articles/10/10/26/apples_steve_jobs_raged_at_steve_ballmer_when_microsoft_bought_halo

Locke, Vince. "The Power of Ludonarrativity: *Halo* as Participatory Myth." In *The Play Versus Story Divide in Game Studies: Critical
Essays*, edited by Mathew Wilhelm Kapell, 86—96. Jefferson, NC: McFarland, 2016.

McLaughlin, Rus. "IGN Presents: The History of *Halo*." *IGN*, last updated July 10, 2012, http://www.ign.com/articles/2012/07/11
/ign-presents-the-history-of-halo-2

Qureshi, Usman. "*Halo* Was Originally Introduced by Steve Jobs as a Mac Exclusive." *iPhone in Canada*, http://www.iphone
incanada.ca/news/steve-jobs-introduces-halo-game-for-mac/

DENSHA DE GO! CONTROLLER (2002)

Ashcroft, Brian. "The Most Amazing Train Game to Hit Japanese Arcades This Year." *Kotaku*, posted November 8, 2017, https://
kotaku.com/the-most-amazing-train-game-to-hit-japanese-arcades-thi-1820244880

Humphries, Matthew. "Taito Has Created the Ultimate Train Driving Arcade Cabinet." *Geek.com*, posted August 9, 2016, https://
www.geek.com/tech/taito-has-created-the-ultimate-train-driving-arcade-cabinet-1665269/

Munro, Scott. "*Densha de Go!*" Kilted Moose's games blog, posted March 1, 2009, http://kiltedmoose.blogspot.com/2009/03/densha-de-go.html

"Sony PlayStation 2 *Densha de Go!* Controller," on The Strong's official website, http://www.museumofplay.org/online-collections/22/43/110.2219

WORLD OF WARCRAFT (2004)

Clayman, David. "The History of Blizzard." IGN, posted October 21, 2010, http://www.ign.com/articles/2010/10/22/the-history-of-blizzard

"ECTS 2001: *World of Warcraft* Announced." *Gamespot,* posted September 4, 2001, https://www.gamespot.com/articles/ects-2001-world-of-warcraft-announced/1100-2810134/

Fahey, Rob. "The Making of *World of Warcraft.*" *Eurogamer.net*, posted August 11, 2009, http://www.eurogamer.net/articles/the-making-of-world-of-warcraft-article

Nardi, Bonnie A. *My Life as a Night Elf Priest: An Anthropological Account of "World of Warcraft."* Ann Arbor, MI: University of Michigan Press, 2010.

Walker, Alex. "This Year, the Original *Neverwinter Nights* Turns 25." *Kotaku AU,* posted January 28, 2016, https://www.kotaku.com.au/2016/01/this-year-the-original-neverwinter-nights-turns-25/

"*World of Warcraft* Retired Server Blade: Barthilas Realm," on The Strong's official website, http://www.museumofplay.org/online-collections/22/53/111.7039

WII REMOTE (2006)

Brain, Marshall. "How the Wii Works." *How Stuff Works*, https://electronics.howstuffworks.com/wii.htm

Hurley, Andrew. *Diners, Bowling Alleys, and Trailer Parks: Chasing the American Dream in Postwar Consumer Culture.* New York: Basic Books, 2001.

Jones, Steven E. and George K. Thiruvathukal. *Codename Revolution: The Nintendo Wii Platform.* Cambridge, MA: MIT Press, 2012.

Juul, Jesper. *A Casual Revolution: Reinventing Video Games and Their Players.* Cambridge, MA: MIT Press, 2012.

Reimer, Jeremy. "How the Wii Was Born." *Ars Technica*, posted October 1, 2006, https://arstechnica.com/gadgets/2006/10/wii-2/

CALL OF DUTY: MODERN WARFARE 2 (2009)

Dyson, Jon-Paul. "Playing the 'Good War.'" *Play Stuff Blog,* posted June 23, 2017, http://www.museumofplay.org/blog/chegheads/2017/06/playing-the-good-war

Entertainment Software Association, *Essential Facts About the Computer and Video Game Industry.* 2017.

Saucier, Jeremy K. "Calls of Duty: The World War II Combat Video Game and the Construction of the 'Next Great Generation.'" In *The War of My Generation: Youth Culture and the War on Terror*, edited by David Kieran, 128–143. New Brunswick, NJ: Rutgers University Press, 2015.

MINECRAFT (2011)

Dyson, Jon-Paul. "*Minecraft* and the Building Blocks of Fun." *Play Stuff Blog*, posted April 4, 2012, http://www.museumofplay.org/blog/chegheads/2012/04/minecraft-and-the-building-blocks-of-fun

Garrelts, Nate. *Understanding Minecraft: Essays on Play, Community and Possibilities.* Jefferson, NC: McFarland & Company, 2014.

Goldberg, Daniel and Linus Larsson. "The Amazingly Unlikely Story of How *Minecraft* Was Born." *Wired*, posted November 5, 2013, https://www.wired.com/2013/11/minecraft-book/

Nesbit, Edith. *The Magic City.* New York: Macmillan, 1910.

SKYLANDERS (2011)

Campbell, Colin. "Toys for Bob and the Story behind *Skylanders.*" *Polygon*, posted April 16, 2014, https://www.polygon.com/2014/4/16/5614716/skylanders-story-toys-for-bob-skylanders-swap-force

Clark, Willie. "How They Make the Toys for *Skylanders*, *Disney Infinity* and *Shovel Knight.*" *Polygon*, posted January 27. 2016, https://www.polygon.com/features/2016/1/27/10811024/manufacturing-skylanders-disney-infinity-shovel-knight

Maloof, Blake. "Alt.GDC: Developing *Skylanders*' Innovative 'Portal of Power.'" *Make:*, posted March 13, 2012, https://makezine.com/2012/03/13/alt-gdc-developing-skylanders-innovative-portal-of-power/

Owczarski, Kimberly A. "'Toys with Brains': *Skylanders* and the Growth of the Toys-To-Life Market." In *Articulating the Action Figure: Essays on Toys and Their Messages*, edited by Jonathan Alexandratos, 135–151. Jefferson, NC: McFarland, 2017.

NANCY DREW: TOMB OF THE LOST QUEEN (2012)

Cassell, Justine and Henry Jenkins. *From Barbie to "Mortal Kombat": Gender and Computer Games*. Cambridge, MA: MIT Press, 1998.

"Rachel—Rest in Peace." *My Journey Through Nancy Drew* (blog), posted March 13, 2012, http://myjourneythroughnancydrew. blogspot.com/2012/03/rachel-rest-in-peace-her-interactive.html

"Rachel E. Vaughn." *The Daily News Online,* posted March 13, 2012, http://tdn.com/lifestyles/announcements/obituaries/rachel-e-vaughn/article_59756072—6d1d-11e1-b2cf-001871e3ce6c.html

POKÉMON GO (2016)

Andrews, Travis M. "*Pokémon Go*: the April Fools' Joke That Became a Global Obsession." *Washington Post*, posted July 13, 2016, https://www.washingtonpost.com/news/morning-mix/wp/2016/07/13/pokemon-go-the-april-fools-joke-that-became-a -global-obsession/?utm_term=.d0a85cbe9155

Belluscio, Lynne. "Pigs in Clover." *Le Roy Pennysaver & News,* posted May 4, 2014, http://www.leroyhistoricalsociety.org /assets/050414---pigs-in-clover.pdf

Dreyfus, Emily, Brian Barrett, Kevin McFarland, Emma Ellis, Jacke Muncy, and Chris Kohler. "The Weekend *Pokémon Go* Took over America." *Wired*, posted July 11, 2016, https://www.wired.com/2016/07/weekend-pokemon-go-took-america/

Dyson, Jon-Paul. "A Short History of Mobile Games." *Play Stuff Blog*, posted May 3, 2013, http://www.museumofplay.org/blog /play-stuff/2013/05/a-short-history-of-mobile-games

Lopez, German. "*Pokémon Go*, Explained in Fewer than 400 Words." *Vox*, last updated July 14, 2016, https://www.vox .com/2016/7/12/12159304/pokemon-go-game-ios-android

Polansky, Lana. "The World's Most Dangerous Game: *Pokémon*'s Strange History with Moral Panics." *Vice*, posted September 5, 2016, https://www.vice.com/sv/article/yvepdx/pokemon-go-moral-panics-satanism-infosec

Warner, Claire. "How Does *Pokémon Go* Work? Here's Everything We Know about the Tech behind the Augmented Reality Fad." *Bustle*, posted July 13, 2016, https://www.bustle.com/articles/172317-how-does-pokemon-go-work-heres-everything-we -know-about-the-tech-behind-the-augmented-reality

THAT DRAGON, CANCER (2016)

Parkin, Simon. "A Father's Video Game About His Son's Terminal Cancer." *New Yorker*, July 22, 2015, https://www.newyorker .com/culture/culture-desk/a-video-game-about-terminal-cancer

Suellentrop, Chris. "This Video Game Will Break Your Heart." *New York Times*, February 5, 2016, https://www.nytimes .com/2016/02/06/arts/that-dragon-cancer-video-game-will-break-your-heart.html

Tanz, Jason. "Playing for Time." *Wired*, January 2016, https://www.wired.com/2016/01/that-dragon-cancer/

Credits

Unless otherwise noted, all photographs represent objects from The Strong's permanent collection. Nintendo properties are trademarks and copyrights of Nintendo.

Pg. 4, 6: "Tennis for Two" hardware recreation. Courtesy of Brookhaven National Laboratory.

Pg. 8: Printout of John Burgeson's baseball simulation. Gift of John Burgeson.

Pg. 12-13, 14: Digi-Comp computer. Gift of Louise French.

Pg. 16: Printout of the *Sumerian Game*. Gift of Alexandra Johnson and Devin Monnens.

Pg. 20-21: Recreation of Ralph Baer's Brown Box. Gift of Ralph Baer.

Pg. 32: *The Oregon Trail* video game. Gift of Matthew Zappia.

Pg. 54, 59: David Ahl's book *101 BASIC Computer Games*. Courtesy of David Ahl.

Pg. 76: Fairchild Channel F *Math Quiz* prototype cartridge. Gift of Marc Lawson.

Pg. 79: Gerald A. Lawson Fairchild employee badge. Gift of Marc Lawson.

Pg. 92: Mattel *Football* handheld game. Gift of Darwin Bromley.

Pg. 96: *Zork* map. Gift of Steven Meretzky.

Pg. 100: *Zork I* computer game. Gift of Phil Chmielewski.

Pg. 102: *Simon* production model. Gift of Ralph Baer.

Pg. 106: *Space Invaders* arcade game. Gift of Mike Wallace.

Pg. 110: *Adventureland* cassette with baby bottle liner package. Gift of Scott Adams.

Pg. 126-127: Light anti-tank weapon. Gift of Ralph Baer.

Pg. 150: *River Raid* video game. Gift of Carol Shaw.

Pg. 153: River Raiders patch. Gift of Carol Shaw.

Pg. 154: *E.T. the Extra-Terrestrial* landfill cartridge. Gift of the City of Alamogordo, New Mexico.

Pg. 166: *Pinball Construction Set* game. Gift of Tony Van.

Pg. 168: Apple II computer and disk drive used by Bill Budge to program *Pinball Construction Set*. Gift of Bill Budge.

Pg. 172: Roberta Williams's handwritten notes for the game *King's Quest*. Courtesy of Ken and Roberta Williams.

Pg. 182-183: Cutout Nintendo Entertainment System console. Gift of Nintendo of America.

Pg. 185: R.O.B. the Robotic Operating Buddy. Gift of Nintendo of America.

Pg. 194: Homemade Hylian Shield from *The Legend of Zelda*. Gift of Nicholas Bell.

Pg. 198: Nintendo Entertainment System Hands Free controller. Gift of Nintendo of America.

Pg. 202-203: *Prince of Persia* rotoscoping photos. Gift of Jordan Mechner.

Pg. 234: *Myst* video game. Gift of Doug Carlston.

Pg. 248: Will Wright's design notebooks for *The Sims*. Gift of Will Wright.

Pg. 254: Sony PlayStation 2 test and debugging unit for Stormfront Studios. Gift of Don Daglow.

Pg. 280: Nintendo Wii-mote. Gift of Raiford Guins.

Pg. 284-285: Autographed *Call of Duty: Modern Warfare 2 - Prestige Edition* video game. Gift of Thomas and Charles Wiederhold.

Pg. 296: *Skylanders: Spyro's Adventure* prototype portal and figure. Gift of Activision.

Pg. 300: Thank you card written to Her Interactive by the parents of Rachel Vaughn. Gift of Her Interactive.

Index

DEY ST.

HarperCollins books may be purchased for educational, business, or sales promotional use. For information, please email the Special Markets Department at SPsales@harpercollins.com.

FIRST EDITION

Designed by Michelle Crowe

Library of Congress Cataloging-in-Publication Data has been applied for.

ISBN 978-0-06-283869-8

18 19 20 21 22   LSC   10 9 8 7 6 5 4 3 2 1